High Crimes and Misdemeanors

High Crimes and Misdemeanors

"Wherefore Richard M. Nixon ...Warrants Impeachment"

The Dramatic Story of the Rodino Committee

By HOWARD FIELDS

W · W · NORTON & COMPANY · INC ·   *New York*

Copyright © 1978 by W. W. Norton & Company, Inc. All rights reserved. Published simultaneously in Canada by George J. McLeod Limited, Toronto. Printed in the United States of America.

First Edition

Library of Congress Cataloging in Publication Data

Fields, Howard.
    High crimes and misdemeanors.

    Includes index.
    1. Nixon, Richard Milhous, 1913–   —Impeachment.
2. Watergate Affair, 1972–   3. Rodino, Peter W.
4. United States. Congress. House. Committee on the
Judiciary.   I. Title.
KF5076.N5F5   328.73′07′453   78–4502
ISBN 0–393–05681–3

designed by Paula Wiener
1 2 3 4 5 6 7 8 9 0

To Cheryl, my wife, who suffered through my reporting of the story, suffered through my writing of the book, and then suffered through her editing of the manuscript.

Contents

Acknowledgments

Although the majority of the book is based upon my daily reporting of the story of impeachment for more than a year, special thanks must be given to those who helped me flesh out the behind-the-scenes activity—Peter Rodino, Bob McClory, Ray Thornton, Dick Cates, Jerry Zeifman, and Francis O'Brien. And thanks, too, to Wayne Kelley of *Congressional Quarterly* for the use of one of Washington's finest news libraries.

Introduction

Thirty-eight men and women, members of the House Judiciary Committee, were on the very special "jury" in the fall of 1973 when an accumulation of events dictated that President Richard M. Nixon should be subjected to impeachment proceedings. For nine months, those thirty-eight people sat at the vortex of swirling animosities, partialities, influences, and interests, the emotions which Alexander Hamilton had predicted would surround an impeachment inquiry.

There had been only one impeachment of a president, that of Andrew Johnson in 1868. By 1973, the history books had come to agree that it was a shameful, politically motivated, tasteless event in American history. When the process of impeaching Nixon began, many people in the United States feared history was about to repeat itself.

There had been eleven other impeachments voted by the U.S. House of Representatives, the last in 1936. Nearly all of them were of federal judges. Nearly every case had been handled in a different manner. There were few precedents the House could use when it decided it would have to determine if Nixon should be impeached.

The Constitution didn't help. It mentioned impeachment only four times:

Article I; Section 2, clause 5: "The House of Representatives shall choose their Speaker and other Officers; and shall have the sole Power of Impeachment."

Article I; Section 3, clauses 6 and 7: "The Senate shall have the sole Power to try all Impeachments. When sitting for that Purpose, they shall be on Oath of Affirmation. When the President of the United States is tried, the Chief Justice shall preside: And no Person shall be convicted without the Concurrence of two thirds of the Members present.

"Judgment in Cases of Impeachment shall not extend further than to removal from Office, and disqualification to hold and enjoy any Office of honor, Trust or Profit under the United States: but the Party convicted shall nevertheless be liable and subject to Indictment, Trial, Judgment and Punishment, according to Law."

Article II; Section 2, clause 1: "The President . . . shall have Power to grant Reprieves and Pardons for Offences against the United States, except in Cases of Impeachment."

Article III; Section 4: "The President, Vice President and all civil Officers of the United States, shall be removed from Office on Impeachment for, and Conviction of, Treason, Bribery, or other high Crimes and Misdemeanors."

Simply put, those words meant that if the U.S. House of Representatives determined the president had committed an impeachable offense, it could vote by a simple majority to impeach him. And "impeach" means only "to accuse." The case would have to be tried in the Senate, which could convict him on a two-thirds vote and remove him from office.

In the impeachment process, some observers have drawn the analogy that the committee designated to do the preliminary work for the House acts as an investigator, the House as a grand jury, and the Senate as jury and judge.

But the process is unlike a grand jury proceeding because the same people who investigate also serve as grand jurors and prosecutors. When grand jurors in an ordinary criminal case return a verdict, their work is done. They don't have to justify their decision and they can return, generally unaffected, to their daily routine. In impeachment, the decision could be the most important decision of many political careers, which if wrong—sometimes even if right—can haunt politicians for the rest of their lives.

So there is no accurate analogy for the impeachment process. It is unique.

Given the political ramifications of the process, the uniqueness of it, the lack of precedents and the animosities and partialities within and without the House Judiciary Committee and its staff, the story of the inquiry into the impeachment of President Nixon emerges as one of emotion, conflict, indecision, compromise, eloquence, courage, and drama.

Despite his innate sense of fairness and awareness of political realities, the committee's chairman, Peter Rodino, chose not to use the power he had. His tendency to mediate disputing factions within the committee membership and inquiry staff rather than exert strong leadership nearly doomed the process several times. Yet it probably would have failed in any other hands.

Only the collision of diverse personalities and the coincidental timing of other events enabled the committee to steer the correct course.

It would appear that other units of government dealing with Watergate—the special prosecutor, the Senate Watergate Committee, and the courts—were more decisive. But the Judiciary Committee was the only body with the constitutional authority to begin the process of removing Richard M. Nixon from office.

This is, then, a historical account of one of the most important moments in recent American history. If it destroys some notions about the heroes and the fumblers who emerged during the impeachment inquiry, so be it.

Howard Fields

High Crimes and Misdemeanors

Genesis

In May 1971, a Pentagon employee named Daniel Ellsberg gave the *New York Times* a copy of a classified Defense Department study of the Vietnam war, a candid report outlining mistaken predictions and U.S. blunders in waging it. The study became known as the "Pentagon Papers."

The White House of President Richard M. Nixon was incensed.

Ellsberg was indicted shortly after on a charge of illegal possession of classified documents, but the Pentagon Papers were only the first of a series of leaks concerning national security issues. The White House suspected other Ellsberg leaks. Nixon ordered a unit formed to plug the leaks. The unit became known as the "White House plumbers."

Their first assignment was to find out what they could about Ellsberg to discredit him before his trial started. Two men were hired for the dirty work by Egil "Bud" Krogh, a White House employee heading the plumbers: E. Howard Hunt and G. Gordon Liddy.

Dr. Lewis J. Fielding, a Beverly Hills psychiatrist, had treated Ellsberg two years earlier. On August 25, 1971, Hunt and Liddy broke into Fielding's office on a reconnaissance mission. They returned on September 4 with three cohorts and watched as the trio entered Fielding's office in an unsuccessful attempt to get his files on Ellsberg.

The plumbers unit was disbanded a few months later. Hunt and Liddy were transferred to the Committee to Re-Elect the President (CREEP). Nixon already was gearing up for his campaign for a second term.

CREEP was headed by an eager young White House staffer named Jeb Stuart Magruder until Attorney General John Mitchell could make the transition to campaign manager. Part of the campaign budget the inexperienced Magruder had been given was for intelligence. For that he was assigned Hunt and Liddy.

The Hunt/Liddy operations included several projects in 1972. One was to plant listening devices in the telephones of officials at Democratic party headquarters in the Watergate office building. The bugs were planted during a break-in on Memorial Day weekend, and another recruit was stationed in a room of the Howard Johnson Motel across Virginia Avenue to pick up the signals and record what he heard.

One of the bugs wasn't working properly, so Liddy and Hunt directed a second break-in, using as cohorts James McCord, Bernard Barker, Virgilio Gonzalez, Eugenio Martinez, and Frank Sturgis. All but McCord were from Florida and had anti-Castro Cuban connections. The break-in took place on the night of June 17, 1972. The five were caught in the offices and Hunt and Liddy were arrested later. All seven were tried and convicted the following January.

Despite the efforts of U.S. District Court Judge John J. Sirica, and because of no effort by the Justice Department's three prosecutors, the trial revealed no higher involvement.

Richard Nixon had won reelection in November 1972, by one of the largest margins in history, but the news media were not deterred.

Washington Post reporters Bob Woodward and Carl Bernstein, then assigned to the newspaper's local desk, began covering what was to become known as "Watergate." Through the rest of 1972 and well into 1973, their stories periodically brought new revelations of administration wrongdoing beyond the Watergate break-in.

CHAPTER I

Personalities

Peter Wallace Rodino recalled reading in a newspaper just as the impeachment inquiry was moving into high gear: "One false move and Pete Rodino's in trouble, two and the country's in trouble."

"My God, when you think . . ." his voice trailed off.

At the beginning of the inquiry, Senator John Stennis (D-Miss.) visited Rodino and told him "something that really was frightening," Rodino remembered. He quoted Stennis: "You know, there are times in the life of our country when men are called upon. Somehow fate just selects someone. And I honestly believe that fate selected you to do this job."

"And I thought, my God . . ." Rodino said.

And before impeachment got off the ground, when the leaders of the House could ignore the pressures no longer and assigned to his committee the task of considering impeachment, Rodino's response was, "Why to me? Why me, Pete Rodino?"

In those autumn days of 1973, Rodino was a little man, both in stature and reputation. He had been a member of the House for twenty-five years, quite satisfied to serve his New Jersey constituents and do his work on the House Judiciary Committee without notoriety. Standing five feet six, hair more white than gray, and given to wearing dark, pin-stripe suits and white shirts, the sixty-four-year-old, raspy-voiced Pete Rodino was anything but impressive. He was no orator, he tended to be repetitious in extemporaneous statements, he was ill at ease with people he didn't know well, and really had not displayed the leadership that would attract national attention.

He was so unconcerned about international affairs that on the floor of the House he usually went along with whatever the administration or the House leadership wanted. His committee had no jurisdiction in world affairs, and he was one of the last liberal Democrats to oppose the Vietnam war. Except for occasional attention to civil rights, constitutional amendments, and national holidays, the Judiciary Committee dealt with dry legal matters about which the general public cared little. Rodino was obscure. There are many men like that in Congress, but generally they are party hacks who continue to be reelected by an apathetic constituency. They usually create a niche for themselves on noncontroversial committees like Rules, Post Office, or one of the myriad Appropriations subcommittees where they don't have to do much and won't be held to account for it.

Rodino was as obscure as the hacks, but he wasn't in the same class.

Although his committee didn't get much attention, he had a working regimen for years from 9:00 A.M. to seven or eight at night in Washington, mostly Tuesday through Thursday. Friday through Monday he would be in his home district in Newark, New Jersey, where he held local office hours and spent the evenings and weekend at home. His family stayed in Newark; in Washington he was a bachelor in an efficiency apartment near the Capitol and had nothing to do but work.

In 1973, Rodino, because of seniority and for no other reason, inherited the chairmanship of the Judiciary Committee. That might have put a little more pressure on him than he had felt in previous years, but not so much that he couldn't handle it easily.

After serving for years under the domineering chairmanship of Emanuel Celler, Rodino had his own ideas of how the Judiciary Committee should proceed. But he was still getting his feet wet as the possibility of impeachment began to gain credibility during the Senate Watergate Committee's hearings in the late spring of 1973.

Rodino is well-read and a student of history, so he began to review the only precedents for a presidential impeachment. They all concerned the 1868 impeachment of Andrew Johnson and there was precious little available. What Rodino read soured him on the whole matter. The material didn't help him to face the task with any knowledge, except of what not to do in impeachment. He decided that the Johnson impeachment was an intolerably partisan affair.

One of Rodino's greatest talents was the ability to ignore matters he didn't wish to face. He officially ignored a resolution to impeach Nixon introduced by Representative Robert Drinan (D-Mass.) on July 31, 1973, but quietly allowed his chief counsel, Jerome Zeifman, to do some research on impeachment for the committee—just in case.

Even so, Rodino had convinced himself, as much through wishful thinking as anything else, that impeachment would not happen. He was truly awed and frightened by the prospect of having to oversee the impeachment of the president of the United States. It was the last thing he wanted to face. Rodino was the type of person who always sought a compromise rather than a confrontation. To him, impeachment would be the last resort. He had been in the House long enough to know that "once the process begins, you will never stop it."

Rodino's critics would call him indecisive; his supporters would say he was cautious, deliberate. He was, in fact, all of those things.

And if Rodino was frightened by the prospect of leading an impeachment inquiry, so were most people who knew him or knew of him. He offered no comfort to those who perceived him to have the fate of the country in his hands.

All anyone knew was that he had chaired the Immigration Subcommittee of Judiciary for several years. Immigration wasn't an important subject then except to ethnic congressmen like Rodino, an Italian. He had gotten Columbus Day declared a national holiday, but as an Italian representing a large Italian constituency, the effort didn't elicit cheers for statesmanship. Rodino was proudest of managing the landmark open-housing bill through twelve rough days on the House floor in the 1960s. But he had gotten the assignment by default, when then–Judiciary Chairman Celler became ill and the job fell to Rodino as second in seniority.

Besides his generally lackluster record, part of the queasy feeling about Pete Rodino's leading impeachment had to do with where he came from. He represented Newark, where political corruption was the order of the day. One of his New Jersey colleagues had been convicted of having organized crime connections, and another, with whom Rodino had roomed in his early days in Congress, was under indictment for similar activities. How clean could Rodino be, coming from the machine-politics climate of Newark?

As it turned out, Rodino was clean. Even that, however, elicited questions from some cynics about how bright the guy could be if even organized crime didn't bother with him.

Rodino had squeaked through a frightening primary fight in the spring of 1972 and faced another in 1974. He was more concerned about reelection and getting help with the management of the Judiciary Committee than he was with the outside chance he'd have to lead an impeachment inquiry. When he interviewed and subsequently hired Francis O'Brien, formerly on the staff of New York Mayor John V. Lindsay, as his administrative assistant in August 1973, impeachment was barely touched upon, and then only as one of those things irresponsible people were talking about.

Even when the suspicions about Vice-President Spiro Agnew first became public in mid-August, Rodino sought to dismiss any talk of impeachment or any other major role for his committee in the still unraveling Watergate scandal.

But Agnew dragged Rodino onto the national stage by appealing directly to the House leaders to try him on impeachment charges. It was his contention that as the vice-president, he could not be tried on any charges until he was impeached and removed from office. As confirmed by his later "no contest" plea and resignation, he obviously thought he would have a better chance in the political arena than in the courts of justice.

When the prospect of Nixon's impeachment later became a reality, the press began taking a close look at Rodino, someone it hadn't had much contact with. Spurred by tips, innuendoes, and suggestions from Nixon people after the "Saturday Night Massacre," the press began probing Rodino's background. They found nothing incriminating. But other probes into his personality developed a sharper picture of him.

One news account quoted colleagues describing Rodino variously as "the most industrious man I ever saw . . . seems relaxed and confident . . . not flashy, but solid . . . experienced, fairly intelligent, not much of a self-starter . . . a low profile, so far untested." Anywhere but in Washington most of those comments would be considered compliments. But one has to consider where they were spoken—in the town of ready backslappers, lawmakers who always say the nicest thing they can about their colleagues when they know it is going to be on the record. Those words were, in reality, diplomatic ones aimed at implying "not much confidence in him."

Rodino had his own description of his reputation:

"I suppose having been one of four hundred and thirty-five for a long period of time . . . I'd never been the type of individual that was looking for plaudits and a pat on the back. I was gratified to know that some of the things I had done over the years had achieved at least that purpose that I thought I was here for," he said. "I worked industriously and diligently as a member of Congress. I sought no other award than that I was able to do something and make a contribution."

Rodino valued his reputation for fairness—the appearance of it as well as the fact of it. He had hanging on his wall before impeachment began a framed photograph autographed by Richard Nixon, commemorating his signing of one of Rodino's bills. Fearing a visiting news reporter or someone else would note the absence of the photograph and read some signal into it, Rodino kept it in place until Nixon had resigned and left town and the books were closed on impeachment.

Rodino also was an extremely patriotic individual—not in the sense of "my country right or wrong," but in the sense of "democracy is the best form of government and must be protected."

With the benefit of hindsight, some congressional observers concluded that it was that view, however corny and trite, that allowed impeachment to succeed. When they considered the pressures, the timing of events, the decisions which proved later to be the only correct ones and which allowed the impeachment inquiry to survive, they broke into a cold sweat at the thought of how easily it could have been someone besides Rodino in charge, someone who might have charged into the task like a bull, and fallen into all the traps that lay ahead. This impeachment had to be led by caution, patience, reasoning, and quiet determination.

Rodino is the son of an Italian immigrant, Pelligrino Rodino, who came to the United States in 1900 and raised his three children by working in a Newark leather factory, as a cabinet maker, carpenter, and toolmaker.

Like most Italian and other immigrants of those days, the elder Rodino, who Anglicized his given name to Peter, took as gospel the material he was learning to earn his citizenship papers. He had a great deal of respect for the U.S. Constitution and the Declaration of Independence. His elder son, Peter, Jr., who lived through the trauma of seeing his mother die of tuberculosis when he was five, became close to his father and his father instilled in him a respect for democracy.

With a raspy throat brought on by a bout with diphtheria, Peter, Jr., imitated Demosthenes by speaking in a park with pebbles in his mouth. He worked his way through Dana College and the New Jersey Law School, both now part of Rutgers University, by working for railroads, as an insurance salesman, factory worker, researcher, and welfare worker. He also taught public speaking and citizenship at the YMCA. He got his law degree in 1937. But he also had dreams of becoming a poet, and once worked with Anthony Petalino, a composer and musician. True to his Italian heritage, he became an opera buff.

During World War II, he served with the First Armored Division in Africa and Italy, staying behind in Italy after the war to work for restoration of the royal family. He organized a letter-writing campaign for the postwar relief of his ancestral country and was decorated by King Umberto in 1945.

"I look back to the first speech that I made to a group of people when I sought the office. I talked about the Declaration of Independence and the phrase, 'the pursuit of happiness,' 'the inalienable right,' and I thought that those weren't just high-sounding words or great rhetoric, but somehow or other that we ought to be able to take this and translate it into action and each one doing a part, we could make life just a little bit better."

He continued: "And I felt that as long as I was able to do this, I was frankly very gratified that I was doing what made me happy."

Platitudes in most mouths. But Rodino really believed those words. He would even take time out from his harried impeachment schedule to deliver brief lectures to visiting elementary and high-school students in his committee hearing room or on the steps of the Capitol. He had a total awe and respect for the Constitution and the democratic form of government.

Rodino's personality and cautious method of operation, the enormity of the project and the emotion-charged atmosphere of the times spelled trouble enough for the Judiciary Committee's impeachment inquiry.

No less of a problem was its make-up. By tradition, all members of the committee are lawyers. Beyond that, the membership included a myriad of political beliefs and experiences, personalities, geographic and educational backgrounds—just about every factor which could cause trouble. The members were all politicians, and they had their own particular problems with their districts. For some, the political leanings of their constituencies conflicted with their own thinking about impeachment. For others, the ideologies only served to radicalize their thinking.

The committee membership also tended to be more liberal than other House committees.

The leadership of the committee had to take all of those factors about the committee members into account in conducting the inquiry. So did the public, in its perception of, and confidence in, the committee.

Of the thirty-eight representatives on the committee and a staff of more than a hundred, impeachment was to pivot around the thoughts and actions of six Democrats, including Rodino, seven Republicans, and six men who were not members of Congress.

The Democrats:

WALTER FLOWERS, Democrat of Alabama, was pure Alabama. He was born there, reared there, educated there. He had been an ardent supporter of George Wallace. He was elected to Congress for the first time in 1968 on the strength of the white vote in his west-central Alabama district. Whites outnumbered blacks there, 60 percent to 40 percent.

Flowers displayed loyalty to the Confederate flag. He wore white shoes, which in the early seventies were a code in Congress meaning "good ole boy" southerner, either Democrat or Republican.

Despite his background, Flowers had less of a knee-jerk attitude about current events than his fellow Dixiecrats. At forty, he had been in Congress for three terms. During 1973 he voted with President Nixon on half the issues measured by *Congressional Quarterly*. Most of his fellow southern Democrats had a higher percentage of pro-Nixon votes in their records.

Flowers, then, could be classified as a moderate conservative, but at the time impeachment proceedings began, he would have voted on Nixon's side if a quick vote had been taken.

Flowers perceived his district to be comprised of Nixon supporters. Not so much because they supported the man himself, but because they revered the office and held the occupant of the office as somewhat sacrosanct. The district did, however, give Nixon his lowest percentage of support in Alabama in 1972—64 percent versus Flowers's own 85 percent of the vote.

Flowers was born in Greenville, Alabama, April 12, 1933, and was reared in Tuscaloosa. He got his law degree from the University of Alabama in 1957. In Tuscaloosa he joined the usual civic organizations while he built his own law practice.

JACK BROOKS would have voted to impeach Nixon if the vote were taken on January 21, 1969, the day after Nixon was first inaugurated. It wouldn't look good to have done it on the same day, Brooks might have said, "let the son-of-a-bitch have one good day."

Brooks had been President Lyndon Johnson's best friend in the House and even patterned himself after the former president. They came out of the same mold. Brooks was a cigar-chomping, fast-talking Texan, who liked to use whatever power he had and liked cracking heads. He was gregarious and his humor and language were salty.

Out of the public eye and among people he trusted, he often would do a little dance of glee when something tickled him and he often could be caught singing in the House corridors.

Brooks was chairman of the Government Operations Subcommittee on Government Activities, waiting to head the full committee with the retirement of the chairman the following year. Brooks used his subcommittee to conduct an in-depth investigation into government money spent on improving Nixon's homes in Key Biscayne, Florida, and San Clemente, California. His panel discovered that seventeen million dollars were spent on the homes and the expenditures became a Nixon scandal second only to Watergate.

Brooks's cigar tipped skyward in his mouth as he chomped on it during the impeachment deliberations. He spat out invectives and relished watching his colleagues squirm over impeachment.

He was surprisingly liberal for a congressman from Beaumont, Texas, although he talked more liberal than he voted. Fifty-one at the time of impeachment, he had been a congressman since the age of twenty-nine.

DON EDWARDS, at fifty-eight, was most often described as urbane, suave, gallant, and reasoned. He was more liberal than most of his liberal colleagues, but while their adoption of liberal viewpoints often was automatic, Edwards was thoughtful, someone who could back up his opinion with persuasive reasoning.

He was one of four former FBI men on the committee. He had served the agency in 1940 and 1941, just before he joined the navy.

Edwards had been a national chairman of the liberal-oriented Americans for Democratic Action. The ADA still gave him a perfect liberal voting record. He was first elected to Congress in 1962, representing the blue-collar suburbs between Oakland and San Jose, California.

A divorcé, he had a reputation as having a way with women, but was still considered one of Congress's hardest working members. He had made a fortune before being elected to Congress as president of a title insurance company.

Edwards was ready early on to vote for impeachment, and he would have been able to make a very good, constitutional case in defense of his vote.

JAMES MANN, fifty-three, was born and reared in Greenville, South Carolina, and had represented his district, a mountain area near the North Carolina border, since 1968.

He was considered the most conservative of the Democrats on the House Judiciary Committee, more conservative even than a few of the panel's Republicans. He had to be to get elected. South Carolina gave Nixon an overall 71 percent majority in 1972, but 78 percent of Mann's district voted for Nixon. Mann supported Nixon on 59 percent of the measurable votes in 1973.

But Mann was a reasoned conservative, whose natural inclination to support Nixon was tempered by the fact that he just didn't like Nixon. Except in politics, they were opposites. Mann was courtly, smooth, genteel. He moved and thought in the same fashion—deliberately. It would be hard to imagine Mann ever rushing to get somewhere or spewing forth obscenities about political opponents. He generally avoided reporters during impeachment, shunning the limelight and maintaining an air of discreet silence.

He was a Phi Beta Kappa at The Citadel, emerged from World War II as a lieutenant colonel at the age of twenty-five and was graduated magna cum laude from South Carolina Law School. He was a state legislator, prosecuting attorney, and lawyer in private practice until he was elected to Congress.

RAY THORNTON was the least conservative of the three southern Democrats on the committee. His district had the largest black population in Arkansas.

He kept his own counsel, refraining from making any public statements on impeachment during the inquiry. He was the most likely of the three southerners to vote for it.

Thornton was an enigma to most of his colleagues, rarely showing any emotion. Part of the reason was that he didn't like serving on the Judiciary Committee. His first committee choice as a freshman in Congress had been to serve on the Agriculture Committee, of far more importance to his southern Arkansas district.

At age forty-five, he already had served as a state attorney general and a prosecuting attorney.

The Republicans:

TOM RAILSBACK represented the north-central Illinois district bordered by the Mississippi River. The district was largely rural, with encroaching industrial areas along the river. Railsback enjoyed broad-based support from farmers and labor unions.

As a Republican he was termed a moderate. He was, however, probably the most liberal Republican on the committee. Railsback, at forty-one, had served his district for six years.

Railsback joined his father's law firm after getting his law degree from Northwestern University in 1957, was elected to the Illinois Legislature in 1962, and to Congress in 1966. He could be counted on for support about half the time by the Nixon White House.

Although Railsback had an open mind about impeachment when it was first being considered, he was very much a political animal and worried whether he could be reelected if he voted to impeach Nixon. He had obvious anxieties about the decision that faced him.

Railsback also was troubled during the inquiry by a throat injury he suffered during a handball game in the House gymnasium early in the impeachment proceedings. It had caused irreparable damage to his vocal cords, forcing him to speak in a hoarse whisper.

Railsback was a member of the Chowder and Marching Society, a group of Republican congressmen that picked one new member each year from among promising young Republicans. Nixon was a member.

ROBERT McCLORY, representing the district north and west of Chicago, was considered an opportunist, and many of his decisions were discounted because of that perception.

But McClory also was more intelligent than he was given credit for and operated by a strict set of principles. He ranked about midway in the conservative-liberal spectrum of committee Republicans.

McClory was aware of the way news judgments were made, and attempted to get press attention whenever he could, even to the extent of openly briefing reporters on confidential meetings. That occurred early in the impeachment proceedings, but soon McClory was dropped when reporters learned their information was not very exclusive.

McClory asserted himself and took command of the Republican side when the passive ranking Republican, Edward Hutchinson of Michigan, left a vacuum. He clearly relished the role of briefing reporters on the GOP positions. Early in the proceedings, McClory saw himself as a defender of Nixon.

An avid skiier, tennis player, and scuba diver, McClory looked ten to fifteen years younger than his sixty-five. A Christian Scientist, he believed in a healthy body untainted by alcohol and nicotine. He was well-traveled, mostly on congressional junkets, and had an appreciation for art.

McClory came from a wealthy family from Riverside, Illinois. Educated in Switzerland and at Dartmouth, he received his law degree from Chicago-Kent College of Law in 1932. He was elected to the Illinois House in 1950, State Senate in 1952, and to the U.S. Congress in 1962.

CHARLES WIGGINS served many of the people who first sent Richard M. Nixon to Washington as their congressman in 1946. His district included the eastern, very conservative, blue-collar section of Los Angeles County, Orange County, and Whittier, Nixon's birthplace.

Wiggins's political views weren't that much different from Nixon's, but his intellect and sense of principle were.

Widely regarded as having the best legal mind on the committee, if not being its most intelligent member, Wiggins also was quiet, articulate, persuasive, easy-going, and candid. Most of all, he loved the law.

A colleague advised a reporter early on to watch Wiggins. If Wiggins could be convinced to vote for impeachment, he said, it would be unanimous. If Wiggins stood steadfast, most of the other Republicans also were likely to.

Wiggins took a narrow view of impeachment into the proceedings. It had to be based solely on criminality, and the evidence presented against Nixon would have to be presented just as it would in a court of law. That also meant that some evidence was likely not to be admissible.

Approaching forty-six at the beginning of impeachment, Wiggins had been a member of Congress since 1967. He had served in both World War II and Korea.

WILLIAM COHEN had just turned thirty-three and yet, besides being a freshman congressman, he already had experience as a mayor, city councilman, assistant county attorney, and law instructor.

He was a poet and amateur baseball player who had hiked half his state of Maine seeking votes to Congress. His jut-jawed, blue-eyed good looks, experience, and self-confidence made him the Republican party's fastest rising young star.

But Cohen also was one of the party's most liberal members in Congress. He supported Nixon on only about half the votes in 1973. He had won election the previous year by only a 54 percent margin, replacing a Democrat who moved over to the Senate. His district was very fluid politically and Cohen knew he was in trouble the following year regardless of how he voted; Nixon had carried his district by a greater margin than Cohen had.

But despite that, Cohen was perceived early as a likely vote for impeachment on the committee, the only one on the Republican side.

M. CALDWELL BUTLER was one of the most conservative members of the committee, reflecting his district surrounding Roanoke, Virginia, where he was born forty-eight years earlier, the son of a doctor. Most of his political career—nine years of it—had been spent as a state legislator in Richmond, the old capital of the Confederacy.

His chinless face, lanky frame, and gawky movements gave Butler a birdlike quality that didn't seem to fit his imperious manner. But he was a man of principle who would not accept unprincipled behavior by the administration.

As impeachment began, most observers considered Butler the least likely to vote to impeach the president. Nixon had carried Butler's district with 73 percent of the vote, while Butler mustered less than 55 percent on his freshman try. Butler's district gave Nixon his biggest margin in Virginia.

To the older members of the committee, Butler had to prove himself far more than other GOP freshmen; he had replaced Richard Poff, a highly respected and popular member of the committee who resigned his seat to accept a judgeship.

HAMILTON FISH was the closest thing to a congressman serving by divine right. He practically inherited his district, which stretched along the Hudson River north of Manhattan.

His great-grandfather, the original Hamilton Fish, represented the district from 1843–45, his grandfather from 1909–11, and his father from 1919–45. His father was a reactionary Republican who supported Nixon during impeachment, spouting such diehard phrases as, "Let he who is without sin cast the first stone."

Fish won the seat in 1968 after defeating a challenger in the Republican primary. The challenger then ran on the Conservative party ticket but dropped out later—after it appeared their split would throw the election to the Democrat—having won a promise from Fish that he would try to get the conservative a federal appointment in Washington if he won. He got him a job in the Treasury Department.

The conservative challenger was named G. Gordon Liddy and Liddy later moved from Treasury to the White House to the original "Plumbers" unit. The incident was a constant embarrassment to Fish, but he accepted jibes about it in a genial manner.

Because of his father's reputation, the younger Fish was automatically branded a conservative. But he was one of the most liberal Republicans on the committee, one of only two who had voted against Nixon more than they had voted with him during 1973.

Born in Washington, D.C., while his father was in Congress, Fish had served as a vice consul in Ireland and as a congressional adviser to the U.S. mission to the United Nations before being elected to Congress himself.

EDWARD HUTCHINSON, the ranking Republican on the committee, was old before his time. He was only fifty-nine, but anyone who didn't know that would have guessed him to be in his seventies, his manner and speech were so ponderous. When he talked, he gave the listener the impression he suffered from chronic indigestion.

Not many people understood Hutchinson. Although he had been a member of Congress since 1963, few of his colleagues knew he was a self-made millionaire.

Hutchinson had had an active past. He was elected to the Michigan House in 1946, became a state senator in 1951, and, in 1961, vice-president of the Michigan Constitutional Convention. While in the state legislature, he was considered a leader in the operation of the state.

He replaced the retired Clare Hoffman, a twenty-six–year conservative veteran of the House, and had no qualms about describing himself as a conservative in the Hoffman mold.

But his conservative outlook and his extreme loyalty to the Republican party were misunderstood. He was often thought to be a Nixon loyalist, which he was not.

Hutchinson also was the closest thing to a constitutional expert on the committee. He made common-sense interpretations of the Constitution and never got involved in the fine art of worrying over the different meanings which could be applied to words and phrases.

He brought a no-nonsense approach to everything he dealt with. He was extremely practical and would not deal in internecine squabbling. He viewed impeachment as a frivolous undertaking, with dangerous overtones.

Hutchinson also had the arch-conservative's paranoid view of the press. He saw reporters as the irresponsible enemy. Until impeachment, he never thought he had to deign to talk to reporters. After impeachment began, he came around slowly, after his colleagues convinced him it was good for the Republicans to get their side across.

Hutchinson was as reluctant as Rodino, if not more so, to face impeachment. Hutchinson was one of that group of congressmen who were quite content to ease their way into retirement and who saw no purpose in leading any charge for legislation. He shunned the limelight and arranged to work regular hours without getting involved in controversies.

He became ranking Republican on the committee even though he joined the panel the same time as McClory. A toss of the coin determined who would be more senior than the other.

The Staff:

JOHN DOAR was inscrutable and unflappable as the impeachment inquiry's special counsel. Imperious and taciturn, his usual response to questions was "nope" or "yep." He certainly wasn't glib.

Doar, fifty-two, had strong, early ties to the Republican party. Born in Minneapolis and raised in New Richmond, just across the border in Wisconsin, he got his law degree from the University of California at Berkeley in 1949, and returned to New Richmond to join his father in the firm of Doar and Knowles. The Knowles family had long been powers in the Wisconsin GOP and produced one of its most popular governors.

In 1960, Representative Melvin R. Laird, then GOP leader of the House, got Doar a prestigious job in the Justice Department, near the end of the Eisenhower administration.

Doar was hired as first assistant to the assistant attorney general for the Civil Rights Division. In that job he recommended that all domestic intelligence activities be coordinated in the Justice Department except for the CIA, which at that time was indulging illegally in domestic intelligence. In 1954, the Justice Department had entered into an illegal agreement with the CIA to overlook the agency's domestic activities.

When President Kennedy took over the administration, Doar stayed on in the same post. Burke Marshall headed the division then, and Bobby Kennedy was attorney general.

When the civil rights movement began in the South, the Justice Department came under a great deal of pressure. A camaraderie under stress developed between Doar, Marshall, and Kennedy, and Doar's GOP background began to blur.

In June 1963, Doar gained national recognition for holding back the police and wading into a group of black demonstrators gathering in the streets of Jackson, Mississippi after the funeral of slain civil rights leader Medgar Evers. Doar had spent many of the previous months in the South and he shouted to the mob, ''My name is John Doar and anybody around here knows I stand for what is right.'' The crowd dispersed.

Doar also was in the South—he often chartered planes or hitched rides on government planes to get to the action as quickly as possible—during the freedom rides in Montgomery, Alabama, and James Meredith's desegregation of the University of Mississippi in 1962.

Doar got his first real taste of work with the House Judiciary Committee in 1964 when it was drafting the Civil Rights Act. The following year, after Bobby Kennedy had been elected senator from New York and Burke Marshall left the Justice Department, Doar was named chief of the Civil Rights Division.

As civil rights chief, Doar conducted the prosecution of the three men accused of slaying three civil rights workers in Mississippi. He had never conducted a prosecution before and observers felt he would have bungled the whole case had not the judge, Frank Johnson, helped Doar along. Johnson later was to be named by President Carter to head the FBI, but withdrew for health reasons.

As a senator, Bobby Kennedy had developed a pet project for rebuilding the Bedford-Stuyvesant area of Brooklyn, often called the nation's largest poverty pocket. When the Bedford-Stuyvesant Development and Services Corporation was set up, Kennedy asked Doar to serve as its president. Doar left the Justice Department in 1967.

Doar was a hard worker and expected the same of his staff. "John would be out interviewing people before breakfast and long after dark," said a man who served under Doar.

But Doar was no more of a legal theorist or planner than he was a prosecutor. Doar's forte was gathering facts. "He was the best fact man I ever knew," an associate said. Doar had his people digging into minute court records to turn up all possible evidence before taking a case to court.

A recent divorcé, Doar could devote long hours to the impeachment inquiry after he was named its special counsel.

JEROME ZEIFMAN had been chief counsel of another subcommittee before Rodino became chairman of the full committee at the beginning of 1973. When Rodino moved up, so did Zeifman, as chief counsel to the entire committee.

Zeifman knew his way around on the Hill, having worked for various committees for sixteen years. He was an avid liberal, distrusted the Justice Department and let it be known from the beginning that he would like to get his hands on impeachment.

Zeifman, forty-eight, was a Harvard and New York University Law School graduate with a speciality in tax matters. It was his tax expertise that had brought him to the House in 1957 to work on the Joint Taxation Committee. He later worked for Representative Ed Willis (D-La.), head of a tax subcommittee of the Commerce Committee, but also chairman of the notorious House Un-American Activities Committee.

Through those contacts, Zeifman was able to work equally well with conservatives and liberals, Democrats and Republicans. It proved to be a help when he moved over to Judiciary later.

Although Rodino intended that Zeifman would have overall responsibility for the impeachment inquiry, as well as regular staff duties, Zeifman was increasingly left out of the inquiry as he began to disagree more and more with the procedure that Doar was designing.

RICHARD CATES, who led the inquiry staff before Doar and stayed on as a chief aide, was an aggressive eager beaver. At forty-eight, Cates had been a senior partner in the Madison, Wisconsin, law firm of Lawton and Cates, long identified with Democratic causes in the state.

Cates was in charge of handling the investigation of the Watergate cover-up and fact-finding aspects of the impeachment inquiry work, with title of senior associate special counsel, one of three on the staff.

Cates relished participating in the impeachment process, but his eagerness turned to advocacy and brought him into contention with members and staff. Part of his problem was that he became too closely identified with Zeifman, another impeachment advocate.

Cates had represented both sides—police and students—in the antiwar clashes during the Vietnam war years of the 1960s at the University of Wisconsin at Madison, at the time considered one of the most liberal campuses in the nation and a hotbed of antiwar activism. His colleagues in the legal profession considered Cates an outstanding trial lawyer.

ALBERT JENNER, hired as chief Republican impeachment counsel, was sixty-six but dressed like a thirty-year-old in brightly colored sports jackets or well-tailored suits, always with one of his collection of 300 bow ties.

But Jenner's age had been catching up with him when impeachment was getting underway. He had health problems and had recently had to cut back a bit on his extensive legal work and speaking schedule. It was his health that had kept him from having the job Doar got.

Jenner felt the job as chief GOP counsel on the impeachment inquiry would be less rigorous than that of special counsel, so he accepted. His reputation had been built on his skills as a trial lawyer and his ego was massive, he would not allow himself to be boxed into defending a losing cause.

Jenner was nominally a Republican, one who registered as such and contributed to GOP coffers, but who also supported Democrats if they happened to be good friends whom he admired. One was Senator Adlai E. Stevenson (D-Ill.).

Several times Jenner had interrupted his forty-two–year career to accept public service assignments. He headed the prestigious Chicago law firm of Jenner and Block.

Jenner was senior counsel to the Warren Commission, which investigated the assassination of President Kennedy. At the end of the 1960s he served on the President's National Commission on Causes and Prevention of Violence in the United States. He also served on several Supreme Court advisory committees and was an active leader of the American Bar Association.

But Jenner was far more liberal than the men who hired him—the Republicans on the Judiciary Committee.

SAM GARRISON, a Republican impeachment counsel, was as conservative as most of the Republicans and became Jenner's chief antagonist. He was as strong an advocate against impeachment as Zeifman and Cates were for it. A young phenomenon, Garrison was only thirty-two at the time he joined the staff.

Garrison, who later became the deputy minority counsel on the inquiry staff, was freed for the job when Spiro Agnew quit the vice-presidency. Garrison had been Agnew's special assistant, serving as a liaison with Congress.

Despite his youth, Garrison already could list among his credentials having been commonwealth attorney for his native city of Roanoke, associate minority counsel on the Judiciary Committee, and Agnew's assistant.

Garrison was another eager beaver, a somewhat haughty person who was more loyalist than lawyer.

FRANCIS O'BRIEN was more like a surrogate son to Peter Rodino than he was the congressman's administrative assistant. With Doar, the three formed a triumvirate, plotting moves in the impeachment inquiry by themselves, often with no outside advice except for that given by secret confidants.

At thirty-one, O'Brien was hired from the staff of New York Mayor John V. Lindsay, where O'Brien had headed a staff handling relations with the black community.

A fast-talker with a New York accent, O'Brien's primary job during impeachment developed into that of a press secretary for the impeachment inquiry. He was a bachelor.

The President's Counsel:

JAMES ST. CLAIR had sat beside Joseph Welch when he defended the U.S. Army against Senator Joseph McCarthy's charges. During televised hearings in 1954, Welch destroyed McCarthy politically. Welch had brought St. Clair with him from his prestigious Boston firm to help out in the hearings.

St. Clair, who had returned to the firm of Hale and Dorr, was approached in 1973 by Archibald Cox, then the special prosecutor looking into Watergate. St. Clair was a Republican and Cox wanted a staff prosecutor who had a GOP background and could lend the prosecution force a bipartisan tone. St. Clair turned him down because he thought it would tie him up too long.

St. Clair had a reputation as one of the best trial lawyers in the business. He conducted Nixon's defense just as he would have an ordinary court trial, stalling, withholding damaging evidence as long as he could, and attempting to narrow the focus of the charges against the president.

At the same time, however, St. Clair took the view that impeachment was essentially a political process.

St. Clair, fifty-three, had received his education at the University of Illinois and Harvard Law. He was a thorough lawyer and, like Doar, a good researcher. His forte was thought to be in courtroom finagling.

As were Doar and Jenner, St. Clair reportedly had been on a White House list of possible replacements for Cox as special prosecutor after the "Saturday Night Massacre" forced the House to kick off the impeachment proceeding.

Although St. Clair was a registered Republican and would defend Nixon, much of his reputation was built around liberal causes. He had defended William Sloane Coffin, the Yale chaplain tried on charges stemming from antiwar demonstrations in 1968. Four years after the Army-McCarthy hearings, St. Clair had defended a Harvard professor who refused to name alleged Communist sympathizers on the faculty.

St. Clair took over the defense of Nixon at the beginning of 1974, believing in the president's innocence while proclaiming that it was his job to defend the office of the presidency, not its occupant.

But St. Clair had come to Nixon's attention because of another client he had been retained by that fall—Charles Colson, Nixon's special counsel. Although St. Clair wound up doing almost no work for Colson, he had been retained by Colson because Colson faced the possibility of being indicted in the Watergate case.

There were twenty-five members of the House Judiciary committee in addition to those listed above—fifteen other Democrats and ten other Republicans.

In addition to the 6 key staff members, there were 101 persons who worked on the impeachment inquiry. Five were investigators, borrowed from the General Accounting Office. Forty-three were lawyers. Four of the lawyers were black, 3 were women.

The average age of the lawyers was thirty-three, slightly older on the GOP staff—thirty-six—than on the Democratic staff—thirty-two. Jenner was the oldest at sixty-six; the youngest—two of them—were twenty-five.

Three other people played key roles in the impeachment, although far behind the scenes. They had no official status and their relationship with Rodino and the staff was never made public, primarily because their associations were anti-Nixon, were embarrassing, or would damage the credibility of an impartial impeachment inquiry.

The three were: Burke Marshall, Doar's superior at Justice, a long-time Kennedy man and Doar's confidant during the inquiry; Clark Clifford, a powerful Washington lawyer who had been President Johnson's defense secretary and who was frequently consulted by Zeifman; and Bernard Hellring, a Newark lawyer and long-time Rodino confidant who spoke to Rodino for hours each day.

CHAPTER II

Prelude

Emanuel Celler had been chairman of the Judiciary Committee for twenty years before he was unseated in the 1972 primary in Brooklyn. He had been one of the old school of autocratic chairmen in the House of Representatives, wielding all the power himself, delegating it only when and where it suited him. No one grew tall in his shadow.

Celler had been beaten by a political unknown within his own party. Rodino faced the same likelihood in his own hometown of Newark, N.J.

Rodino's Tenth District was 52 percent black. Most of the whites were from ethnic backgrounds, including Italian-Americans like Rodino. Rodino had squeaked through in the Democratic primary, defeating two black opponents. He was aided tremendously when two blacks ran against him, thus splitting the black opposition. He got a plurality that time, but there was no promise he would the next time.

So, early in 1973 Rodino was still frightened that he might be serving his last term. Not only had a black already announced he would oppose him next time around, another Italian also had announced he'd run. They were causing Rodino all sorts of headaches.

The black, the Black Muslim playwright Imamu Amiri Baraka (LeRoi Jones), was making headway toward polarizing the blacks against Rodino. Anthony J. Imperiale was chaining himself to fences, getting national news coverage for his charges that Rodino was avoiding

Newark housing problems. He was sponsoring Michael Giordano to challenge Rodino's seat. For several weeks, Rodino was even afraid to make his usual trips home because of the political brickbats he would face.

Since the courts had ordered redistricting in New Jersey, Rodino thought his only chance of being reelected lay in getting his district redrawn so he would have only part of Newark itself, with the rest of the district composed of white suburban areas.

But the American Civil Liberties Union and other liberal organizations were challenging the tactic because they felt Newark, being 52 percent black, should have a black representative in Congress.

Jerome Zeifman, Rodino's chief counsel, had strong ties to the ACLU and other liberal groups. So Rodino instructed Zeifman to seek out the ACLU director, Charles Morgan, impress upon him Rodino's good qualities and get him to soften his opposition to Rodino's redistricting ploys.

When Zeifman and Morgan had lunch together in March 1973, Morgan insisted upon talking about impeachment. He had been retained by the Democratic State Chairmen, a subgroup of the Democratic National Committee that had an employee in the national committee headquarters at the time of the Watergate break-in. That group's phone was among the telephones bugged and there were press reports that some of the Watergate bugging devices had picked up conversations about arrangements for sexual companions for visiting state chairmen. Morgan had sought to intercede in the original Watergate seven trial in January as a lawyer for the state chairmen.

While Zeifman tried to talk to Morgan about Rodino's virtues, Morgan insisted on telling Zeifman about his suspicions that Watergate was being covered up by the Justice Department's prosecutors and that it should lead to impeachment proceedings against Nixon.

Not long before that, Rodino and Zeifman had had another clue of revelations to come when they received an unexpected visit from Richard Kleindienst, then attorney general.

About the most urgent issue the Judiciary Committee faced early in 1973 was what to do about restructuring or eliminating the Law Enforcement Assistance Administration (LEAA), the government agency that parceled out federal funds to state and local law enforcement agencies for various police projects.

Kleindienst sought the appointment to discuss the upcoming LEAA hearings and Rodino, Zeifman, and Kleindienst met in Rodino's office in February.

When the three sat down, Kleindienst asked if Rodino would agree to give the administration two more weeks before its witnesses had to come to the Hill to testify on the LEAA legislation. The committee had been considering postponing the hearings, so Rodino happily acceded to Kleindienst's request. The exchange, plus discussion of a few other matters of mutual interest, took only a few minutes. Rodino then asked Kleindienst how he was getting along as attorney general.

Kleindienst replied, "Let me tell you something, Pete. You have no idea what I'm going through, because every Friday when I come home from the office, I tell my wife, 'Darling, we got through another week without getting indicted.'

"Let me tell you something, Pete. If I can get out of this mess with my skin intact, I don't care if I ever practice law again. I'd be happy to go back to Phoenix and pump gas if I could do it with my skin intact."

Rodino took the comment as a joke and laughed. Kleindienst laughed and so did Zeifman. But after Kleindienst departed, Zeifman said to Rodino, "Jesus Christ, do you know that was the attorney general of the United States? And you know, I know he meant that."

Zeifman interpreted Kleindienst's remark as an attempt to give Rodino a message. Rodino never considered the remark as anything other than a joke.

A few other approaches were made to Rodino by lawyers and citizens groups that spring, all interested in impeachment. Rodino dismissed them all as overly eager.

But Zeifman and Frank Polk, the chief Republican counsel on the committee, had served opposite one another for several years and had a close working relationship despite their partisan differences.

They began discussing the possibility of impeachment as spring began. They agreed that perhaps the talk of impeachment was not all that premature and that it was up to them to get the committee prepared.

The pressure of time and other duties prevented much headway in their research, until Congress recessed for ten days at Easter. Zeifman checked out some books from the committee storerooms in the basement of the Rayburn House Office Building and looked first at the material the committee had gathered three years earlier when it considered Gerald R. Ford's proposal that the House impeach Supreme Court Justice William O. Douglas.

While Zeifman read, Nixon's counsel, John Dean, whose discussions with Justice Department prosecutors were then the subject of several leaks, issued a prophetic press release in Washington. ''. . . Some may hope or think that I will become a scapegoat in the Watergate case. Anyone who believes this does not know me, know the true facts [*sic*] nor understand our system of government.''

The same day, Richard Kleindienst disqualified himself from further involvement in Watergate because he had decided, after getting briefings on the progress of his department's investigations of the case, that too many of the persons mentioned in connection with Watergate were personal or professional friends.

During the spring of 1973, Congress went about its routine legislative duties while Nixon's three-month-old second administration showed its first signs of crumbling. Revelations of new Watergate details were like air rushing into a balloon. The balloon was growing larger.

By late April, the Ellsberg trial was under way in Los Angeles.

John Dean had known about both the Ellsberg and Watergate break-ins. For two weeks, he had been talking to Justice Department prosecutors looking into Watergate.

On April 26, Jeb Magruder resigned because his Watergate involvement was embarrassing the Commerce Department where he worked and had ruined his chances for confirmation to a higher post he was in line for. His resignation was the first trickle in what became a flood of resignations by Nixon loyalists.

The following day in Los Angeles, Judge W. Matthew Byrne, Jr., presiding over Ellsberg's trial on the documents charge, disclosed evidence obtained by the Justice Department investigators. The evidence showed that E. Howard Hunt and G. Gordon Liddy, already convicted for the Watergate break-in, also had directed the burglary of Lewis Fielding's office.

The same day, L. Patrick Gray III, filling in as FBI chief since the death of J. Edgar Hoover the previous May, announced his resignation. He resigned the day after news stories disclosed he had destroyed some fake documents that Hunt had created for use in the 1972 campaign. Gray had destroyed the material on orders from Dean and Nixon's chief domestic adviser, John Ehrlichman. In his resignation statement, Gray cited the embarrassment those allegations caused the bureau.

Nixon spent the weekend at the presidential retreat at Camp David in the Catoctin Mountains of Maryland. He was still there on Monday when his press secretary, Ron Ziegler, mounted a podium in the White House press room.

He announced that Attorney General Richard Kleindienst, Nixon's chief of staff, H. R. "Bob" Haldeman, and Ehrlichman had resigned. In their resignation letters, Haldeman said his implication in Watergate was diverting too much of his attention, and Ehrlichman cited the embarrassment his alleged involvement was causing the Nixon administration. In reality, the resignations were designed to take the heat off Nixon.

John Dean had been fired, Ziegler said, and he added that Nixon would deliver a televised address that evening.

The stunning announcement was carried, accompanied by attention-getting bells, on the wires of Associated Press and United Press International. A teletype ticker of each service was located in the Speaker's Lobby of the House of Representatives, a gathering place for members just off the floor.

Representative John Moss (D-Calif.), an irascible man who had few friends because of his overbearing manner, read the report on the tickers. Like other members of the House, Moss had been worried and enraged by the revelations of White House–connected wrong-doing that had been tumbling out during the past several months.

Now the Watergate case appeared to have reached the highest levels of the White House, only one step short of the president himself. There was a growing likelihood Nixon was involved. If so, Moss reasoned, it was a case for the House to consider, and the House was not prepared.

Angered, Moss sought out Speaker Carl Albert to urge him to get some sort of committee inquiry started.

Albert gave no indication of what he would do. Moss got the clear impression the always reticent Albert wouldn't do anything. So Moss wrote a petition calling for creation of an impeachment committee and posted it in the members' cloakrooms. The petitions posted there usually were ones to discharge a bill from a committee over the objections of the panel's chairman. As such, their secrecy was sacrosanct.

Representative Bella Abzug (D-N.Y.), though unwelcomed by him, joined Moss in the effort. But the initial reaction from other House members was lukewarm. Up to that time, few congressmen could be found who would even pronounce the word "impeach" in public, much less give any clue that they favored it or anything leading to it.

Soon after the Moss petition was posted, Democratic Leader Thomas P. "Tip" O'Neill was asked about the still little-known Moss effort. Impeachment talk was premature, he said, although "the time could come when such a committee should be set up."

Rodino was approached by colleagues who tried to engage him in casual conversation about impeachment, but Rodino also dismissed the talk as premature. It was almost as if talking about it would make it a reality.

Other members discussed the possibility of having a special House committee formed to study the impeachment matter.

Suddenly, impeachment had become something Congress had to think about even if it didn't intend to do anything.

After the initial crescendo, however, the sounds of impeachment died. Moss continued gathering signatures on his petition but would not reveal how many he had. He didn't have many.

The Congressional Research Service of the Library of Congress received at least fifty queries from members during the first week after the April 30 resignations bombshell, all asking for impeachment background. But the members did it quietly and the service would not reveal who made the inquiries.

Actions occurring on other fronts kept alive the question of President Nixon's survivability.

Bud Krogh, the director of the original plumbers group, and minor figures who had a more tenuous connection with Watergate—David Young, Gordon Strachan, Robert Odle, and Kenneth Rietz—added their names to the administration's resignation rolls in early May.

On May 1, with only five senators present, the Senate decided by voice vote to ask Nixon to appoint a special prosecutor from outside government to investigate Watergate. The following day, several members of the Senate Judiciary Committee announced they would hold up Nixon's appointment of Elliot Richardson to replace Richard Kleindienst as attorney general until Richardson, at the time the acting attorney general, appointed a special prosecutor.

On May 18, Richardson named Archibald Cox and gave his guarantee the prosecutor would be independent of executive branch controls. Richardson then was confirmed as attorney general.

Less than six months later, the relationship of the appointment of a special prosecutor to Richardson's confirmation would play a key role in getting impeachment off the ground.

In mid-May, the Senate Watergate Committee opened its first round of nationally televised hearings. Within a week, Nixon issued a four-thousand word explanation of Watergate, acknowledging that he had formed the plumbers unit in the aftermath of the Pentagon Papers disclosure and that there had been a White House cover-up of Watergate. But he had no part in that cover-up, he said.

Representative Paul N. "Pete" McCloskey, a California Republican who had challenged Nixon's renomination the previous year because of the Vietnam war, invited his colleagues to join him on the House floor on June 6 in a special discussion of Nixon's statement, saying it raised such serious constitutional questions that it justified a discussion of impeachment.

Nixon supporters engaged in parliamentary maneuvering to prevent the special discussion by McCloskey then, but it was held the following week, with eleven members participating. None called for impeachment. Reticence on impeachment wasn't confined to Rodino and the House leadership.

During the late spring and early summer, leaks from the Senate Watergate Committee staff conducting interviews of prospective witnesses, leaks from grand jury proceedings and announcements of pending indictments kept the Watergate story on front pages even when the Senate committee's hearings faltered.

Nixon already was denying publicly that he would resign and constantly was denying his knowledge of, or complicity in, the Watergate break-in and its cover-up.

Opinion polls taken on an almost weekly basis were showing a steady erosion of Nixon's popularity and of public trust in him. The balloon grew larger. The House averted its eyes.

The last week of June was dominated by John Dean, who had been granted immunity by the Senate Watergate Committee to tell what he knew of the Watergate cover-up. He became the first witness to implicate Nixon in the cover-up, recalling dates and events in such detail he cast doubts on Nixon's innocence even in the minds of some of the president's supporters.

Jerry Zeifman and Frank Polk watched the televised hearings that week with special interest. Both had worked with Dean when he held the job on the Judiciary Committee Polk now held.

Zeifman told Polk that as far as he was concerned, Dean's testimony was the clincher. Nixon must have known of the cover-up, he concluded. He discussed his conclusion with Polk because both knew from their knowledge of Dean that he was an extremely ambitious person. As such Dean always had made sure he got full credit for everything he did for any member of the committee, by letting them know every move he made. That also meant he wouldn't take the rap alone for any mistakes.

Zeifman and Polk knew of times when Dean had taken memos written by lower-ranking committee staffers and put his name on them if he liked them, before handing them on to the member.

Zeifman told Polk, "I know damn well that if Dean had his fingers in the cover-up, John's mentality is such that he made goddamn certain that the president would know that John Dean was covering his [Nixon's] ass. John Dean is not that loyal to anybody or anything other than his own career."

What Dean related at the hearing about his activities in Watergate fit Dean's pattern of sharing culpability. Zeifman and Polk also agreed that from an institutional point of view, when a previously anonymous person, as Dean had been, is suddenly snatched from low on the list of authority and thrust out front, it is because that person is going to have to take the blame. Dean was almost certainly telling the truth, they reasoned.

Zeifman told Gary Hymel, Majority Leader O'Neill's administrative assistant, of their conclusion and asked him to relay it to O'Neill, because Zeifman was convinced impeachment was imminent.

Rodino, with the concurrence of Edward Hutchinson, the committee's ranking Republican, reluctantly decided to allow the first tentative step toward impeachment. Polk and Zeifman would visit Archibald Cox to determine what Cox might be doing in relation to the president's involvement in Watergate. But the visit had to be made in utmost secrecy, Rodino warned.

Cox assured the two emissaries that he wasn't investigating Nixon, that his charge was to investigate criminal conduct. Anything related to the president would come out only as ancillary information connected with other investigations, he said. But he agreed it would be his responsibility to notify the House, "if I get a whiff of anything." At the time he had no such sign.

The same day, the pair from House Judiciary visited Sam Dash, the chief counsel for the Senate Watergate Committee. Dash reminded them that his committee was specifically barred—by an amendment introduced by Senator Edward M. Kennedy when the panel was established—from investigating the president. It had been formed only to look into abuses of campaign financing.

Dash also said that before any impeachment-related information the committee gathered could be turned over to the House, the Senate panel would have to have a request, in writing, from Rodino.

It was clear then, that no one was investigating presidential involvement in anything that could be construed as impeachable offenses. None of the probes going on addressed themselves to that issue. Unless an impeachment inquiry were conducted by the House, the chances were the public would never know, except by implication, about the president's guilt or innocence.

On July 16, shortly after the Zeifman and Polk conversations with Cox and Dash, one of the biggest bombshells of Watergate exploded.

Alexander Butterfield, who had been an aide in the White House, revealed at the Senate hearings that Nixon had tape-recorded conversations and telephone calls in his White House offices since early in 1971.

For the first time, although they could never be sure their contents would ever be disclosed, those interested in the Watergate case and possible presidential culpability knew that evidence probably existed to answer their nagging questions. The day after Butterfield's testimony, the Senate Watergate Committee asked Nixon for the tapes.

Shortly after that, on July 23, Nixon became the first president since Thomas Jefferson to be served with a subpoena. And Nixon got three. Two came from the Senate panel and the third from the special prosecutor. All asked for tapes and papers in connection with the Watergate case. The special prosecutor subpoena specified nine different tapes he wanted.

The walls of the Watergate balloon were becoming thinner.

Rodino didn't make a public reference to impeachment until a member of his committee, Robert Drinan (D-Mass.), forced him to.

Drinan was a Jesuit priest who had been dean of Boston College Law School before being elected to Congress in 1970. Wearing his clerical garb, Drinan introduced the first impeachment resolution against Richard Nixon on July 31, 1973. No one else joined him in it. Most of his colleagues were still deaf to the word "impeachment."

Drinan's impeachment resolution was simple. It contained no suggested articles. It said: "Resolved, that Richard M. Nixon, President of the United States, is impeached of high crimes and misdemeanors."

It had been revealed in early June that another minor White House figure, Tom Charles Huston, had drafted, and Nixon had signed, a plan for a secret White House intelligence unit to conduct illegal break-ins, postal surveillance, and other criminal activities. Then came the Butterfield revelation about the tapes.

Congress had been smarting all year from Nixon's refusal to spend various funds Congress had appropriated. Court cases consistently overturned Nixon's impoundments. Drinan was still rankled about the Vietnam war and seized upon the disclosure three years earlier that the United States had secretly been bombing Cambodia, at a time it was supposed to be a neutral nation.

All these actions were cited by Drinan to justify his impeachment resolution. A simple impeachment statement, without articles, was all that technically was needed for impeachment. Under House procedures, something of that magnitude was considered a "privileged resolution," which could be brought up on the floor at any time and a vote demanded.

The leadership had feared a move like Drinan's would result from the growing hostility in the House against Nixon. The leadership also feared the Republicans might bring up the motion to short-circuit the impeachment process.

To be sure the House didn't act precipitously by forcing an impeachment vote that would almost certainly be defeated overwhelmingly and thus damage the prospects for any future impeachment proceeding, the leadership had arranged that one of its number would be on the floor at all times. That member would counter with a motion to refer the matter to a committee.

Realistically, articles and the evidence to back them were necessary to sell a majority of the House on impeachment and to be able to prosecute the president in a Senate trial. Drinan knew that, too, and said he just wanted hearings on his resolution.

So when Drinan introduced his resolution, it was quickly referred to the Judiciary Committee. Rodino viewed the Drinan bill as an outgrowth of his pique over Vietnam and was willing to ignore it. But Rodino was inundated with so many press queries, that the next day he and Zeifman fashioned his first press release on impeachment, concluding:

At this time, no formal action on the Drinan resolution is scheduled. Removal from office of the president, or any other federal official, is an extraordinary remedy. Extraordinary remedies are applied only under extraordinary circumstances. As legal historians have noted, impeachment must be viewed as "a sword of Goliath" which ought not be brandished lightly. As a result, only the most careful, the most sensitive, and the most thoughtful deliberation will precede any action taken by the Committee on Judiciary.

The press release was correctly interpreted to mean that Rodino would sit on the resolution.

Zeifman had been collecting all of the public material coming out of the Senate Watergate hearings and the published reports about the special prosecutor's investigation. He had finished compiling impeachment precedents and was ready to have them published in one of those dull beige-bound paperback books Congress prints as official documents.

But Rodino wouldn't let him publish it. He feared that the mere publication would be construed as an attack on Nixon. It wasn't that Rodino wanted to protect Nixon. He actually disliked him. Nixon had slighted Rodino, a proud man, at a White House event honoring a visiting Italian dignitary when Nixon gave a speech mentioning distinguished Italian-Americans present, including Senator John Pastore (D-R.I.), and finished without mentioning Rodino's name. But that slight wasn't enough to push him into anything approaching an impeachment posture.

Nonetheless, Drinan's resolution put "impeachment" on official paper. That act seemed to bring the subject closer to reality. Rodino decided he had better do some reading. He chose Michael Benedict's *The Impeachment and Trial of Andrew Johnson* to read on the shuttle between Washington and Newark. Rodino was still an obscure congressman then, but he blanched when a seatmate saw the title and remarked, "Oh, that's quite interesting, to be reading that at this time." Rodino had carried the book aboard in a large brown envelope with his name in the corner. He moved his hand to cover the name, lest the man connect him with imminent impeachment proceedings. Rodino replaced the book jacket with plain brown paper after that.

Rodino's hopes that he could avoid an impeachment investigation received a blow when he read the *Wall Street Journal* the day before he and the rest of Congress were to leave on a month-long vacation.

The newspaper revealed on August 6 that a federal prosecutor was investigating Vice President Spiro Agnew on possible charges of bribery, extortion, and tax fraud.

Agnew had been Nixon's front man, making speeches around the country in defense of the embattled president. Nixon didn't have much more help than that. His own White House appeared to be under siege and his credibility almost nonexistent. And now Agnew himself was tainted.

Rodino and Francis O'Brien, his new administrative assistant, discussed the news just before Rodino left, and they decided that while it further damaged confidence in the administration, it would not be enough to spark impeachment.

Rodino spent the recess, as was his custom, dividing his time between his home in Newark and his house on the Atlantic Ocean shore near Long Branch, New Jersey. Every week or so he might make a trip to Washington to conduct some office work.

It was impossible to leave the woes of Watergate behind him, though, and the Agnew case was attracting more attention.

The Senate Watergate Committee had suspended its hearings with the congressional recess, but Watergate then moved into the courts where the committee and the special prosecutor's office pressed their subpoenas for Nixon's tapes. Nixon's lawyers were claiming the conversations were protected by the principle of executive privilege and the case bounced from court to court.

Nixon felt compelled to make a nationally televised speech in mid-August to defend himself against the accusations raised by the Senate Watergate hearings. A national poll showed presidential popularity had dropped to its lowest point in more than twenty years. It was in that mood that Nixon held his first press conference in five months, the first to be televised live in more than a year. It was held in the Rose Garden of the White House late in the afternoon of a steamy August 22.

Rodino was in Washington that day, so he and O'Brien watched the news conference on a television set in Rodino's office. Probably through wishful thinking more than anything else, Rodino expected that the news conference had been called because Nixon could no longer tolerate the national crisis that was still building. He would have to clear the air once and for all and end the nation's preoccupation with Watergate.

What Rodino saw at the news conference greatly disappointed him and gave him a sense of foreboding about impeachment he had not felt before. Nixon opened his news conference with a major announcement, that Secretary of State William Rogers was resigning, to be replaced by Henry Kissinger, his White House adviser on foreign affairs.

But almost the entire news conference was about Watergate, with this major foreign policy decision virtually ignored. Still Nixon "toughed it out," dodging direct answers to questions and twisting some previous revelations to reflect more flatteringly on him. He said, though, that he accepted full responsibility for Watergate. One of his questioners asked whether, if he were a member of Congress, he would favor impeachment proceedings against a president who had violated his oath to faithfully execute the laws by authorizing a burglary of the office of Daniel Ellsberg's psychiatrist?

Nixon replied that he would favor impeachment if the oath of office had been violated, but added that the Supreme Court had indicated in a previous decision that the president had inherent power to protect the national security, even if it had to be done with burglaries. He said that Presidents Johnson and Kennedy had authorized hundreds of "burglaries of this type" when they were in office and "there was no talk of impeachment. . . ."

It already had been fairly well established by that point that the Los Angeles burglary had little, if anything, to do with national security.

The news conference angered Rodino. Nixon could have reduced the building crisis and at the same time lifted the threat of impeachment proceedings off Rodino's shoulders.

Rodino's opinion and reaction were now being sought. He didn't know how to handle the attention. O'Brien had no experience with public relations either, other than by osmosis while serving on Lindsay's staff.

The evening after the Nixon news conference, radio station WINS in New York arranged to interview Rodino live on a talk show. Nervous and ill at ease, Rodino started off the live portion by saying, "Hello, Mr. Wins."

Rodino returned to Washington with the rest of Congress shortly after Labor Day to find the Watergate scandal still brewing, the revelations still mounting. Just the week before, U.S. District Court Judge John J. Sirica had ordered Nixon to give the special prosecutor's office the tapes it had subpoenaed.

As members filed into the House on September 5, they could read on the news tickers that a grand jury in Los Angeles had indicted four persons in connection with the Ellsberg break-in. No names were divulged, but almost immediately it became known that Nixon's number two man, John Ehrlichman, was one.

The following week, Nixon's lawyer, Charles Alan Wright, told an appeals court considering a Nixon appeal of Sirica's order that the president could not be forced by law to give up the tapes. Without deciding on Sirica's ruling, the higher court ordered the two disputing parties to compromise. They returned to the court a week later, however, and said they couldn't.

Two weeks later, Agnew went to the Capitol to formally request Speaker Carl Albert to have the House begin impeachment proceedings against him so he could clear his name. He contended that a vice-president, like the president, could not be indicted before he was impeached.

Rodino and the House leadership were called into the meeting, but would give Agnew no immediate answer. After hours of indecision the group decided, on the basis of research Zeifman had done following a tip that Agnew was about to make the move, that the House would reject Agnew's request and not begin the proceedings.

Their argument was based on a suspicion that because the statute of limitations was nearing on the charges against Agnew, he was trying to shift the matter to the House where he knew it would languish until the charges expired. He was gambling the House would vote against impeaching him, they judged, and they agreed it probably would. Zeifman argued that the matter especially should not be referred to the Judiciary Committee, because the mere acceptance of jurisdiction could cloud the central issue of whether a vice-president was indictable before he was impeached.

The haggling among House leaders, Rodino, and Judiciary staff members over what should have been simple issues raised by Agnew's request, consumed more than a hundred man-hours. That was the outfit that Nixon's men would later label a "lynch mob."

Although the House leadership had refused the bait, the Agnew question had given Rodino the excuse to authorize publication of "Impeachment—Selected Materials," which Zeifman had compiled earlier. With the addition of two vice-presidential impeachment precedents to justify it, the book was published.

On October 6, the Justice Department issued an opinion saying that a vice-president could be indicted before he was impeached, but a president had to be impeached first. Most constitutional scholars judged that a bunch of hogwash. Rodino agreed with the scholarly view, that both could be indicted first because no one was above the law.

On October 10, the day after Zeifman's book was distributed, Spiro T. Agnew resigned. He announced it in the afternoon after pleading "no contest" to a tax fraud charge against him in federal court in Baltimore.

Almost immediately, Secret Service agents took up positions outside the offices of Speaker Carl Albert, next in line of succession to the presidency.

It was the first time since President Kennedy was assassinated in 1963 that the Speaker of the House stood next in line. Albert didn't like it. There was no way that he would ever agree to be president.

Rodino didn't like it either. It dragged him back onto the national stage. He was on the Judiciary Committee in 1965 when, in the aftermath of the Kennedy assassination and Vice-President Lyndon Johnson's accession to the presidency, the panel drafted what became the Twenty-fifth Amendment changing the Constitution to allow for appointment of a vice-president whenever a vacancy occurred.

The amendment had not been tested. It was written primarily to cover the possibility that the president would be either physically or mentally unable to discharge his duties, and it arranged for the procedure a vice-president could use to take over until the president was able to resume his duties.

Only one brief part of the four-part amendment covered the Agnew case: "Whenever there is a vacancy in the office of the vice president, the president shall nominate a vice president who shall take office upon confirmation by a majority vote of both houses of Congress."

There was never any doubt the confirmation job would go to the Judiciary Committee. The staff got busy with research on the matter even before Nixon appointed Agnew's successor, House GOP Leader Gerald R. Ford, on October 12.

Most of the controversy concerning the vice-presidential confirmation proceedings centered around demands from liberal Democrats that Ford not be confirmed until the House determined whether Nixon was impeachable. Their argument was that a man who might be impeached should not be allowed to pick his own successor. That, however, was rejected by both the House and the Judiciary leadership. After a closed-door meeting on the Ford confirmation issue, Rodino emerged to tell reporters that confirmation was not likely before November, but that it would not be delayed, especially not for the still unlikely event of impeachment proceedings against Nixon.

Although Agnew's troubles momentarily diverted attention from him, Nixon's Watergate troubles were still climbing toward a crisis stage.

After the special prosecutor's office and the White House said on September 20 that they were unable to reach the compromise the appeals court had ordered, the court considered Sirica's ruling on its merits. The higher court upheld Sirica's order and directed Nixon on October 12 to turn over nine tapes to Sirica, so he could determine if Nixon's claims of executive privilege had any merit before the tapes were given to special Prosecutor Cox for presentation to the Watergate grand jury.

Talk then began about the likelihood that Nixon would take his case to the U.S. Supreme Court. Four days later, Melvin R. Laird, who had replaced John Ehrlichman as domestic adviser, told reporters he had advised Nixon that if the Supreme Court ruled against him and he defied the Supreme Court order, he would face impeachment. But Laird, a former member of the House Republican leadership, added that he also had predicted impeachment would fail.

Instead of taking the issue to the Supreme Court, however, Nixon fashioned a compromise during the weekend. He told Cox the compromise was his final offer and ordered Cox to stop his court action for Nixon tapes and papers.

Nixon's offer was that he would have summaries of the tapes prepared and then turn the tapes over to seventy-two-year-old Senator John Stennis (D-Miss.) to verify the summaries. After the summaries were verified, they would be turned over to Cox and the tapes returned to the White House and locked up.

Cox would not agree to the compromise. The stand-off became critical on October 19, because that was the last day the White House could appeal the appellate court's decision to the Supreme Court.

By the end of the day, the White House announced it would not appeal and revealed the compromise offer Nixon had relayed to Cox, accompanied by his order that Cox subpoena no more tapes.

Stennis appeared in his Senate office Saturday, October 20, and told reporters gathered there of the compromise and his understanding that he had "the absolute promise of a free hand." He seemed satisfied he could do the job without encumbrances. But Stennis's statements were premature.

Cox also took his case to the press that day, staging a rare Saturday afternoon news conference carried on live television from the National Press Club. He told the assembled reporters he would not accept Nixon's compromise. He was an officer of the court and a representative of the grand jury, he said, and as such felt it was his duty "to bring to the court's attention what seems to me to be noncompliance" with a lower court order. He would return to court and press the matter, he said, regardless of Nixon's orders to the contrary.

Elliot Richardson, the attorney general, had given the Senate assurances in his confirmation hearings—after getting the same assurances from Nixon—that the special prosecutor he chose would be totally independent. That meant he could take a case against the president to the Supreme Court if he chose. Richardson told that to Nixon. Nixon ordered him to fire Cox in light of Cox's afternoon news conference. Richardson said he could not do so without violating his promise to the Senate. Richardson offered his resignation as he was expected to do and Nixon accepted immediately.

William Ruckelshaus, Richardson's chief deputy, then became acting attorney general. He was ordered to fire Cox. He said he could not. He was fired.

Next in line was Robert Bork, the solicitor general. He was ordered to fire Cox. He did.

Washington had been alive with rumors all day. So the news media were primed and ready when at 8:25 P.M., White House Press Secretary Ron Ziegler mounted the podium in the press room and announced the details of what instantly became known as the "Saturday Night Massacre."

The wholesale exodus from the Nixon administration in the spring had caused a momentary ripple in impeachment sentiment. After the "Saturday Night Massacre," the world listened attentively when the word "impeachment" was spoken.

CHAPTER III

Massacre

Archibald Cox greeted his firing with a message: "Whether ours shall continue to be a government of laws and not of men is now for Congress and ultimately the American people" to decide.

On that Saturday night, October 20, 1973, it appeared Congress and the American people already had lost.

At the same time Ziegler was outlining the massacre to the press, including the firings, the abolition of the office of special prosecutor—although that decision was rescinded later—and that Nixon had ordered the special prosecutor's offices sealed, directives were sifting down from the White House to FBI agents. They were to go to Cox's ninth-floor headquarters in a downtown office building to "secure the offices."

It was Veterans' Day weekend and many Washingtonians had left town. Peter Rodino was at his beach house. Francis O'Brien was in his New York apartment. Jerry Zeifman was at his mountain home near Front Royal, Virginia.

The special prosecutor's headquarters were in chaos when the FBI agents arrived. Most of Cox's staff had gathered there that evening, and there was well-justified suspicion the FBI was there to confiscate the files and arrange for their disappearance.

But the FBI agents' orders were just to seal the offices to be sure nothing was removed. In any case, Cox's staff could not countermand the orders, no matter how strong their suspicions. No one knew his status or how to handle the situation. Staff members started making telephone calls seeking help and/or advice.

Philip Lacovara, one of Cox's chief aides, was one. Among those he called was Zeifman. Before Zeifman had left for the mountains that day, he and Lacovara had discussed what to do with the files in the special prosecutor's office if Cox were fired. Since neither man knew exactly what would happen after the firing, they reached no decision.

Normally a calm, quiet person, Lacovara was highly excited when he reached Zeifman late Saturday night. The operator told Zeifman she had an emergency call for him. Lacovara came on the line, fear in his voice. He said, ''I'm in the office of the special prosecutor. The FBI has just entered. And they're armed. This may be the end of the republic. You've gotta do something.''

Zeifman was an excitable person. He usually was intrigued by internecine political maneuvering, but he was panicked by Lacovara's call. He tried without success to reach House Speaker Carl Albert, Majority Leader Tip O'Neill, and Rodino. He got through to O'Brien and shouted that the FBI was going into the special prosecutor's offices at gunpoint to remove the files. ''Jesus, they're taking over the government,'' he said. O'Brien said he would try to get Rodino.

Zeifman tried to call Lacovara back but couldn't get through to him. He considered—but rejected as useless—driving back to Washington and marching into the special prosecutor's office, presenting himself as chief counsel of the Judiciary Committee and demanding the files not be removed. He didn't know at the time the FBI was there to prevent their removal.

Rodino was watching television that night when announcers broke in with bulletins about the firing of Cox. As Judiciary Committee chairman, Rodino's first thoughts were about the safety of the documents the special prosecutor's office had compiled and about replacing Cox, since several bills calling for an independent special prosecutor were before the committee.

When O'Brien got through to him and related Zeifman's urgent call and the concern about Cox's files, Rodino ordered O'Brien to contact congressional leaders for him so he could discuss what to do, especially about a new prosecutor.

Rodino called the special prosecutor's office, seeking Cox. Cox had remained at his home in suburban Virginia that evening, but Rodino got through to Henry Ruth, Cox's chief deputy, and told him he was going to "fire off a letter to the attorney general immediately, or the deputy attorney general or the acting attorney general, Bork, or whoever," about guaranteeing the security of the documents.

On Sunday, word came the FBI was not attempting to remove Cox's files. Nonetheless, Rodino ordered O'Brien and Zeifman back to Washington to prepare him a statement on impeachment and to draw up plans for how the committee should proceed from there. Although Rodino never made a conscious decision to initiate the process he had shunned for so long, his instructions assumed that impeachment proceedings were now a foregone conclusion.

When Rodino arrived in Washington Sunday evening, he gathered his staff and they drafted a letter to Acting Attorney General Robert Bork insisting that he take proper action to preserve the special prosecutor's files.

House Speaker Albert was not a strong leader. But the national reaction to the "Saturday Night Massacre" was overwhelming. Literally hundreds of thousands of telegrams and telephone calls were flooding into Washington, most of them against Nixon.

Albert called all of the key House Democrats who were in town to a meeting in his office on Monday morning.

Referral of impeachment to the Judiciary Committee was not automatic. Others in Congress already had been thinking about the matter and were pressing for the assignment to be given to some other committee or for establishment of a special one. The reasons given included a lack of confidence in Rodino's ability to handle something as big as impeachment and his ability to handle the Ford confirmation and impeachment at the same time.

As the meeting began, there was no discussion of whether an impeachment inquiry would be set up. The question was the forum—Judiciary or a select committee.

Albert argued against establishing a select committee. He had a special problem, he said. As Speaker, it would be his duty to choose the Democrats to serve on such a panel. Choosing them would put him in an untenable position. He would be choosing members of a committee that could be deciding, in effect, whether to make him president.

Rodino said Democrats on his committee had decided in a caucus the previous week that the Ford confirmation would come first in the event of an impeachment move. Albert agreed. Until Ford was confirmed, Albert was "a heart-beat away" from the presidency and he didn't like the situation.

Albert's brief speech became emotional. His only ambition in life, he said, was to serve as Speaker of the U.S. House of Representatives. He had achieved that goal, he had no other. He did not under any circumstances want to be president. Beyond his own personal problems, Albert said, the country would be leaderless if it had no vice-president and the president were consumed with a trial in the Senate.

Albert asked Rodino if he thought he could handle the Ford confirmation and then begin the impeachment probe. Rodino said he thought he could. It was a "Catch-22" for him. Rodino didn't have any great desire to handle impeachment, but he didn't want to give up any jurisdiction over it.

The discussion in Albert's office dragged on for three hours as the leaders agonized over every little nuance of undertaking an impeachment proceeding. They even agonized over what to call it, finally agreeing that they should soft-pedal the imminent action and not use any potentially incendiary words like "impeachment trial" or "impeachment hearings." Their decisions still had to be endorsed by the Democratic Steering and Policy Committee, set to meet the next morning. If that group agreed, Albert told Rodino, he would want Rodino to be ready with an announcement at the speaker's regular prenoon news conference the next day.

As Albert's meeting was going on, Representative Jerome Waldie was holding a news conference. A member of the Judiciary Committee since 1966 and candidate for the 1974 Democratic gubernatorial nomination in California, Waldie told reporters that when the congressional session resumed the next day, he would introduce an article of impeachment against Nixon.

Rodino called his staff together that evening to begin work on the statement for Albert's news conference. An old friend, Joseph Califano, a Washington lawyer, Lyndon Johnson crony, and fellow Italian-American, showed up at the office to help in the drafting.

Rodino feared that the American people didn't understand that his committee's activity was only the first step in a long procedure that might or might not lead to removing Nixon from office. The most his panel could do would be to recommend that Nixon be impeached and tried in the Senate. The wording ended up with only a reference to "preparation for impeachment proceedings."

The next morning, the nearly two dozen members of the Steering and Policy Committee agreed that Rodino's panel should begin preparations for an impeachment investigation.

Albert and Rodino went back to Albert's office and watched the farewell speech of former Attorney General Elliot Richardson, which was being carried on live television, as were most things dealing with the "massacre." As they watched, Richardson announced the content of the Saturday letters he and Nixon had exchanged, and Richardson delivered an emotional speech about the integrity of the governmental process.

Albert turned from the TV set and said Nixon had gone too far. He had tried to talk to Nixon several times to explain to him the hot water he was getting into, especially in his relations with Congress, and had been ignored, Albert said. Congress was just going to have to begin standing up to him, he said.

Rodino and Albert went to Albert's ceremonial office to hold his daily news conference. They announced the leadership decisions and Rodino read the statement he had so carefully prepared the night before.

As they finished, the bells rang throughout the House side of the Capitol announcing the start of the session. Reporters crowded the press gallery, spectators the visitors' galleries, and members the floor. Normally the beginning of a session was sparsely attended. That day more than 100 of the 435 members showed up.

As he had promised, Waldie walked up to the clerk's desk and deposited his six-page impeachment resolution. Albert, sitting in the speaker's chair, referred the resolution to the Judiciary Committee.

Seven other members of the House also introduced impeachment resolutions that day. They ranged in size and content from Waldie's six-page resolution to the sixteen-word resolutions of Representatives Ken Hechler (D-W. Va.) and Parren Mitchell (D-Md.): "Resolved, That Richard M. Nixon, President of the United States, is impeached of high crimes and misdemeanors." Other resolutions would follow.

It was widely reported at the time that there were more than two dozen impeachment resolutions introduced, but in reality there were only seven different ones introduced by a total of fourteen members. Plagiarizing by reintroducing the same resolution with different co-sponsors led to the inflated figure.

One of those who introduced a resolution was Representative Thomas L. Ashley (D-Ohio). His great-grandfather, James M. Ashley, had served the same Ohio district and was known as "the original impeacher" because of his repeated attempts to impeach President Andrew Johnson, in 1866 and 1867. In a speech on the House floor, Ashley said his and his great-grandfather's impeachment efforts differed because his ancestor's were political and unwarranted whereas efforts to unseat Nixon were based on a solid, legal foundation.

Others who introduced resolutions, and some of those who didn't, gave brief speeches at the beginning of the session to denounce Nixon's actions of the previous Saturday. A few members rose in support of Nixon. One, Dan Kuykendall (R-Tenn.), got to his feet and warned his colleagues "to go slow and not be part of a legislative lynch mob." To emphasize his point, he raised a hangman's noose high above his head "as a symbol of your action."

Nixon's Watergate lawyer, Charles Alan Wright, was in the U.S. District Court at the foot of Capitol Hill at the same hour, telling Judge John J. Sirica that Nixon had capitulated, that he would release the tapes the special prosecutor had subpoenaed.

J. Fred Buzhardt, the chief White House counsel, was on the Hill spreading the word to the Republican leadership. In a one-hour meeting, he outlined the president's compliance with the two-month-old court order.

Assistant GOP Leader Les Arends of Illinois happily told reporters, "The President no longer can be accused of impeachable offenses. He's wiped that out."

Arends was wrong. Nixon's compliance hadn't changed a thing. It came too late. A poll of all those who had introduced impeachment resolutions earlier in the day said so, members of the Judiciary Committee said so, and even the House Democratic leadership said so. Democratic Leader O'Neill conceded, however, that Nixon's compliance would dampen impeachment cries.

Among those saying it changed nothing was Rodino. His statement at the news conference earlier "still stands," he said, and the inquiry would begin.

Rodino called his committee staff members together in Jerry Zeifman's office that night to decide what to do next. He told them that despite any actions Nixon might take, the inquiry would proceed until there was a decision that impeachable offenses had or had not been committed. They shouldn't be misled by Nixon's decision to surrender the tapes, he said. The tapes did not comprise, nor respond to, the bases for all of the impeachment allegations. Archibald Cox had been fired and the Senate Watergate Committee had turned up a lot of questions, the answers to which would not be found on the tapes.

Rodino also urged staff members to be extremely careful in what they said, either privately or publicly. The impeachment of a president was an extremely serious matter, and the committee must not be caught responding to what might be mere public relations gimmicks by critics or supporters of Nixon. He said the public must never believe that Judiciary was moving precipitously into impeachment. The public must be convinced that impeachment, if it came, was voted fairly, carefully, thoughtfully.

The normally reticent Rodino had become more courageous since he was handed the Ford confirmation assignment. He had gotten used to being a national figure and he found he liked it.

At the lengthy Tuesday night meeting, Rodino and the staff reviewed some of the problems they would confront in impeachment. The primary problem was to dovetail that inquiry with the two other large assignments the committee had—the Ford confirmation and bills to establish a permanent and independent office of special prosecutor. It was decided the special prosecutor bills would be referred to the subcommittee headed by Rep. William Hungate (D-Mo.).

The Ford confirmation would be speeded up if possible. The impeachment matter would require extremely delicate handling, but some initial groundwork had to be laid.

Albert already had assured Rodino he could have whatever he needed in the way of staff, facilities and money to conduct an impeachment inquiry. The committee staff already was stretched thin, so Rodino had to begin making plans to hire more people on a temporary basis for the inquiry. Zeifman already was working on getting investigators from the General Accounting Office, Congress's investigative arm, and was lining up possible recruits from other congressional committees. But time was the big problem and some changes would have to be made in the rules under which the committee operated.

First, the rules required that no meeting of the committee could be held without forty-eight hours prior notice to all members. Unless that were eliminated, the committee would be severely hampered. The other problem was that each subpoena the committee wanted to issue had to be approved by a majority of committee members. Rodino envisioned a stack of subpoenas that would have to be issued for both the Ford and impeachment hearings. Rodino and the staff decided Rodino would seek to have the power vested in himself alone.

Rodino said he had talked with Edward Hutchinson, the ranking Republican on the committee, earlier that day and that Hutchinson had no objection to Rodino's having sole subpoena authority. Hutchinson would rather not bother with it anyhow.

Rodino said that one problem the committee had with impeachment was the same one it faced in confirming a vice-president. There were no precedents. Records were very poor about how the Johnson impeachment case progressed before it got to the House floor. The committee would be flying by the seat of its pants in both cases.

Some subgroup of the committee would have to be formed to make decisions about the initial stage of the inquiry, he decided. Rodino suggested that one might be formed of the chairmen and ranking Republicans on each of the seven subcommittees, plus Jack Brooks (D-Tex.), who was the third-ranking Democrat on the committee, but who did not head a subcommittee because he was in line to become chairman of the House Government Operations Committee when the chairman resigned the following year.

The Democratic half of the proposed ad hoc committee was set to meet behind closed doors the next day, so after the general staff meeting, Zeifman, O'Brien, and Rodino went to Rodino's office to draft the statement he expected to issue after the Democrats met. When the three got there, an aide told them the committee had received four hundred telegrams responding to Nixon's tape offer. They all said to impeach him anyhow.

When Rodino presented his outline to the top committee Democrats and later to all twenty-one Democrats the next day, there was no disagreement. He called in the reporters waiting outside the committee room and released his statement saying, "I have initiated a broadscale investigation to be conducted by an expanded staff that will be assembled immediately."

He emphasized that the committee would collect whatever material other congressional committees had relevant to impeachment and would not use any employees of other government agencies. The statement wound up with Rodino's refusal to cancel the inquiry due to Nixon's release of the tapes on Tuesday:

. . . The committee is charged with the responsibility of acting on the various resolutions of impeachment and to develop procedures to determine whether there is a reasonable basis for the charges brought in the House of Representatives that the President has committed high crimes and misdemeanors.

Two floors above the committee room, Republicans on the committee held their own caucus in Ed Hutchinson's office. They didn't like being shut out of the decision-making process and didn't care for some of the decisions the Democrats were making.

They agreed unanimously to oppose elimination of the forty-eight–hour notice rule and also the vesting of sole subpoena power in Rodino. But they didn't suggest Rodino share it with Hutchinson. Their position was that the full committee should vote on each subpoena, regardless of the time that would involve.

The decisions by the separate caucuses promised the partisan fight over impeachment that Rodino had feared all week. It would be fought the following Tuesday when the committee held its first full meeting since the post-massacre impeachment resolutions were introduced.

Frank Polk, the chief Republican counsel on the committee, usually sat in on the Republican caucuses. Zeifman sat in on the Democratic ones. They had made it a practice since the beginning of the year to keep each other informed of the other party's activities. Neither believed it was in the best interest of the committee to have the two sides act in ignorance of the other's positions.

They conferred about what each caucus had decided that day, and Zeifman reported to Rodino. Rodino feared the inquiry would get off to a partisan start, so he discussed first with Zeifman, and then O'Brien, the advisability of pressing for sole subpoena authority. They reached no conclusion.

At the same time, reporters had cornered Hutchinson near the House floor. He had been pushed by his people at the Republican caucus and now told reporters that he had discussed the impeachment proceedings with Rodino but had not said he was willing to have subpoena power vested solely in Rodino.

When Rodino walked by, reporters told him of the remark and asked his reaction. Rodino said that perhaps he should have a talk with Hutchinson. He went into the House chamber and sat down beside Hutchinson on the Republican side. Hutchinson told him about the GOP caucus demands for a sharing of the subpoena power. Otherwise, he said, there would be a partisan split the following Tuesday.

Rodino didn't know what to do. His Democrats now were adamant about having the power vested in Rodino alone. They didn't want to allow the Republicans any opportunity to obstruct the inquiry. Jack Brooks had led that argument.

The next day Zeifman arrived at his office to find a note saying Brooks wanted to see him immediately. Zeifman went to Brooks's office and was ushered in.

"Ziffman, sit down," Brooks said in his most imperious tone, deliberately mispronouncing Zeifman's name. "Let me tell you something. You'd better be straight with me because if you're not straight with me, I'll fuck you like you've never been fucked before."

Zeifman didn't know Brooks very well, and after seventeen years he knew his own position as a staff member in Congress. But Brooks's attitude incensed him and he shot back that "you can't fuck me because I'm prepared to walk out of this goddamned place any hour of the day."

He would be straight with Brooks, Zeifman told him, but only because that was his style.

Brooks smiled and offered Zeifman a cigar. Brooks told him he didn't like the plodding progress of the committee under Rodino's leadership. He sensed that he had a cohort in the impatient Zeifman. He did.

Adding to his concern was that morning's news. During the night President Nixon had placed American troops on an unexplained worldwide alert because of what he claimed were dangerous developments in the Middle East.

Brooks feared the president might be acting irrationally. He thought the Judiciary Committee was dragging its feet on impeachment and had to do something to challenge the president's apparent view that he had unlimited power.

The two men tried to figure out some initiative the committee could take that would be supported by the full committee. They decided that the least political charge against Nixon in the impeachment resolutions introduced earlier that week was the one charging Nixon with evasion of income taxes. Nixon couldn't claim any national security defense against that. They decided Rodino should send a courteous letter to the president, asking him to produce his income tax records for the past several years for the impeachment investigation. Zeifman and Brooks would have the letter typed and presented to Rodino for his signature.

They felt the move was harmless enough. Ford had willingly given the same committee his tax records for its confirmation hearings. It would be an affirmative step by the committee on impeachment.

Rodino refused to sign the letter when Zeifman handed it to him. At the time, Representative Wilbur Mills (D-Ark.), chairman of the House Ways and Means Committee, was looking into the tax charges and Rodino said he wanted to wait until Mills finished his investigation.

The same day, the seeds of a GOP offensive were sown when Representative Tom Railsback (R-Ill.) began criticizing Rodino and the committee Democrats publicly for making decisions without consulting the Republicans. He said the Republicans' primary concern was that "this so-called broadscale investigation could turn into a wholesale fishing expedition."

Representative Robert McClory (R-Ill.) chimed in with accusations that Rodino's decisions to date had been "arbitrary and partisan." It looked, he said, as if Rodino were "going to take over the role of special prosecutor and everything else. We don't need that right now." Other Republican members of the committee joined the chorus of criticism.

This was not the way Rodino had expected things to turn out. He really wanted to conduct the impeachment inquiry in as bipartisan and fair a manner as possible.

Renewed interest in impeachment that week had led newspapers and magazines to critique the impeachment of Andrew Johnson in 1868. What they found was what Rodino had found in his own reading. He did not want to go down in history as one who led another unfair political fight to oust a president from office.

Even worse than that, from Rodino's standpoint, news media profiles about him kept bringing up possible associations with organized crime and his connections with former New Jersey politicians then serving time in jail on extortion and other charges. Most pointed out that Rodino had emerged clean from a close inspection, but these constant sinister references to innocent past associations were getting him down.

Rodino and others suspected that the impetus for those reports had come from the White House. It didn't help Rodino's mood any when the staff that Archibald Cox left behind and Assistant Attorney General Henry Petersen together filed a motion in U.S. District Court asking the court to take possession of the special prosecutor's files and not give them to anyone else. Rodino had been considering asking for those files himself.

And members of Rodino's committee began squabbling over who would serve on a subgroup, such as a subcommittee, handling the initial impeachment matters. The decisions to that point had been little more than housekeeping matters, but big decisions would have to be made soon.

The week was proving a disaster. In an effort to at least get the Republicans off his back, Rodino instructed Zeifman to draw up a proposal for him to present to his Democrats the following week. The proposal would have him share subpoena power with Hutchinson. Tired and frustrated, Rodino left for Newark on Friday to spend his usual weekend back home in his district.

The Republicans kept up their attack on the Democrats for shared authority when Congress resumed the following Monday. House Republicans decided in a caucus that since a just-completed FBI report found Gerald Ford about as clean as any politician could be, there was no reason he couldn't be confirmed almost immediately.

Tom Railsback emerged from the caucus to raise the spectre of a witch hunt by the Democrats and warn that "they're going to have a fight on their hands" if the Nixon impeachment investigation and Ford confirmation were not done judiciously and fairly.

Democrats on the committee also caucused, and they convinced Rodino that he didn't have to share the subpoena power with Hutchinson, that the Republicans were just lining up ways they could obstruct the impeachment inquiry. Democrats had the votes to win, why not use them? Jack Brooks insisted that the Democrats not give in to the Republicans.

Much of the rest of Rodino's day was spent with his staff members working out a lengthy opening statement for the next day's committee session, the first since the impeachment resolutions were filed. The statement said Rodino had received 27,634 letters and wires since the resolutions, all urging some action on impeachment. That didn't count thousands of other wires and letters that had not been opened and counted.

Referring to Nixon's order of the previous week, putting American troops on worldwide alert, and the public's cynical response to it, Rodino's statement said:

> The legitimacy of executive authority has not undergone this type of stress since the Civil War. And last week we were given an awful glimpse of what it means when the president's credibility is questioned, and what it could mean if his authority to lead were in doubt with our allies and our adversaries.
>
> This crisis of executive authority is embodied in the legislation and resolutions the Speaker has referred to us. Personally, I do not believe this crisis in authority can be permitted to continue. . . . It is our responsibility to make determinations that will contribute to the stabilization of government.

Rodino also said the inquiry would seek information already gathered by other congressional committees "before attempting to generate new material." He said Zeifman was preparing a "carefully drawn resolution" that would be presented to the entire House "to strictly define the subpoena authorities of this committee respecting these investigations" so there would be no questions about scrupulous adherence to "constitutional and procedural parameters."

Rodino also responded to Railsback's charges, stating his own aversion to a "witch hunt."

The sole subpoena authority he was seeking that day, he said, would not be widely exercised. "If any occasion arises where I feel the need to use this authority, I will of course consult fully with Mr. Hutchinson," he added, to mollify GOP objections.

By a vote of 21–17, the exact breakdown of Democrats and Republicans, respectively, the committee turned down Republican Railsback's amendment requiring the subpoena power to be shared with Hutchinson. By the same margin the panel then voted to invest in Rodino the sole subpoena authority.

But a Republican amendment to compromise on elimination of the forty-eight–hour rule for prior notice of a committee session and make it twenty-four hours instead was adopted by the committee.

The vote on subpoena power had been the first concerning impeachment, however, and the precise partisan split bode ill for the bipartisanship Rodino had promised for the inquiry.

Throughout November, the House Judiciary Committee was concerned with passing bills to create an independent office of special prosecutor, extend the life of the Watergate grand jury, and confirm Gerald Ford to be vice-president.

The impeachment questions foremost in Rodino's mind during that month were two—how to handle the inquiry on a procedural basis and whom to hire as a special counsel.

Although the committee was preoccupied with the Ford confirmation during November, it was under pressure to take action on impeachment. Nothing major could be done about impeachment until the Ford matter was disposed of, but some of the rudimentary decisions could be made.

They included forming a basic staff to gather impeachment-related material and research the procedural aspects of impeachment, determining whether the inquiry would be handled by an augmented committee staff or an entirely separate and independent one, and then deciding what type and how many people would be appointed to it and where they would work. Decisions also would have to be made on some outline of an inquiry schedule.

All that was housekeeping, but the press was hungry for news about impeachment and the fifteen most senior committee members, whom Rodino had chosen to rely on for those initial-stage decisions, got to stand in front of the television cameras almost daily to announce what had been discussed.

The committee had an unusually large number of freshmen—eleven—and sophomores—six. Many had been elected by narrow margins and feared they might lose their reelection bids in 1974. Exposure on impeachment, therefore, was extremely important to them.

As the committee approached the point where it would finish with the Ford confirmation and turn its full-time attention to impeachment, the junior Democrats became increasingly aware they were being left out of impeachment. The junior Republicans didn't find it in their favor to be associated with impeachment, so they didn't mind being left out.

Rodino had grown comfortable with using the fifteen-man ad hoc arrangement. He could share responsibility with fourteen others; it was less likely that mistakes would be made by a group of eight Democrats and seven Republicans. He proposed to make that the official group for making all future preliminary decisions for the committee. The group would make the housekeeping decisions by itself and work out the proposals the full committee would have to act upon.

That idea landed on the junior Democratic members like a bomb and threatened to open yet another rift in the committee before it got well into impeachment. The previous rifts had been Republicans versus Democrats, now Rodino had a Democratic squabble on his hands. How the matter would be handled became the most burning issue in the committee even while it was still immersed in the Ford confirmation hearings. Committee members were anxious to know which of them would be involved in impeachment more than the others.

As soon as the committee sent the Ford nomination to the full House in early December, the members began to focus even more on impeachment.

Zeifman prodded Rodino. His staff had been gathering all the public material relevant to impeachment, but he argued that the inquiry should soon begin taking testimony from witnesses. Since House rules required that committee members be allowed to question all witnesses, he felt it would be necessary to have the questioning done at a subcommittee level, rather than opening the questioning to thirty-eight members who would not have time to question witnesses thoroughly and ask logical follow-up questions.

Rodino agreed, but would not take the responsibility for selecting the members who would serve on the subcommittee. He wanted to use his ad hoc group, but feared the junior members' animosities toward that format might become uncontrollable.

Some of the more temperamental junior Democrats on the committee—Charles Rangel of New York, Jerry Waldie of California, Robert Drinan of Massachusetts, Elizabeth Holtzman of New York, John Seiberling of Ohio, and Ed Mezvinsky of Iowa—rebelled. They wanted a role. Rodino and Zeifman acting together were unable to calm them.

Rodino put off a decision even longer, depressed at the shallowness he had witnessed in his members on a subject of vast national importance. But top committee staff people began pressing Rodino to bite the bullet and name a subcommittee. They felt that time was ripe and their time was being wasted.

Rodino had grown stronger, had grown inured to criticism, but still wasn't strong enough to exercise his prerogatives as chairman. He hadn't even chosen a special counsel.

Rodino's greatest strength was becoming his greatest weakness—his willingness to confer and consult with everyone ad nauseum, to consider every possible alternative for so long that eventually there was no need for decisions because events had taken over and dictated things themselves.

At a Democratic caucus, Holtzman, the Brooklyn Democrat who had ousted the committee's former chairman, Emanuel Celler, fought for the committee to be divided into seven task forces, each with its own staff and assigned "a piece of Nixon" to investigate. Each would hold its own public hearings. Rodino finally rejected that on grounds the panel wasn't even close to deciding what charges to look into, much less to assign tasks to subcommittees. And all those task forces would turn the inquiry into a seven-ring circus, he felt.

Republican Railsback pressed for a nine-member ad hoc advisory group, and GOP committee members decided in a mid-December caucus to back that plan. But by that time Rodino had decided it wasn't going to be feasible to break the committee into formal subgroups.

Rodino was still determined to mollify the Republicans, however, so he finally decided he would share as much responsibility as possible without letting control of the process out of his hands. He knew that if the impeachment was going to be accepted by the people, it could not be sent to the House floor on a party-line committee vote of twenty-one Democrats against seventeen Republicans.

Giving the Republicans as much chance to participate as he could would help cultivate the votes he wouldn't go to an impeachment vote without. He was going to let everyone speak his or her piece.

But knowing what to do and how to do it were two different matters. His only choice seemed to be to abandon the idea of a subpanel. He would rely on unofficial consultations with his ad hoc advisory group, while letting the full committee participate in all impeachment proceedings, despite the many problems that would entail. He decided, then, there would be no official subgroup.

By the end of 1973, Rodino's decision-making process thus evolved into discussing matters first with Jerry Zeifman and/or Francis O'Brien; then the Democratic subcommittee chairmen; then his ad hoc advisory group; then the entire Democratic side of the committee; and, finally, the entire committee.

That way Rodino's proposals gained acceptance or were refined as they went up the ladder. The method also tended to head off any challenges to his decisions or his authority. He used the same method to find a special counsel for the impeachment inquiry.

By early November, Zeifman had gathered a tiny staff, borrowing five investigators from the General Accounting Office, plus about a dozen persons from other committees on Capitol Hill. In selecting the basic staff, Zeifman had ruled out anyone from the executive branch, including the FBI, and anyone who worked for a law firm that represented any Watergate defendants. He felt that eliminated most Washington law firms and many in New York.

Zeifman had a list of more than two dozen persons he would like to hire for the impeachment inquiry and had tagged several members of the committee staff to work on it. But he was reluctant to hire many people before a decision had been made on whom they would work for—the special counsel. And Zeifman couldn't put his committee staff selections to work on impeachment because they were involved at the time on the Ford confirmation hearings.

Rodino had decided by early November that, as Senator Sam Ervin had done with the Senate Watergate Committee—a special panel set up to look into campaign financing violations—he would go outside standing committees for his impeachment staff. He reasoned that the committee should be as nonpartisan in appearance as in fact. If he used existing Judiciary Committee staff, the inquiry would appear to be a partisan undertaking, since there existed a Democratic and a Republican staff, both used to making political decisions.

During the fall, a consensus developed in Democratic caucuses in favor of a ''big name'' for special counsel, someone widely respected like Archibald Cox. Francis O'Brien had the task of finding the ''big name.'' O'Brien tended to act and dress older than his age or politics. He often wore three-piece, pin-striped wool suits, even in the summer. Well-groomed with black horn-rimmed glasses, his demeanor and looks made him appear older than his thirty-two years. He was also glib, and it was that glibness and adroitness under pressure that helped catapult him into his very influential job.

But O'Brien still was young, had not had that much experience in Washington and was not a lawyer, so he could count all the ''big name'' lawyers he had ever heard of on one hand. Yet he had to choose one who would conduct an inquiry into the impeachment of the president of the United States.

He didn't know where to begin. Obviously, his first task was to collect recommendations. Rodino told him to start by writing letters over the chairman's signature to every law school in the country asking the deans for suggestions. O'Brien also asked other members of Congress, committee staffers, and even reporters for recommendations.

Since the person selected would direct the daily conduct of the inquiry and would have a great deal of influence on how it turned out, Rodino said he was very concerned the final choice be "objective, professional, have all the integrity in the world, have courage, [be] the kind of person who has some experience in this direction and preferably, I hope he might be an independent Republican." Rodino added that the special counsel should not have a political reputation and should be old enough that he couldn't trade on an impeachment reputation for political advantage, like a district attorney might after winning a big case. But given that, the candidate should not be so old that he couldn't put in the long, hard hours that would be required. Rodino's last demand was that O'Brien not consider anyone who had made a public statement on impeachment one way or the other.

O'Brien figured he also should add the criteria of being able to get along with Congress and being willing to take a back seat and let the members receive the glory. The person also had to be able to get along with Rodino, and O'Brien wasn't sure what type of person that would be.

Initial checks on the names were made by calling law professors and judges in the areas where the candidates worked. Clark Clifford advised Zeifman on some of the names.

A key person in the selection process was an old friend of Rodino's from Newark, a fellow attorney named Bernard Hellring, who had close connections with Harvard Law School. Hellring's name had never been associated with Rodino's in the press, so he was an ideal person to make contacts on a subject as sensitive as choosing a special counsel for impeachment.

Hellring, fifty-seven, had been a confidant of Rodino's throughout his congressional career. Rodino had discussed with him many of the major decisions he had to make as Judiciary Committee chairman and as a candidate for reelection. The consultations continued throughout impeachment, as Hellring kept Rodino informed of the political nuances at home.

Many of the decisions Rodino had made concerning the early parts of the impeachment inquiry were made after consultation with Hellring. It was Hellring who helped him decide on the qualifications he should seek in a special counsel, although Hellring also advised against the special counsel idea. He thought Rodino should just beef up the current Judiciary Committee staff. He had talked with Zeifman for hours over the past several years, felt close to Zeifman, and had confidence in his ability to handle the matter.

The Hellring association was a closely guarded secret in Rodino's office, because his staff feared the administration would attempt to dig up dirt about Hellring to try to smear Rodino and thus reduce the credibility of the committee's work. The fears were based on the fact that Hellring was Hugh J. Addonizio's lawyer. Addonizio had been a Newark representative in Congress along with Rodino in the 1950s. They were close friends and, like several other members who left their families at home, shared an apartment in Washington. Addonizio ran for mayor of Newark in 1962 and won. He was seeking his third four-year term in 1970 when he was indicted on extortion conspiracy charges, for joining four codefendants in shaking down city contractors for $1.4 million. Addonizio lost his reelection bid and was convicted and sentenced to prison. Suspicions that Addonizio was a Mafia figure never died. Hellring was still Addonizio's lawyer as impeachment got under way, filing appeals for him and trying to get his sentences reduced or reversed. The prosecutor in the Addonizio case was a Republican named Frederick Lacey, who had been appointed to the job by President Nixon in 1969. Two years later, Nixon appointed him a federal judge in the Newark district. If Hellring's connections with Rodino were exposed, then the entire Mafia–New Jersey corruption issue would be raised about Rodino again. Rodino had not always been that sensitive about those ties. He had once put Addonizio's son on his district payroll.

Although his committee matters were foremost in Rodino's mind during the fall of 1973, his district problems had not been forgotten. He had no idea what impeachment would portend for him. As far as he knew the issue could wash out in a few weeks, could be a hit or a dud, and either ending would affect his reputation. He was still concerned about making points with the blacks and others back home. Why not let impeachment help him out?

He had O'Brien put Lacey, fifty-three, at the top of his list, against the advice of both Zeifman and O'Brien. It would be political suicide, both nationally and at home, for him to hire as his special counsel someone who was from his own district and whose appointment would prompt stories dredging up Lacey's connections with Addonizio and all the old suspicions that Rodino was somehow connected with the Mafia or at least with persons of questionable character.

Still Rodino persisted. He wasn't insisting that O'Brien choose Lacey as his top choice, just that he be on the list of those under consideration. To humor Rodino, O'Brien kept Lacey at the top of his list, with no intention of ever clearing him for the job.

A person who would be pushed strongly for the job of special counsel, however, was right under O'Brien's nose.

The fact the Judiciary Committee was sending queries to law schools across the nation was reported in newspaper stories. Richard Cates read the story on his four-hundred-acre farm just outside Madison, Wisconsin. Cates had been practicing law in Madison for more than twenty years and had taught for most of that time at the University of Wisconsin Law School. Cates had built a reputation throughout Wisconsin as a sharp trial lawyer and thought that might be just what an impeachment inquiry would need.

Cates didn't look like a high-powered lawyer. Tall with sandy, stringy hair and the cauliflower ears, crooked nose, and nasal twang of a prizefighter, Cates was more at home in denims than he was in a suit.

He called George Bunn, Wisconsin's law dean, and asked him to put his name on the list if he felt Cates were qualified for the job of special counsel. Bunn did, and sent Rodino a copy of Cates's resume.

Among the things it listed was the fact Cates had served one term as a Democrat in the Wisconsin Legislature and in 1968 had served as campaign manager for Representative Robert Kastenmeier, in 1973 the fourth-ranking Democrat on the Judiciary Committee. He and Kastenmeier were old friends.

Not satisfied to sit back and wait for a response, Cates took advantage of a lawyers' meeting in Washington early in November to drop in on Kastenmeier and tell him of his desire to serve in some capacity on the impeachment inquiry.

Kastenmeier liked the idea of Cates working on impeachment and called Zeifman.

Zeifman and other influential committee staffers were used to getting calls from congressmen saying, ''There's a guy from my district in my office. He's looking for a job. Please interview him. You don't have to hire him. Interview him as a courtesy.'' Zeifman agreed to see Cates.

In many ways, Zeifman and Cates were alike. Both were types who liked to shoot the bull. Both used street language and were very straightforward. Cates felt comfortable with Zeifman because Zeifman was a casual, even sloppy, dresser. Zeifman had been trying to lose weight for the past year and most of his suits were outsized. The two men were about the same age, lawyers, had grown up in New York, and been educated at prestigious eastern schools—Zeifman at Harvard, Cates at Dartmouth.

They were very dissimilar, though, in that Zeifman was somewhat of a bureaucrat and was extremely loyal to the institution of Congress, having worked there for sixteen years. Cates was not a corporation man, preferring the independence of working for himself. He had thrown off his eastern heritage and had begun to spend less of his time practicing law and more working on his farm.

But their feet-on-the-desk talk and rumpled casualness attracted them to each other and they became instant friends and confidants. Cates's statement to Zeifman, ''I have the courage to wear my heart on my sleeve, so you'll always know how I feel about things,'' impressed Zeifman, because Zeifman saw himself the same way.

After Cates left the office, Zeifman called Bernie Hellring, who already was checking the backgrounds of people on O'Brien's list, and told him to add Cates's name. Then Zeifman contacted Rodino and told him he had a very good prospect for the impeachment inquiry, someone who was willing to work in any capacity and would be willing to start soon to begin the spadework. Rodino agreed to meet him, and Zeifman called Cates at his hotel the next day to arrange the interview.

Cates's interview with Rodino was quite a switch from his talk with Zeifman. Cates didn't feel comfortable with Rodino. One of those rarities among politicians, Rodino did not have a gift of gab and his sense of humor was shallow. Rodino couldn't let his hair down. His gray-and-white mane, three-piece, pin-stripes, and stiff manner seemed to command a rigid decorum.

Cates generally called everyone he met by a first name but didn't feel comfortable doing that with Rodino, so he addressed him with the very stiff, ''Mr. Congressman.''

Cates didn't think the interview went well. He thought O'Brien, who also was present, received him cooly. O'Brien resented the fact that influential friends of Cates were backing him. In addition to a contact from Kastenmeier, O'Brien also had received a call from Senator Gaylord Nelson, a very good friend of Cates's law partner, John Lawton.

To O'Brien, all that and the coincidence of Cates being in Washington that week and available for an instant interview smacked too much of old-fashioned politicking and influence-trading. He opposed the hiring of Cates and fought bitterly against it.

After receiving good reports from Hellring, Rodino told Zeifman he could hire Cates. No mention was made of Cates as a possible candidate for special counsel.

Cates joined the tiny impeachment inquiry staff as its director on November 19, at $36,000 a year. He had an understanding that he would stay for only six months.

Zeifman had rented an apartment for Cates at the Coronet Hotel just beyond the congressional complex on Capitol Hill. He gave Cates all the material relevant to impeachment that he had gathered, including the first nine volumes of the Senate Watergate Committee hearings, which had just resumed. Cates was the inquiry's first lawyer, working with the five GAO investigators and a handful of clerical workers.

O'Brien, meanwhile, was continuing his search for a special counsel. Although Rodino obviously leaned that way, it had not been officially decided that there would be a special counsel, only that a search would be made for one. Rodino was still considering the possibility the inquiry would be conducted by the regular committee staff, augmented by about fifty temporary workers.

Hellring was still against the special counsel idea and pressed his opinion on Zeifman. Zeifman vacillated. O'Brien interpreted Zeifman's vacillation as indecision about whether Zeifman wanted the special counsel job for himself. Zeifman did want to run the impeachment inquiry, of that there was no doubt. He had been led to believe by Rodino, however, that if a special counsel were hired that Zeifman would still be in command. But it also was obvious that the special counsel was going to get all of the publicity.

O'Brien had worked for Rodino for three months, long enough to realize that Rodino rarely made flat statements. His instructions always were in the form of indications the listener had to discern from his convoluted speech. O'Brien, of course, would have to take the blame if something went wrong, because he could not say that Rodino told him specifically to do something. O'Brien assumed, thus, that since Rodino instructed him to conduct a search for a special counsel, that meant he did not want Zeifman in that post. O'Brien was correct.

Rodino didn't consider Zeifman the type of person he wanted for the special counsel job. He wanted the inquiry staff separate from the committee staff for political reasons. He also knew how strongly Zeifman felt about impeachment.

Zeifman also was one of those anonymous government employees who do much of the work that makes the person who employs them look good. He hadn't the national stature that Rodino was seeking in a special counsel. Cates also didn't have the national reputation O'Brien was looking for; he was too political, had too many Democratic ties. But after Cates had been hired, O'Brien feared that Cates would move into the job of special counsel by default. Zeifman pressed for Cates as chief counsel. O'Brien resisted. Both pushed their view on Rodino. It was the first major blow-up between O'Brien and Zeifman and the rift was never to heal.

Using the nearly two hundred recommendations he had gathered from law school deans and others and comparing their resumes with the qualities that Rodino had demanded, O'Brien whittled the list of names to a manageable number. He had background checks made on those persons and then reduced the list further to a group of persons he and then Rodino would interview.

O'Brien's older brother, John, helped him in his search, often spending evenings in O'Brien's apartment spreading the lists over the living room floor, trying to put them in categories and arguing over the qualities of the candidates. In spreading out the names on the floor, the O'Brien brothers soon discovered that although he was not at the top of anyone's recommendations, John M. Doar was the name most often listed among the recommendations.

The O'Briens didn't have his resume; they only had his name and a brief outline of his background. Francis assumed that he was only about forty. That would be too young to meet one of the criteria Rodino had set out. Francis discounted him and turned to search through other names. But John protested. "You're crazy, the guy has to be fifty. Add it up." Francis studied the brief biography again, noted that Doar had joined the Justice Department in the Eisenhower years and had been with his father's law firm for ten years before that. He did some quick arithmetic and discovered his brother was correct, Doar had to be about fifty, the right age bracket. Doar's name was returned to the list of possibilities.

By early December, O'Brien had the names down to about a dozen candidates. Six were interviewed for the job. The rest either refused it before the interview or were eventually eliminated for other reasons.

Zeifman read off the list of finalists to Clark Clifford to seek his opinion. On the list was John Doar. Clifford knew of Doar and expressed reservations about considering him for the job because of his closeness to the Kennedy family and to Burke Marshall. His reservations weren't strong, Clifford told Zeifman, but he thought Zeifman should know them.

Burke Marshall had been a close friend and confidant of the Kennedy family, serving as Bobby Kennedy's right arm when he was attorney general in John Kennedy's administration. Doar had been next in command under Marshall in the Civil Rights Division. It also was Marshall who consulted and advised Senator Edward M. Kennedy (D-Mass.) in 1969 in the aftermath of his accident at Chappaquiddick Bridge on Martha's Vineyard.

Zeifman told Clifford that Hellring still thought the impeachment inquiry ought to be handled by a beefed-up committee staff and added that he was coming around to Hellring's view. Clifford responded, "I've never been in a town, park, or public square where there's a monument to a committee." Zeifman might have replied that he hadn't been in one where there was a monument to a special counsel.

In choosing a special counsel, Clifford advised, "remember, university presidents are specialists in climbing the academic ladder, corporate presidents specialize in climbing the corporate ladder and anyone who can rise to become president of the American Bar Association has got to have something wrong with him." Among the finalists on the list were members of each group.

Frederick Lacey was still high on the list, but only to satisfy Rodino's earlier instructions. John Doar was emerging as O'Brien's primary choice at about that time. O'Brien decided he would be interviewed first.

To avoid any leaks that could tie him or the committee directly to a prospect, O'Brien always made his initial approaches to candidates through third parties. To reach Doar, he called A. S. Goldstein, dean of Yale Law School and the person who had first recommended Doar. O'Brien asked Goldstein to contact Doar and, "Ask him one question, just one. Would he accept a call from me?"

Goldstein called back and said Doar would talk with him. O'Brien called Doar and said Rodino would like to meet with him the following week for an exploratory conversation. Doar agreed to come to Washington from New York, where he had just tendered his resignation as head of the Bedford-Stuyvesant Development and Services Corporation.

O'Brien had selected Doar as his first choice, despite the mixed reviews he had received from those contacted about Doar. In addition to Clifford's reports via Zeifman, O'Brien learned Doar was not an easy person to get along with. He was stubborn and did things in his own meticulous and plodding manner. Many of his former Justice Department coworkers had criticized his tendency to demand picayune information they considered time-wasting.

When Doar arrived the first week in December, O'Brien ushered him in, unrecognized, to speak with Rodino, past a reporter who had staked out Rodino's outer office just so he could catch a glimpse of who might be interviewed for the job.

Neither Doar nor Rodino was loquacious. Discussions between them consumed a lot of time. Rodino would use a lot of words to make a simple statement or ask a routine question, and Doar would respond with single-word answers, providing no more information than he was asked to give. Both spoke in riddles. O'Brien felt his job was that of an interpreter for the two men.

In their first conversation, nearly two hours were spent by Rodino discussing Doar's background, his knowledge of the impeachment inquiry, whether he could draw together a competent staff quickly and then manage that staff. The central question on Rodino's mind, however, was whether Doar had made up his mind about Nixon's guilt or innocence of impeachable offenses. Could Doar be fair, Rodino wanted to know. Zeifman sat in on part of the interview and asked Doar questions about his activities in the Justice Department.

Rodino had others to interview for the job, so Doar left without an offer. O'Brien walked him to the elevator and, feeling a bit foolish, asked Doar if there was anything in his past the committee should know about.

Doar began to explain about his divorce, but O'Brien said he already knew about it. Doar offered nothing else. O'Brien told him to call the next day if he was still interested in the post.

Doar did, using no more words than necessary. He said, ''This is the last call you're going to receive from me. I just want to let you know that I'm interested. Goodbye.'' And he hung up.

In the early evening of December 6, 1973, Gerald R. Ford was sworn in as the new vice-president in ceremonies attended by President Nixon on the floor of the House of Representatives.

But Zeifman, who had just finished one job—Ford's confirmation—now had to devote full attention to another—impeachment. He called his first formal staff meeting on impeachment while the ceremonies were being held. Those attending included Frank Polk, Zeifman's GOP counterpart; Dick Cates; Sam Garrison, just hired by the Republicans as Cates's counterpart on the inquiry staff; Dan Cohen, a Judiciary Committee counsel; and John Kennahan, one of the first persons Zeifman had hired after Cates. They all agreed that things had been progressing too slowly and that it was past the time when a special counsel should have been named.

Zeifman decided to throw his support to Doar. Partly, he felt it might hurry matters along, but his judgment also was based on political considerations. He called Rodino at his home in Newark on Saturday, December 8, and urged him to hire Doar. Zeifman told Rodino he thought Doar would be the wisest choice for special counsel because "his appointment would not only be in the best interest of the United States, but would also be in your personal, political interest. Since Doar is a close Kennedy man and is admired by the blacks and the liberals, his appointment would quiet down your political opponents in Newark." Both were acutely aware of Doar's Republican background, nebulous as it was.

Rodino hadn't decided, though. He had a few other people to interview the following week and wouldn't make up his mind until he saw them. He favored others somewhat over Doar, though not strongly.

Bernie Hellring came to Washington from Newark on the following Tuesday evening for a nitty-gritty session on selecting the special counsel. Hellring still wanted Zeifman to handle the inquiry as chief committee counsel. Zeifman said it already was too late for that course.

O'Brien announced to the group that William T. Gossett, a sixty-nine-year-old corporation lawyer in Detroit, a registered Republican, and a former president of the American Bar Association, would not accept the job. He had been on the final list of five people.

Hellring then called Robert Keeton, fifty-four, a Harvard Law professor. Keeton agreed to meet with Zeifman and Rodino two days later for an interview. Also remaining on the list of finalists were the ever-present Lacey, and Albert Jenner, a Chicago attorney who had gained national attention for his service on several presidentially appointed commissions.

Keeton's interview with Rodino on Thursday established, however, that he hadn't tried a case since the early 1950s. Jenner's health would be a problem since he could only contribute a few days a week to the impeachment inquiry and would not be able to stand a constant grind. Rodino had learned on his trip back to Newark the previous weekend that the Italian-Americans would never forgive him if he chose Lacey, the man who had prosecuted one of their own, Hugh Addonizio. Lacey finally was eliminated.

By week's end, it was clear that Doar was the final candidate. But Rodino wanted more checks on Doar just to be sure. He was concerned about his Kennedy ties. He wanted to know if Ted Kennedy had any information about Doar, but didn't want an open approach from the committee to Kennedy. He told Zeifman to contact R. Sargent Shriver, husband of one of Kennedy's sisters, and have him contact Kennedy. Zeifman did and Shriver suggested that Cyrus Vance, later to become President Carter's secretary of state, be considered.

During the weekend, Rodino decided on Doar without having heard from Shriver. The interview had clinched it. Doar was not an overbearing personality, so Rodino didn't feel threatened. He sensed a compatibility. He called O'Brien and had him advise Doar he was under serious consideration. Rodino wanted him in Washington on Tuesday. Doar would later learn that that was as much of a job offer as he was going to get.

Rodino wanted to tell Doar he had the job in front of Zeifman and Cates in order to build the idea in the minds of all three that they were to work as a team on impeachment. The meeting took place in Rodino's office on Tuesday, December 18, but Doar already knew he had the job. It had been obvious from all the arrangements that had been made. O'Brien had booked him in for an indefinite stay at the Carroll Arms Hotel behind the Senate office buildings.

The job was never formally offered. It was just assumed by all parties that Doar had the job. Rodino introduced Doar to Cates and then gave à little speech to Doar.

"It's not going to be easy, but if the facts show that Nixon is not guilty of impeachable offenses, I'm going to have the courage to say it. I know it won't be the popular thing to do, but it has to be done if that is the case.

"Bring all the facts before us, the exculpatory and the inculpatory, weigh them and give them to us so we can make the judgment," Rodino said, emphasizing the "we." The members of the committee would glean the relevant from the irrelevant, he said. "You put it together for us so we can evaluate it."

Rodino told Doar he was to follow those same guidelines in hiring the rest of his staff. His final warning to Doar, which was to be relayed to any prospective employee, was that, "If at any time before the facts are in that need to be in, you indicate or suggest that you are an advocate, I'm going to fire you then and there. No one can make a judgment as to whether Nixon is to be impeached except members of the committee. We will look to you for a presentation of the facts and legal advice."

After Rodino's brief speech, as the group chatted, Doar slipped and referred to himself as "chief counsel," Zeifman's title. Rodino corrected him. He told him he would be known as a "special counsel" and Zeifman would have overall responsibility for the inquiry.

Doar suggested that he go to Newark during the Christmas recess at the end of the week to discuss some problems with Rodino, but Rodino said that wouldn't be necessary, that he should confer with Zeifman instead. He said he had confidence and trust in Zeifman, who knew Capitol Hill and would be heading the impeachment inquiry without a special counsel if he had not had other responsibilities as chief counsel.

Doar replied, "That's fine; I think it's important that we have a team."

Cates had heard about Doar being interviewed and strongly urged Zeifman to promote the hiring of Doar. Cates's preferences, however, were personal. He had been working with a young staff, was far from home and his farm and family and was lonely for someone of his own age and experience to talk to. He knew Doar was a former Wisconsinite and thought they would have a great time together.

It was not to be. The harmony was short-lived. Doar was going to have problems with Zeifman and Cates.

By the day Doar became special counsel, December 18, 1973, more than seven months before the vote on impeachment, Cates felt he had gathered enough evidence to impeach Nixon.

Cates had told Zeifman nearly two weeks earlier that he had enough evidence to convict Nixon of conspiracy to obstruct justice.

He said: "My God, if this wasn't the president of the United States and I couldn't secure a conviction, they could take my license. It is horrendously solid."

CHAPTER IV

Movement

By the time Dick Cates arrived in Jerry Zeifman's office for his first day of work on impeachment on November 19, 1973, Zeifman had neatly stacked up on a leather-covered couch all of the Watergate-related information he had been gathering since spring. Added to the pile was the material Zeifman's five General Accounting Office investigators had collected. There was nothing new in any of it. It had all been public before.

But for the first time since the Watergate break-in almost fifteen months earlier, someone was going to study the information with an eye to the president's involvement, ignoring any crimes that may have been committed by somebody else. Included in the stack of material were the first nine volumes—all that had been published to date—of the Senate Watergate Committee hearings.

Before Cates got to town, the House already had approved one million dollars for the committee's investigation. A total of twenty-six persons had been hired or assigned—mostly clerks, typists, and secretaries, as well as an office manager. The committee had acquired two extra suites in the Capitol complex.

Cates chose to spend his first week of work in his Coronet Hotel apartment. Since all he would be doing was reading and making notes, he didn't need the office surroundings and did need the peace and quiet. The first thing he turned to were the fifteen separate impeachment resolutions that had been introduced to that point. Next in the stack were the allegations written into some of the resolutions and referred to generally in others, so he looked into material related to the allegations. The Congressional Research Service, an arm of the Library of Congress, had prepared sample articles of impeachment based upon the resolutions introduced. They provided the scope of the impeachment case for Cates.

As he worked day and night for the first six days—including Thanksgiving—Cates also read a rough draft of charges against Nixon that had been compiled by a public interest law firm set up by consumer advocate Ralph Nader and headed by William Dobrovir. It cited twenty-eight counts of criminal acts committed by Nixon or his aides in connection with Watergate, as well as other allegations of impeachable offenses Nixon had committed. The allegations ran the gamut from malicious mischief to extortion, blackmail, and bribery. The draft also made a case for the principle of holding a boss responsible for the acts of his underlings.

The Dobrovir brief's value to Cates was its outline of the allegations. It listed them all with the supporting evidence and helped to draw the case into a comprehensible package. Cates otherwise would have been left to wade through all sorts of material unrelated to Nixon in order to find the few items that were related.

By the end of the first six days Cates was able to divide the case into four categories: the cover-up, political contributions, personal finances, and a catch-all of federal statutes Nixon was alleged to have broken.

By itself, the Watergate cover-up category was a mass of disjointed facts that had to be assembled to be understood. Cates hadn't done that yet, but already the cover-up subject, when added to the other three categories, raised grave questions about the responsibility of the leader in following the law. And Cates saw in the final catch-all category the beginning of a new standard for presidential activity.

With those four categories in hand a week later, Cates visited Zeifman and asked him for people to direct the investigation of each of the categories. Bill Dixon and Bill Trainor from the Judiciary staff were lent to him. The trio went to dinner in a Capitol Hill restaurant and discussed Cates's four categories. The men wouldn't be available immediately but were expected to be released to Cates within two weeks, after the Ford confirmation was completed. Dixon had worked on the political contributions aspect of the Ford investigation and chose to handle that category for Cates. Trainor, whom Cates felt had more drive than Dixon, took the cover-up. Cates assigned to Dixon a GAO investigator who had done some work on contributions. Robert Murphy, one of the persons Zeifman had gotten from the GAO, was assigned to head the probe of Nixon's personal finances. Zeifman had just hired Jared Stamell, a lawyer in the Justice Department who had graduated from Harvard two years earlier. Cates assigned him to the fourth, catch-all category.

Although Cates was fascinated with the fourth category on presidential violations of federal law, he felt because of the mass of detail and contradictory evidence involved, that he should concentrate on helping Trainor with the cover-up investigation.

The other members of the investigative staff, drawn from the pool Zeifman was hiring daily, were assigned to the four leaders. Cates assigned one of the nine volumes of Senate Watergate testimony to each member of the cover-up staff and asked them to form a legal digest—weeding out the pertinent parts of the transcripts.

Soon, Cates abandoned the Coronet office and moved into a suite on the sixth floor of the Congressional Hotel, which had just been acquired by Congress and was right behind the row of three House office buildings. With his staff in place, he began holding weekly meetings of the category chiefs.

The facts related to the allegations against Nixon were not easily comprehensible, and still resembled a jigsaw puzzle. Cates decided the staff should learn to weave the facts into logical narratives. As more information was gathered, a clear picture would begin to emerge.

Cates read and reread the Senate Watergate testimony, comparing the answers to the questions, the patterns of responses given by various Watergate witnesses. He felt confident after a few weeks that he could, without a transcript, respond to the questions just as someone like John Ehrlichman, Nixon's domestic adviser, responded when he was before the Watergate Committee. The intimate knowledge of the transcripts showed him that Ehrlichman had been dissembling and that others probably were lying.

Before December, Cates was able to tell the staff, pounding on his desk for emphasis, "Look, what we're finding is seventy, eighty, ninety, one hundred pieces of proof, all of which have one thesis, that all of these acts are done to cover up the guilt of other people. The way I try a lawsuit is that if we've got seventy pieces of proof that all show actions to conceal, to cover up, to hide, the other guy's got to have an explanation for every goddamn one."

For example, he noted, during a news conference in San Clemente, California, August 22, Nixon had been asked about what he had told John Dean on March 21, 1973. Dean had testified he told Nixon that day of blackmail attempts by some of the seven men arrested for the Watergate break-in. Dean said Nixon had offered clemency. Nixon gave his version of the long conversation Dean had referred to and said he had told Dean, "It's wrong, it won't work, we can't give clemency."

Citing that, Cates told his staff, "Supposin' you're innocent; just suppose you're innocent. And let's say you're the president of Coca-Cola or just some corner grocery store. The guy comes in and says, 'They want us to pay seventy-five thousand to Hunt.' What do you say? You say, 'Tell that son of a bitch to fry his ass. Who the hell does he think he is?' " Cates said, flailing his arms as he got into the role.

"I mean, Jesus, what is your response? . . . You're innocent as hell and you can show how you can withstand blackmail. But when you start having a conversation and you're talking . . . here's a president of the United States telling the world what he told to Dean. He said it wouldn't work." Cates broke out laughing.

"What the hell. The president may have an explanation for everything that happens. But he has to win on them all, because if he loses on one, there's trouble."

Cates turned to the June 23, 1972, tape made in Nixon's Oval Office. Neither that nor the March 21 tape had been produced by the White House, but John Dean and others testified to the dates, and White House logs that Nixon had released revealed that Nixon had conversations on those days with certain aides. Cates reviewed the Senate Watergate testimony about the flow of money to the Watergate burglars via Mexico and the reason the White House tried to get the FBI to stop trying to trace the money. On June 23, Cates said, "Nixon said he thought that there might be some CIA involvement in Mexico. Okay, he has an excuse. Then Ehrlichman specifically testified that on the seventh of July he's walking down the beach with the president and he brought up the idea of clemency for these seven guys. My analysis of that—Jesus Christ, what is Ehrlichman's job? Does he watch the criminal pages and then go into the president and say, 'Jesus, there was a hold-up over on Fiftieth, you'll be wanting to give the guy clemency?' ''

''All right, they've got an explanation,'' for their involvement in both matters, ''but the problem is if you don't believe that explanation, then you believe he's in the cover-up.''

At that point, near the end of November, Cates wasn't really concerned about getting Nixon's tapes. He was a lawyer used to trying lawsuits in which circumstantial evidence sometimes could be better than the ''smoking gun.'' He told his staff, ''You can figure out what's on those tapes by just figuring out all the [events] that took place beforehand.''

Cates wanted witnesses. Through skillful questioning, he felt, he could draw out the truth and fill in all the gaps in the narratives. ''If you get the tapes, you get a windfall, but there's no sense worrying over what you don't have.''

He said, more quietly now, ''I don't think I ever could have seen displayed by circumstantial evidence a more compelling case than what took place on June twenty-third. The president had to know. He had to have something on the CIA. He just had to know.''

It had occurred suddenly to Cates one day as he plowed through the Senate testimony that the only person who could have tied the Watergate break-in to the White House from the summer of 1972 to early 1973 was G. Gordon Liddy, the ringleader of the break-in. It was apparent that Liddy wasn't about to say a word about it. He had vowed he would stand on a street corner and be shot before he would talk. ''They're solid as a rock'' on Watergate, Cates realized. The White House didn't have to pay $75,000 for the break-in. E. Howard Hunt, Liddy's second-in-command, didn't have the details of the ties to the White House, only Liddy had them. But it was Hunt who was demanding money and getting it, through the president's personal lawyer. The money wasn't being paid out of the goodness of someone's heart.

"Jesus Christ, Cates," he shouted. "They're paying off because Hunt's got them by the short hair on non-Watergate stuff."

He returned to events prior to the Watergate break-in. John Mitchell had recounted "White House horrors" to the Senate committee. In addition to the break-in of the office of Daniel Ellsberg's psychiatrist, Mitchell had listed the following: whisking Dita Beard, an International Telephone and Telegraph (ITT) lobbyist, out of town when she was a key witness in a scandal involving ITT and the 1972 GOP convention site; falsifying State Department cables alleging that President Kennedy wanted South Vietnamese President Ngo Dinh Diem assassinated; numerous bugging operations; planting a firebomb in the Brookings Institution in Washington; "and a lot of miscellaneous matters with respect to Chappaquiddick."

When Cates plugged the "White House horrors" into the cover-up to conceal the White House involvement in the Watergate break-in, it answered his question, "Why was the concealment necessary?" Everything fit then.

Cates reviewed other Senate Watergate testimony. The jigsaw puzzle seemed to put itself together.

Three days after the Watergate break-in, on June 20, 1972 Nixon's chief of staff, Bob Haldeman, met with Dean, Ehrlichman, John Mitchell, and then–Attorney General Richard Kleindienst, to discuss the break-in. Haldeman met later with Nixon and admitted the break-in was discussed. Then Ehrlichman met with Nixon. He admitted they discussed Watergate. The same day, Liddy met with two top aides to Mitchell on the reelection committee and revealed all the White House horror stories. The two then met with Mitchell and told him. Nixon made a dictabelt recording that day outlining a conversation he had with Mitchell.

On June 21, Ehrlichman ordered acting FBI Director Patrick Gray to work closely with Dean on Gray's Watergate investigation. Ehrlichman and Dean then discussed the contents of Howard Hunt's White House safe. Haldeman had ordered the contents destroyed because they outlined the White House horrors. Dean met with Gray, who told the White House counsel that the FBI had traced laundered money from the Watergate burglars back to a businessman and that Gray suspected the CIA was involved. Dean told that to Haldeman.

On June 23, Haldeman met with Nixon and told him of Dean's conversation with Gray. Nixon directed Haldeman, according to Haldeman testimony, to meet with CIA Director Richard Helms and his deputy, Vernon Walters, and Ehrlichman and find out if there was any CIA involvement in Watergate and whether an FBI investigation would endanger CIA operations. Haldeman said Nixon wanted him to express concern about the possibility of disclosure of CIA operations and the "White House plumbers" activity in pre-Watergate activities. Then he wanted Walters to meet with Gray and express those concerns and convince the FBI to limit its investigation of Watergate to the break-in itself. At the Nixon-ordered meeting that afternoon, Helms assured the others there was no CIA involvement or danger and that he already had told that to Gray. Then Walters met with Gray and Gray reported back to Dean. Three days later Dean asked Walters for CIA money to pay bail for the Watergate burglars, citing approval by Ehrlichman for the request. Walters also had told Dean a recheck by the CIA found no danger to the CIA in an FBI investigation.

Cates reviewed all of that information with his staff leaders on the morning of November 30. There were all those White House aides working feverishly on a project and Nixon getting reports on it. "He knew what was going on," Cates said, pounding his desk again for emphasis. "And when he knows that's going on and they're doing it for him, how the hell can he say he's not involved?

"You can't be the president of a company and all your men are going out and doing something, and you sit there and say 'I don't know anything about it.' . . . I know human beings well enough to know that unless that son of a bitch comes up with a hell of an explanation, he's in it. And the only explanation he gave was not a hell of an explanation"—his concern that CIA activities would be exposed.

"The logic of the June twenty-third meeting," he said, is that Nixon denies using the CIA to interfere with the FBI investigation while everyone around him is testifying in one form or another about discussions on that subject, some of them involving Nixon. "I wasn't born yesterday.

If I'm being falsely accused, and I have a document that basically will exonerate me, I show it," he said, referring to Nixon's refusal to divulge the June 23 tape. It was not among the nine tapes that the special prosecutor had pressed for in the courts, the action that brought about his firing and the "Saturday Night Massacre." But it could have been volunteered.

"We have all of these kinds of things which establish to any thinking person he's in it. Then we have explanations that don't wash and conduct that just incriminates him more," Cates said. "I'm a trial lawyer. I know what I can do with a certain set of facts, I know what kind of arguments I can make, because in learning my trade I've learned about people. I've had to."

Although Cates had gotten most of his information through a careful reading and rereading of the Senate Watergate Committee transcripts, he was struck by the shallow questioning that was done of its witnesses. Cates didn't appreciate that the information the hearings brought out about the president's involvement was only incidental to the Senate panel's investigation into campaign financing.

He also was not familiar with the artificiality of congressional hearings. It appalled him that a witness could say something to the Senate Watergate Committee that would go unchallenged. He was especially struck by the failure to follow up statements by John Ehrlichman, especially when he would remember some parts of an event but not the parts that might prove incriminating. Cates was used to testing answers by a witness in court. He wanted a chance to ask the questions himself.

Because Cates was alone in town and Zeifman's wife, Donna LeRew, a concert violinist, was busy many evenings, the two men often would get together for dinner or for long discussions at Zeifman's house on Capitol Hill. So Zeifman was well informed on Cates's progress and was convinced Cates had made a case against Nixon. But Cates wanted witnesses he could cross-examine.

On the morning of November 30, 1973, less than two weeks after he had begun the job, Cates went to Zeifman's office to ask him for permission to question some witnesses in the case and, less enthusiastically, to subpoena some White House tapes. After questioning witnesses, he said, he would have all he needed to establish Nixon's complicity in the cover-up. Tapes would make the case even more solid.

The president unlawfully directed the FBI and CIA to obstruct justice, Cates said. What he already had in hand proved that. But any additional information that the committee could obtain concerning the president's knowledge of the prior illegal activity of either of the two intelligence agencies would be extremely relevant. If Nixon had knowledge of prior criminal acts by the FBI or CIA, he could have used that information to put pressure on the agency officials to aid in the Watergate cover-up, Cates reasoned.

Zeifman was cautious. He didn't have the final authority. He was satisfied that Cates knew what he was doing and could wrap up the case with witnesses, but he would still have to sell the idea to Rodino. The question of subpoenaing tapes would be even more sensitive.

Zeifman was aware that Rodino was beginning to assert himself as Judiciary Committee chairman. But he also knew Rodino would be reluctant to make a decision as important as calling witnesses. He asked Cates for material he could use to persuade Rodino. Cates said there were all kinds of holes in the questioning of the Senate Watergate Committee witnesses, particularly by the committee's chief counsel, Samuel Dash.

As an example, Cates chose the crucial period surrounding March 21, 1973, when according to the puzzle he had put together, Nixon had acquiesced in the payment of hush money through Frederick LaRue, John Mitchell's reelection committee assistant, to attorney William Bittman on behalf of his client, Watergate burglar E. Howard Hunt.

"There were some delightful holes, such as LaRue, when Dash was questioning him and Dean has already said he had a conversation with the president on March twenty-first about the payment of seventy-five thousand dollars. And we know that LaRue gave the money to Bittman, but the big fuckin' question is 'when?' He has LaRue on the stand. God, it's the most delightful question because he asked him twice and never does get the date, except LaRue says on or about the twentieth. Well, hell, it's the guts whether it was before or after the conversation with the president and when you get done listening to Dash you don't know.

"The reason I'm interested in witnesses is this is the flesh and blood you may have to use to establish your proof. I really want to get attitudes, demeanors; I want to know what they're going to hang tough with, what they're going to weasel on.

"I want to see Sloan [Hugh Sloan, reelection committee treasurer] early in the game because I want a witness who will give me rundowns on others. In other words, I could talk to him and, in addition to whatever he had to say, I would want to find out what Magruder's [Jeb Magruder, the chief of staff for the reelection committee] attitude was and such and so."

Cates said he didn't want Haldeman or Ehrlichman "or any of that crowd" at that moment. The people he wanted were those who had testified before the Senate Watergate Committee and "whose testimony I've read and who I want to get a feel for. What are their anti–House Judiciary sentiments? Just a reading."

Cates began to tell Zeifman the names of the people he wanted to see, but Zeifman asked him to write a memo. Cates protested. That wasn't the way he worked. He only had nine people he wanted to call. Zeifman could just write them down. Zeifman insisted he needed a memo, so Cates stepped outside Zeifman's office into an anteroom and dictated the memo to Zeifman's secretary. All it said was: "Cates wants to see" and then listed the nine names.

In addition to Sloan, Magruder, and Dean, Cates wanted to question Robert Cushman, a former deputy director of the CIA; Vernon Walters, then deputy director; Henry Petersen, assistant attorney general who headed the Justice Department's Watergate investigation; Gordon Strachan, Haldeman's assistant; Robert Odle, administrator for the reelection committee; and James McCord, leader of the five burglars who actually got inside Democratic headquarters in the Watergate office building.

After Cates left, Zeifman became nervous over the request. Cates was getting in deep when he wanted to call witnesses after less than two weeks on the job and before a special counsel was found. He recounted the conversation to Rodino and handed him Cates's list.

Zeifman and Rodino understood the sensitivity of calling witnesses for a closely watched inquiry like impeachment. It couldn't be done lightly. Zeifman questioned the advisability of calling witnesses without harder evidence than Cates had at that time. If the committee questioned witnesses before it was fully prepared and learned no more than the Senate panel had learned of the president's complicity, then its credibility would have been damaged severely and it would be ridiculed and criticized for acting precipitously.

Rodino was concerned about the effects of Cates's total immersion in the impeachment charges. He suggested the three of them have dinner the following Monday evening at the Monocle Restaurant behind the Senate office buildings.

Cates didn't get a chance to repeat his request to call witnesses to Rodino. The dinner was used to give Cates a short course in the institution of Congress and the federal government. Cates was not trying a lawsuit back home in Madison, they told him. With the circumstantial evidence already in hand, he probably could get a conspiracy conviction against Nixon in any court. But Nixon was the president of the United States. The Constitution provides an explanation of how an errant president must be dealt with.

The men and women who would be deciding the president's fate were not typical jurors, who could make their decision and then return to their normal lives. On Nixon's jury would be sitting 435 men and women in the House of Representatives and 100 men in the Senate. Try as they might to separate themselves from their political surroundings and make a judgment based solely upon the law, their futures could depend on how they decided on Nixon.

The future also depended on how the inquiry was conducted, because Congress's final decision on Nixon would be viewed according to how fairly the impeachment investigation was handled.

The Constitution is very vague on how and for what a president could be removed, they told him. It cites only "treason, bribery, high crimes and misdemeanors" and interpretations about what those charges constituted varied dramatically. The Constitution gave the committee no guidelines on how to conduct the inquiry, and the impeachment of Andrew Johnson a hundred years earlier was no help.

All the members of the committee, then, were flying blind. Too many political careers were at stake to be rushing into impeachment.

One of the reasons Cates would not be chosen as special counsel,

Rodino said, was that the counsel had to have the tact necessary in dealing with a political institution like Congress.

(Cates also was rejected because he told the committee Democrats once that he saw his role as one of trying to make a case for impeachment and to win it for the committee. And Cates had neither the national stature nor the Republican background required.)

The members, as soon as they were relieved of the Ford confirmation burden, would begin throwing their weight around on impeachment, and it was going to be hard to keep them mollified while doing the job correctly, Rodino added. The members would want to decide whether and which witnesses to call.

When trying a lawsuit in Madison, the lawyer need only request an interview with someone or issue a subpoena and then to do it. When it concerned impeachment, each interview of a witness was highly significant and there was little chance of keeping the interview secret.

In that fishbowl atmosphere, the committee had better have a good, solid reason for talking to anyone, be pretty certain of what it would learn and that the result would be favorable to the committee. The entire inquiry could be put out of balance if witnesses were called that early. Not only the public, but the members of Congress, had to be conditioned and stroked before moving, even slowly.

And it would be best not to make any significant moves until the special counsel were chosen, they said. A special counsel such as the one Rodino was looking for would command a great deal of respect and add credibility to committee requests and actions.

Rodino had been in Congress for twenty-five years and he knew the institution intimately. Like the institution, he preferred caution.

Cates left the dinner that night with a new outlook on Congress and a greater appreciation of the need for a special counsel.

On December 19, the day that John Doar was introduced to the committee members as their special counsel, Cates gave his first briefing to the fifteen-member ad hoc advisory group Rodino was still using as an informal subcommittee.

After his dinner at the Monocle, Cates was ready to play it Congress's way, however slow and tedious that might be. In his conversations with members, he would soften his conclusions about Nixon's guilt.

Cates was anxious for Doar to come aboard, for he saw in Doar an ally of a similar age and background. Doar also was someone from outside Congress, so they could help each other through the unfamiliar legislative bureaucracy.

After Doar's appointment was announced to a news conference on December 20, Zeifman took Doar over to one of the rooms the impeachment inquiry staff had in the Congressional Hotel to meet the people he would be working with.

Doar gave a brief speech to the group about the importance of the inquiry and the care and fairness they would have to bring to it.

Zeifman was still chafing from an incident which had occurred just before the news conference. A two-page press release announcing the appointment had been circulated to reporters in the House press gallery before the 10:30 A.M. news conference. Moments later a staff member from Rodino's office returned to the press gallery to take back the release, claiming there was an error in it. When the new release was circulated, the last four paragraphs had been omitted. They had read:

Until Doar's appointment today, the inquiry staff worked directly under supervision of Committee General Counsel Jerome M. Zeifman. Zeifman will retain overall responsibility both for the impeachment inquiry and regular staff activities.

Zeifman had served on the Judiciary Committee for nearly 12 years when he was chosen last January to head the staff.

A Harvard University and New York University Law School graduate, Zeifman previously headed a variety of other congressional investigations.

"Both Zeifman and Doar will work closely with me," said Rodino. "I want to stress that my intention is to proceed in an orderly, lawful, dignified way to carry out my responsibility to prepare the Judiciary Committee to determine what actions, if any, it may wish to take with respect to the impeachment resolutions now pending before me."

When Zeifman asked the author, Francis O'Brien, why those four paragraphs about his having overall responsiblity for the inquiry were dropped in the final release, O'Brien said they comprised the second page of the release and rather than doing that page over to correct an error, it was eliminated. The error was in the last word, he said. It should have read "us" instead of "me."

Zeifman already thought he had detected signals in a meeting with

Doar in Rodino's office the previous day that there might be an effort under way to squeeze him out.

Lois D'Andre, a woman in her early thirties, had been Rodino's closest confidante in Washington for several years. She was the only member of his staff who addressed him as "Peter." She controlled the office. If something happened she didn't like, she would storm into Rodino's office and get her way. She was blamed for having the previous administrative assistant fired, and it was she who had recommended O'Brien, a former classmate, for the job. A close friend, Janet Howard, had gotten the job as office manager of the impeachment inquiry staff.

D'Andre also attended the meeting of the inquiry staff with Doar in the hotel headquarters. As soon as Doar finished his remarks to the assembled group, Zeifman said, "Now, John, what can I do to help?"

Doar replied cooly, "The first thing I want to do is talk to Lois alone." Zeifman was aware of D'Andre's influence with Rodino, so he said, "I prefer to sit in on that conversation." Doar acceded. As Zeifman listened, Doar and D'Andre formulated policies for hiring additional staff members and handling press inquiries. Zeifman was not consulted.

After lunch Zeifman took Doar back to the hotel to meet individually with the staff members, first with the top-ranking staffer, Dick Cates.

Despite his two-week-old lesson on Congress, Cates was anxious to show Doar the work he had done. He wanted an ally for his view that the investigation ought to be pressed, calling witnesses as soon as possible and subpoenaing some of the key White House tapes.

He had been asked to gather the material that Doar should look at first.

Cates started spilling out the case to Doar as he saw it, speaking as one lawyer to another. He had the facts to convict Nixon, Cates told Doar. "You don't have a firecracker here, you have a hell of a howitzer." The only problem, he said, was whether the type of forum they were working in—Congress—could handle the mountain of facts and make a decision based upon them. He handed Doar a foot-high stack of materials to read.

William Dobrovir, who had compiled the cover-up scenario for Ralph Nader's public interest law firm, had disgraced himself publicly just three days earlier. At a cocktail party he played a tape that the White House had turned over to the firm to satisfy its suit alleging that Nixon had given the dairy industry favors in exchange for campaign contributions. The firm's work had been funded by Stewart Mott, a millionaire contributor to liberal Democratic causes. The party incident had made headlines the following day and was the subject of court and White House activity the day before Doar's appointment was announced.

Insensitive to the political ramifications of what he was doing, Cates handed Doar as the first thing he should read to background himself on the Watergate scandal, the Dobrovir brief on twenty-eight criminal charges against Nixon.

"No, I refuse to do that," Doar responded angrily, sweeping aside Cates' proffer. "If the press wants to write a story about my first day on the job, I don't want anyone to be able to tell the press that the first thing I had begun with was the Dobrovir brief."

When Doar calmed down, he explained to Cates, "My responsibility is to go at this on a step-by-step, fair, impartial way. It isn't going to look right. How is it going to look when someone asks me sometime, 'What's the first document that you read?' and I tell them it was Dobrovir's brief?"

He added, "I have to come on fair and impartial. There are an awful lot of sharks in the water."

Doar then met individually with the rest of the staff members, including Bill Dixon, who told Doar he thought the committee should investigate the possibility of criminal bribery charges against Nixon in connection with allegations he gave ambassadorships in exchange for large campaign contributions.

After Doar had made the circuit of staff members, he returned to Cates and complimented him on his staff selection, noting that everyone seemed to be an eager, willing hard worker.

Cates said Dixon was having trouble with the political contributions subject because there was nothing more he could do on it until he could interview some witnesses. Dixon had complained that as matters stood, about all he could do was read the newspapers.

Cates told him his search for an accountant to help them with the personal finances category of the investigation had been resolved by allowing the Joint Committee on Taxation to work on the issue first. Other subjects had been stalled for one reason or another, so the substantive work Cates had to report on was in the Watergate cover-up area, on which Cates specialized. And that case was solid, Cates repeated.

Early that evening, Doar got an appointment with Rodino in the chairman's office. Rodino was still not that comfortable with Doar, whom he hadn't known very long, so he called Zeifman to sit in.

While they were waiting in Rodino's outer office, Doar told Zeifman he wasn't about to buy Cates's understanding of the conspiracy case against Nixon nor Dixon's recommendation on bribery charges against Nixon. Those kinds of criminal charges should be left to the special prosecutor's office or the Watergate committee, Doar indicated. He said he didn't think the inquiry ought to go into those kinds of things.

"In order to go into a tax fraud case against Nixon," Doar said, "we would need a mini Internal Revenue Service."

Zeifman replied that Doar was making too much of a production about the difficulties of conducting an investigation. "Supposing Nixon had engaged in a criminal conspiracy," Zeifman said. "Don't we have an obligation to develop that case?"

At that moment, O'Brien emerged from Rodino's inner office and announced to the two men he was ready to see them. Doar rose and walked into Rodino's office, closing the door behind him. Zeifman stood in the outer office and stewed. Rodino buzzed the receptionist on the intercom and told her to send Zeifman in. Doar apologized to Zeifman, saying, "I didn't mean to exclude you."

Doar repeated to Rodino what he had told Zeifman in the outer office. Rodino agreed that inquiry staff need not duplicate the work that other congressional committees had done.

Zeifman and Doar tried to patch things up between them after that meeting, but relations between the two men already were severely strained and it was only Doar's first day on the job.

And Zeifman was still seething over Lois D'Andre's throwing her weight around and moving in on the impeachment inquiry. The next evening the two had it out in Zeifman's office. Zeifman feared that Rodino still wasn't strong enough to keep D'Andre in her place and had received complaints from her good friend, Janet Howard, that D'Andre was interfering in her administration of the impeachment inquiry offices. Rodino would later get so many complaints about her he would transfer her to his district office in Newark.

Zeifman's relations with O'Brien, Doar, and D'Andre were still tense when Rodino left Washington for the Christmas holidays on December 22, the day after Congress began a month-long recess.

Before he left, Rodino told Zeifman he would be in charge of the committee since all the members would be out of town during the recess. Rodino said he desperately needed a rest, that he was exhausted, so he didn't want to be contacted in Florida, where he and his wife would be visiting their daughter, unless it was a dire emergency. He wouldn't leave his number. He told Zeifman that if an emergency arose, Bernard Hellring would be able to get in touch with him. Use Hellring as a trusted confidant, Rodino instructed.

Rodino's instructions to Doar were that Zeifman was in overall charge, and that in hiring staff members for the inquiry, all persons must be approved by Zeifman before they could be hired.

Rodino also had granted Doar's request that he be allowed to discuss matters with Burke Marshall, his former Justice Department boss. Zeifman objected to Doar going outside Congress, especially to Marshall. He recalled to Rodino the conversation Zeifman had with Clark Clifford, who had warned about Marshall's close relationship with the Kennedy family, a family Nixon saw as enemies and a connection that could destroy the credibility of the impeachment inquiry if it ever became public.

Doar consulted with Marshall frequently during the recess. Despite Zeifman's misgivings about Doar's outside consultations, however, Zeifman talked almost daily with Hellring and sometimes with Clifford.

By the time Doar had been on the job for two weeks, he had decided that he wanted to fire Cates, or at least relegate him to a minor role in the impeachment inquiry. Zeifman blocked the move.

The two also quarreled during the first three weeks of January 1974 over hiring decisions. Zeifman wanted a California expert in tax fraud cases to be hired, but Doar rejected the idea, saying the inquiry had no busines getting into Nixon's taxes.

Doar insisted that he be allowed to hire several friends and relatives for the staff—including Marshall's daughter—and didn't like having to go through Zeifman for permission.

In one conversation, Zeifman told Doar he would need some experienced lawyers, rather than the green kids he had been hiring, if he ever got into interrogating experienced Justice Department officials. Doar replied, "I don't believe in cross-examination. I win cases only on the basis of my witnesses and the other guy's documents." And career Justice officials wouldn't need to testify under oath because they could be relied upon to tell the truth, Doar said.

Zeifman decided the only way to keep Doar from single-handedly dominating the impeachment inquiry was to delay any decisions on his part, especially about giving final approval to hiring proposals, until Rodino returned to town in mid-January.

Jack Brooks, third-ranking Democrat on the committee, had remained in town for the holidays instead of going home to Beaumont, Texas. Zeifman arranged to talk to him on January 3 about the troubles he was having with Doar.

Zeifman and Cates were more Brooks's types of people. He didn't get along with quiet, taciturn people like Doar. His feelings against Doar already had jelled even though they had only met once.

"I have come to some tentative conclusions which I want to share with you," Zeifman told Brooks. "One, Doar is inept as a lawyer. Two, Doar is unwilling to investigate any illegal role that the Department of Justice, the FBI, or the CIA may have played in Watergate, and he's also unwilling to investigate the possibility that the president committed tax fraud. Three, I'm afraid Doar may be deliberately delaying the impeachment for as long as possible."

The last point, Zeifman said, was backed by Doar's connection with Burke Marshall and the Kennedy family and his own suspicion that the person who would benefit most by running against Nixon's administration would be Teddy Kennedy. The closer to the next presidential election in 1976 that the impeachment inquiry could be delayed, the more Kennedy would be helped.

"I don't yet have all of the facts," Zeifman admitted to Brooks. "These conclusions are based partly on facts and mostly on my strong feelings. And I'm not certain if I can trust my feelings."

Brooks leaned back in his chair, bit on his cigar and said, "Goddamn it, you remind me of me. I went to Sam Rayburn once and said the same thing, that I didn't yet have all the facts but I had strong, strong feelings and I didn't know if I could trust my feelings." Brooks said Rayburn replied, "Let me give you some advice. You ought to trust your feelings. If you don't trust your feelings, you'll never survive in Congress. You better trust your feelings or you'll be dead."

Bolstered by Brooks's support, Zeifman went over to the Congressional Hotel to confront Doar and tell him of his misgivings about the way Doar was conducting the inquiry. Doar held firm. He would do it his own way, he said, and would not conduct the investigation that Zeifman wanted him to get into.

Zeifman exploded. "This is a place made up of four hundred and thirty-five members of Congress. They delegate some responsibility to thirty-eight members of the Judiciary Committee, which has a chairman, a general counsel, and now a special counsel. It's not going to be done your way, my way, or the chairman's way. This has something to do with collective judgment and the collective responsibility of the committee, John. That's what this whole place is about and that's what this case is about."

Doar replied, "That's not what the case is about. I'll do it my way."

Zeifman, becoming more heated, then went into the subject of cross-examining witnesses. "Why not cross-examine Haldeman? Why not Ehrlichman? Why not Howard Hunt? Why not Mitchell? How about the president? Why not ask him some questions? We could even go about it politely. Why not just ask him about his income?"

Doar remained stoic and replied quietly, "We shouldn't go into his personal finances; we can't do a tax fraud case."

"Why not?" Zeifman asked. "How about the money in Swiss bank accounts? Shouldn't we investigate that?" Speculation that such accounts existed for Nixon had been the subject of recent Joint Taxation Committee probes.

"No," Doar said. "For us to go into the subject of foreign bank accounts on Nixon's part is too long and too complicated."

Zeifman said as he rose to leave, frustrated, "If we don't who will?"

Cates was having his problems with Doar, although he was trying harder than Zeifman to overlook the differences between them, primarily between their working styles.

Cates had backed off his earlier insistence on quickly calling witnesses and issuing subpoenas, but he was having trouble adjusting to the tidy, neatly arranged atmosphere in which Doar worked.

In a discussion one day, Cates told Doar that his assignment to some of the staff members to prepare background legal briefs on some of the allegations against Nixon was "bullshit. Now I know it has to be done and you have to have those briefs, and I know the strategy, but the fact of the matter is with the kind of proof that is shaping up, you just don't need them."

Cates also was chafing about Doar's dictum that all the staff write memos about anything they had to say. Everything had to be on paper and neatly filed. To coordinate that task, Doar hired an old friend from law school, Joe Woods. Cates didn't adjust well to that arrangement.

Cates told Doar, "I run a helluva shop in Madison and we've never written a fuckin' memo in our lives. I see a guy in the men's room and I say, 'Shit, we gotta do this.' That's the way we run our shop."

Doar was feeling a bit more relaxed around Cates by that time, even though he privately wanted him off the staff. He was afraid Cates would embarrass the inquiry.

Doar told him, "Cates, we've got to get this stuff down, in case you get hit by a truck."

Cates said, "I know that, I understand that. But the fact is I'm not doing this solo. I've got a whole bunch of guys knowing the facts. The problem is they can't articulate them because they don't have the training."

Exasperated in a pleasant sort of way, Doar said, "Cates, this isn't the kind of case you can just shoot the shit about."

Doar tried to be tolerant of Cates's working habits, which he considered very sloppy. He knew that Cates wasn't about to change.

Cates also couldn't work within Doar's dictum that every piece of information the inquiry staff had gathered relevant to impeachment be put down on three-by-five index cards and filed chronologically. It was a massive, time-consuming operation, which Cates saw as ridiculous. Cates spent his own time teaching the new staffers the case as he knew it to that time. The more people hired the greater detail he could assign them to look into, but he was getting frustrated with the pace.

On the other side of the committee, the Republican staff members were having their own problems during January.

After Cates was hired in mid-November to head the impeachment inquiry staff's preliminary work, the Republicans decided they had better have their own person on the staff to protect their interests.

Sam Garrison, a former member of the Judiciary Committee GOP staff and congressional aide to Vice-President Spiro Agnew before he resigned in October, had asked Edward Hutchinson, ranking committee Republican, for a job on the Republican impeachment staff.

By early December, it was clear that the impeachment inquiry, no matter how clean Hutchinson or Rodino might try to keep it, would become embroiled in partisan politics.

After the Republicans had begun complaining that Rodino was making all of the decisions without consulting the minority side, the Republicans elicited a promise from Rodino that Republicans would be hired for the impeachment inquiry panel although he still wanted the staff to be as nonpartisan as possible.

But then Rodino hired the decidedly Democratic Dick Cates to set up an inquiry staff without consulting the Republicans, so they decided they had better pick a Republican for the staff soon to make GOP selections.

On December 10, Garrison was hired. An ambitious youth, the thirty-two-year-old Garrison felt that by getting in on the ground floor, he would be able to become the chief minority counsel on the inquiry staff by default whenever the time came to establish that position.

Garrison worked hard at organizing a staff, combing lists of recommendations in much the same way the Democrats were taking recommendations to form their side.

But after Rodino announced that he had hired John Doar as special counsel for impeachment, the Republicans decided they would have to have someone of equal stature as his GOP counterpart.

On December 19, Rodino's ad hoc advisory group held an informal session. It began with a discussion of whether the impeachment inquiry and the Senate Watergate Committee would be duplicating each other's efforts. Charles Wiggins (R-Calif.) and John Conyers (D-Mich.), normally on opposite sides of any issue, led the talk in favor of the Judiciary Committee asking the Senate Watergate Committee to halt its investigation and leave all the Nixon matters to Judiciary.

The previous day, Bob McClory (R-Ill.) had made a speech on the House floor criticizing the committee's partisan conduct during the previous month. In the speech he also said, "It smacks of partisan politics to refuse to consider a schedule for concluding the committee's work on the impeachment inquiry." Several other committee Republicans joined McClory with similar speeches.

In an effort to defuse the criticism, Rodino told the ad hoc advisory committee that he thought Judiciary could conclude its impeachment inquiry by April, although privately he hadn't the slightest idea when the panel would be through. At that time he had no idea how the inquiry would be conducted, what the committee would need and what it would get.

Rodino then told the group that he was going to hold a news conference the following day to announce he had hired John Doar to be special counsel for the inquiry.

Almost immediately, the Republicans, to whom the hiring was a surprise, complained that Rodino hadn't discussed it with them. They raised the same complaints they had been making for the past month, that the inquiry was being handled on a partisan basis and that the GOP was being excluded from the big decisions. They said Rodino's predecessor, Emanuel Celler, would never have left the Republicans out in the cold that way.

Rodino answered that he had intended to hire the special counsel without consulting them, that the majority Democrats were still responsible for the operation of the committee and that thirty-eight people couldn't be making every decision. Anyhow, he said, Doar was not only nationally known, he was a Republican and they should be happy to have him.

The ranking Republican, Ed Hutchinson harrumphed, "He's no Republican!"

The Republicans weren't mollified. If the Democrats had their own person of stature, then the Republicans would have a counterpart. Tom Railsback (R-Ill.) brought up the name of Albert Jenner. McClory said he also knew Jenner and endorsed Railsback's idea. Rodino told them Jenner had been considered before Doar but had been rejected because he didn't think he could devote full time to the task.

But the Republicans could have Jenner if they wanted him, Rodino said. He reminded them, however, that he did not want any clear partisan breakdown on the staff, that whomever the Republicans hired would have to know that he or she was working for all the members, not just for the GOP side.

Sam Garrison was present at the meeting when Jenner's name was brought up and it became clear the Republicans would make a search for their own nationally known counsel.

Garrison had convinced himself that he would have that job. The next day while Doar's appointment was being announced to the press, Garrison sat down with Cates for a long discussion.

Two months earlier the vice-president for whom he worked had resigned his office in disgrace, Garrison said. He had assumed he was tainted by the same scandal through guilt by association and had hoped for a big score to recover his credibility. Being the chief GOP counsel on impeachment would give him that chance. So he was extremely disappointed when the Republicans turned to someone else. He felt disgraced again. "It's a lot easier on you," to have Doar selected, Garrison told Cates. "You came and you were never going to be number one. You had a specific job. Me, I thought that when I came here this was going to be a chance for me to get rid of the stigma" of having worked for Agnew.

There wasn't much that Cates could say in a situation like that. He tried to dissuade Garrison from being too pessimistic about it. He knew about Jenner, he said, and if Jenner was the man the Republicans chose, then Garrison would be working for a hell of a man and would still be in an important position on an extremely important task.

During the holiday period, Railsback spoke with Jenner about the job. Jenner said he would take it, providing he could spend only part time on it, at least in the early stages. After conferring by telephone with Hutchinson, Railsback told Jenner that would be acceptable.

Hutchinson then telephoned Rodino in Florida and told him of the GOP decision.

Rodino said that was all right with him, but that he wanted to talk with Jenner before the selection was announced because he still had the final say in hiring and he wanted to be sure about Jenner.

Rodino returned to Washington late in the first week of January and met with Jenner. He told Jenner the same things he had told Doar about the importance of appearing impartial on impeachment.

Nine other members of Rodino's fifteen-man advisory group interrupted their vacations to return to Washington for a meeting on January 7. The selection of Jenner was announced at the outset and the panel then spent the next two hours getting a briefing from Doar on the staff's progress.

The staff then numbered forty-two people, including nineteen lawyers, four investigators, seven secretaries, six clerks, three researchers, and three administrative staffers. Six of the lawyers were from the regular committee staff and four of the others, including Jenner, had been hired by the Republicans.

The entire second floor of the Congressional Hotel had been set aside for the impeachment inquiry staff, with extra suites on the third and sixth floors. Security measures were borrowed from the security-conscious special prosecutor's staff, so the second floor was off limits to any persons not specifically authorized to be there. To be sure no one else got in, guards were posted at the second-floor elevators.

Doar told the ad hoc group he had had two conversations with Leon Jaworski, the new special prosecutor, and another with Sam Dash, chief counsel for the Senate Watergate Committee, and had asked both men to turn over to the impeachment inquiry all of the materials they had relevant to Nixon.

Both Jaworski and Dash said they were concerned about the procedures for maintaining the confidentiality of that material which had not been made public. Both were aware the Senate committee had leaked like a sieve and they had no reason to believe the House panel would be any different.

Jaworski, Doar said, advised him that whatever he could give the inquiry also was being given to the Watergate grand jury. And grand juries always held everything given to them in strictest confidence. Before he could turn anything over, Jaworski said, the committee would have to adopt some sort of procedure for maintaining the confidentiality. Even then, Jaworski had said, he wasn't sure he could cooperate.

Doar said he argued that the committee's power to conduct an impeachment inquiry was specified in the Constitution and as such, was superior to all other considerations. Jaworski said he was a servant of the court and had to operate under its rules. He didn't necessarily buy the supreme authority of the inquiry either, he said, and wasn't even satisfied the committee had the power to issue subpoenas since the power han't been voted by the whole House. Beyond the court strictures, Jaworski said, his office was in very touchy negotiations with the White House over material he wanted from Nixon, and the White House was resisting Jaworski partly out of concern about confidentiality.

Because of his problems with Jaworski and Dash, Doar also recommended that the committee set up some elaborate procedures for protecting the confidentiality of the records they obtained and, because of Jaworski's questions about committee authority, seek a subpoena authority directly from the House to clear up any doubts.

The four categories that Cates had set up before he joined the staff, Doar told the group, probably would be further broken down. He was thinking about six categories, he said, taking some of the charges out of the main cover-up category and adding two others, one on domestic intelligence activities ordered by the White House and the other on intelligence activities aimed at the 1972 election campaign under the code name "Operation Gemstone."

Doar also brought up a proposal Rodino had made earlier, that the committee retain constitutional experts as consultants in deciding what were impeachable offenses. Doar, in consultation with Burke Marshall, had decided, and Rodino had approved, having the committee provide some display of movement on impeachment during the early slow months of Doar's investigation by holding televised hearings on the meaning of impeachable offenses.

Jack Brooks ridiculed some of Doar's suggestions at the meeting. First, he said, the committee could take a vote that day and decide to impeach Nixon, because the cover-up of the White House connection with the Watergate break-in was worse than the break-in itself. Second, the committee was not going to get into a position of having to vote on what were impeachable offenses, so there was no sense in conducting hearings on the subject and opening members up to those kinds of pressures. The members will have to make that decision when they vote whether to impeach Nixon, he said. Ed Hutchinson agreed. On the subpoena question, Brooks said there was no problem in deciding the committee already had power to subpoena whatever it wanted for impeachment. It was one of several committees having that standing power and the committee already had voted to vest that authority in Rodino alone.

Rodino replied that he would drop the idea of having hearings on what constituted impeachable offenses. But he still thought the committee members needed some guidelines and a consensus on what such offenses would entail, so he instructed the inquiry staff to issue a report to the committee within the month on what impeachable offenses were.

On the subpoena question, Rodino was satisfied the committee had the power, but lacked specific authority, and he thought the entire House should vote on the question to remove any doubts that could cloud the future validity of the inquiry. He was aware it might reopen the partisan wrangle the committee had engaged in the previous October so to avoid that he would agree to share the subpoena power with Hutchinson. He instructed the inquiry staff to draw up some proposals for maintaining the confidentiality of material and have them ready for a committee vote shortly after the recess ended on January 21.

The Republicans demanded, and Rodino agreed, that the staff would eliminate from its "mountain of material" all but the matters relevant to impeachment and "present to us only the undisputed facts which had been admitted by those involved." The committee members then would decide what else they needed.

In early January 1974, then, three months after the House Judiciary Committee was handed the impeachment assignment, the panel was geared up, staffed, and pointed in the direction of some conclusions about impeachment.

But more pitfalls lay ahead. The day after the meeting of the ad hoc advisory group, the White House began an offensive against impeachment by releasing two "white papers." One was a defense against the allegations that the dairy industry had bought favors with campaign contributions. The other was a defense against the allegation that the administration had issued an antitrust decision favorable to ITT in exchange for contributions to its proposed convention site in San Diego in 1972.

It soon became clear Jaworski and Dash would resist the committee's efforts to get at the White House material given them.

Bert Jenner started off his impeachment career on the wrong foot by injudiciously telling reporters in Chicago that the president could be held accountable for the actions of his aides if those aides committed impeachable offenses. That was the theory advanced by President James Madison, but it was one which had been widely rejected by Republicans. Jenner had said break-ins and wiretapping were two examples of such actions. This statement began the war between Jenner and committee Republicans.

Charles Wiggins (R-Calif.) opened a campaign against some of the allegations against Nixon, calling charges such as impoundment of funds and the bombing of Cambodia—lumped into the catch-all category—frivolous and not worth the committee's time.

He and others also were pressuring Rodino to set a deadline for wrapping up the inquiry. The Republican leadership in the House pressed for limited hearings and a prompt vote, assuming correctly at that time that there were not enough votes on the committee to impeach Nixon. None of the Republicans would have voted for it, and probably half a dozen Democrats would have opposed impeachment if the vote had been taken then.

Vice-President Gerald Ford joined in exerting pressure for a quick vote. Public groups both for Nixon and against him had already been formed to lobby House members on impeachment. Calls for Nixon's resignation were increasing. Some committee members were readying resolutions to have the House force the committee to take steps Rodino did not want it to take, such as setting a deadline for finishing the inquiry and going to court to get evidence Jaworski was withholding.

The pressure was bipartisan. Jack Brooks was sniping at Doar and Rodino's leadership. Democratic Majority Leader "Tip" O'Neill was

hassling Rodino so much about displaying some progress on impeachment that Rodino uncharacteristically lost his temper on the House floor
one day and snapped at O'Neill, "Goddamn it, get the hell off my
back."

For his part, Rodino began his own public relations offensive against
Jaworski's refusal to give the committee the material he had collected
for the grand jury. "If we start from scratch, it could go on from now to
God knows when," Rodino told reporters late in January. He already
had let his "by April" target date slip to the end of April.

Jerry Waldie (D-Calif.), the committee member who introduced the
first impeachment resolution against Nixon after the "Saturday Night
Massacre," threatened to call up his resolution for an immediate vote
on the House floor if Nixon refused to give the committee any material.

A lawyer from Boston joined the White House team to spearhead
Nixon's legal defense, which until then had been vacillating, uncoor-
dinated, and weak. James St. Clair would almost split the committee
down the middle before its inquiry was over, and nearly deny Rodino
the bipartisan vote for or against impeachment that he so badly wanted.

Rodino faced so many unsolved problems, took pressure from so
many sides, and worked so many hours in the early weeks of the new
year that he felt as though he had had no vacation at all.

Since the hectic days began in the fall, he no longer had been able to
maintain his regimen of paddleball three times a week in the House
gymnasium. He was tired, had trouble sleeping, and had returned for
the start of the session on January 21 with what he thought was a virus.

He was in his mid-sixties and knew he wasn't in the kind of shape he
should be.

CHAPTER V

Evidence

When the congressional recess ended on January 21, 1974, it meant the beginning of sixteen- and eighteen-hour work days for Rodino, and he didn't always make it home on weekends. When he did go home, he took along material John Doar had given him to read on the progress of the inquiry. Rodino often closeted himself in his Newark or shore home to read the material, emerging only for meals and brief chats with his family. Since he didn't have time to play paddleball anymore during his work weeks, he had gained weight. To lose it, he quit eating lunch during the week and existed instead on black coffee.

The pressures were rising. The public, the Republicans, the White House, and, because of all of those, the Democratic leadership, were demanding action. The work was being done behind the closely guarded doors of the Congressional Hotel's second floor, so movement was unperceptible.

Everyone involved had his own idea of what should be done and how to do it. Rodino's staff was squabbling, his committee members were unhappy. The committee was supposed to be gathering impeachment evidence but had no more than was in the public domain. How to obtain material and how to protect it were becoming overwhelming issues.

Rodino thought he had picked up a virus infection in Florida. He was becoming increasingly exhausted by the end of each day, and by mid-February began to complain of chest pains, which he hoped were caused by indigestion from irregular and poor eating habits, but which he feared were signs of heart trouble. He was sixty-four and working harder than he ever had.

On February 14, after three weeks of negotiating, bickering, resolving, and deciding, some hurdles had been jumped, but many others loomed. For ninety minutes that day, John Doar and Bert Jenner related to members of the ad hoc advisory group their first discussion with James St. Clair the previous Monday.

As had Special Prosecutor Leon Jaworski and Senate Watergate Committee Counsel Sam Dash, St. Clair had brought up the question of confidentiality of any evidence that might be turned over to the impeachment inquiry. Rodino didn't know how to resolve that problem. The members would insist that they have access to all of the evidence, yet Rodino knew from twenty-five years in the House that he couldn't expect an entire committee to keep the same secrets.

And St. Clair had raised a new problem, Doar and Jenner told the group. He assumed the president would have the right to have counsel present during any evidentiary hearings on impeachment. Since Rodino, Doar, and the members viewed the committee's activities as tantamount to the proceedings of a grand jury, where defendant's counsel is never allowed, they had assumed there was no role for the president's counsel in initial impeachment proceedings. But St. Clair's contention was going to raise a political problem. It would inevitably open new questions about the inquiry's fairness.

That afternoon, Rodino's chest pains became more intense and frequent. They were too persistent to be passed off as indigestion. He also felt more nervous and tired. He became alarmed, and after a break on the House floor, went downstairs to the doctor's office. The doctor sent him out to Bethesda Naval Hospital—members of Congress have VIP privileges in the military hospital—where Rodino was given an electrocardiogram examination and other checks to determine if he had suffered a heart attack.

He hadn't, but the doctors said he needed a rest. They advised him to remain there in the intensive care section of the coronary unit through the weekend.

Francis O'Brien, Rodino's administrative assistant, was still green to congressional practices. He became concerned that if the hospitalization became known, Rodino would lose the impeachment assignment. Rodino was concerned that a revelation of his illness might cause anxieties about his ability to continue. Together they decided to keep the hospital stay a secret and Rodino returned to his grind the following Monday.

The issue of the committee's authority to issue subpoenas was an important question, even though the committee had acted as though no doubt existed by its vote to vest the subpoena power in Rodino acting alone.

No one had challenged the committee's subpoena or its delegation of the power to one person, to that point. But the power hadn't been used in the extremely contentious case of impeachment. The power in impeachment also had to reach the possibility of what the staff had come to call "the big subpoena," one served on the president himself. There was no doubt the subpoena authority would be challenged somewhere and the fight that would result could divert, and possibly cloud, the outcome of the inquiry.

There also was the question of the confidentiality of the inquiry's activities. If the committee had to vote on each subpoena, as it had to do under House rules, the matter would soon become public, and the scope and direction of the inquiry would become known, jeopardizing efforts to negotiate and maneuver quietly behind the scene. Like a prosecutor's probe, the investigation couldn't be very effective if its every move were telegraphed in advance. Even routine subpoenas would take on extraordinary importance in the press.

So Rodino and others felt the subpoena authority had to be vested in one or a select few individuals.

Court participation had to be avoided at all costs, a majority of the committee believed. The power to impeach was vested directly in the House of Representatives by the second section of the first article of the Constitution. To grant court intervention would be to strike at the very heart of the concept of three co-equal branches of government.

Political considerations also were involved. The special prosecutor already was bogged down in a court fight for White House materials; his predecessor had been fired over issuing subpoenas for them. Some committee members wanted all the issues facing the committee, particularly the subpoena issue, clarified by the Supreme Court before beginning the inquiry, but they were a tiny minority.

Speaker Carl Albert, was very concerned that the Judiciary Committee do nothing that would abrogate the House's overriding authority in impeachment, either in fact or in appearance. He had called Jerry Zeifman and John Doar over to his office to give them a lecture on just that issue.

Rodino believed the only way, then, to clarify the committee's power to subpoena and thus its power to vest it in one person was to have the entire House confirm that the power did, indeed, exist in the committee. To bring the matter up again, however, would not only mean a new partisan battle, it also would place the House in a position it didn't want at that time, a vote on an impeachment issue. Its vote two months earlier to give the committee one million dollars for its inquiry was as close as it had wanted to come. Beyond that, there was a risk, however slight, the vote would go against the committee. The committee needed all the backing from the entire House that it could get. The inquiry wasn't going well.

When the committee members returned with the rest of Congress in late January, the Democrats met to go over impeachment issues the committee faced, including action on the subpoena power resolution Doar's staff had drafted by then.

Doar handed out copies of the first draft to the advisory group. It was long, complicated and convoluted, citing court litigation and other matters usually extraneous to congressional procedures.

"You've sent us a subpoena resolution in Sanskrit," Jack Brooks bellowed at Doar, waving the pages in the air.

"Don't you realize, more than forty lawyers worked on this subpoena resolution?" Rodino asked Brooks.

"Yes, Pete, and it looks it," came the rejoinder from Barbara Jordan (D-Tex.).

Brooks asked Doar why he thought it was necessary to write the resolution in such a complicated form.

Still unruffled, Doar responded, "The subpoena power is extremely important, therefore it has to be precisely defined."

Brooks replied sarcastically, "Let me tell you something about power, Mr. Doar. Power is best defined by its exercise."

Doar was instructed to take the resolution back to his staff and return with one more in line with normal congressional resolutions in time for the next Democratic caucus on January 30.

When Doar presented the new draft to that group, Brooks told him, "Well, at least you changed it from Sanskrit to Old English." Brooks offered a much tighter, simpler version one-third as long as Doar's, but his colleagues rejected it.

The relationship between Brooks and Doar was set in cement from that time on. It reached its nadir a few days later when Brooks learned during a closed committee meeting that Doar and an inquiry staffer had participated in a U.S. District Court session. The closed court proceeding was held so lawyers in related cases—including impeachment—could see depositions in the Nader group's lawsuit alleging Nixon traded favors for campaign contributions from the dairy industry. The lawyers present had to stipulate the matters would be kept confidential. In the case of Doar and his aide, that stipulation meant that members of Congress would be bound by the court's dictum. Committee members didn't know about the appearance until a reporter began asking questions. At the next meeting where Doar appeared before the members, Brooks screamed at him for submitting Congress to the jurisdiction of the court right after the committee had held a long discussion about just such action. Doar apologized.

Rodino had even said at the previous meeting that the power of impeachment was so broad that "to engage us in any controversy with the court would be a fatal mistake." He said it not only would divert the committee from impeachment into litigation, but it also would mean that Rodino was unsure and unconvinced that the committee possessed that broad authority and power.

Nevertheless, Rodino had given Doar permission to make the trip to the court and didn't consider that incident as a submission to court jurisdiction in impeachment. Anyhow, he told Brooks after his blow-up, nothing of great importance came of it.

Brooks wasn't satisfied. He launched into a long discourse about

Doar's going off half-cocked believing himself to be equal to the members of the House. Jordan joined Brooks in the rebuke. Brooks returned to his office afterwards and wrote a letter to the court saying in no uncertain terms that he didn't consider himself bound by any court strictures on confidentiality which Doar might have agreed to.

The Republicans also decided to complicate the world of Peter Rodino in late January. Tom Railsback introduced a bill in the House in the form of a petition requiring Jaworski to turn over to the committee whatever evidence he had relating to the possible impeachment of Nixon.

That was one of the avenues Jaworski had suggested to Doar as a means of freeing him from the court strictures. But the Democrats had specifically resisted that route, again because they didn't want to submit to court jurisdiction.

In their own caucus, the committee's Republicans decided to push for an April 30 cut-off date for impeachment proceedings. After all, they said, that was Rodino's target date. They would attempt to attach it as an amendment to the subpoena power resolution three days hence when the committee held its first meeting to consider impeachment.

The Republicans argued that they merely wanted to hold Rodino to his word, even if it had been given in a reckless moment when Rodino considered it easier to name the most-mentioned target date than to continue evading the question of when the inquiry would end.

The bill's chief sponsors, Tom Railsback and Bob McClory, said that if the administration failed to cooperate with the committee, or if Jaworski continued to delay in turning over his material to the committee, the deadline could be extended.

A fight over the issue could jeopardize the decisive vote that Rodino wanted from the House. But other events unrelated to impeachment—the type of good luck the committee would have for the next six months—were taking place.

Public opinion polls were showing that most persons believed Nixon was guilty of at least one of the serious charges against him. A group of electronics experts also concluded that eighteen minutes of blank space on a tape of a conversation Nixon had held with John Mitchell on June 20, 1972, was caused by four or five deliberate erasures. And Nixon's new attorney general, William Saxbe, issued the opinion that in a defense against impeachment, Nixon would have to hire his own defense lawyer; the Justice Department couldn't help him. Then Nixon himself contributed to the committee's good luck.

The Constitution requires that the president report to Congress on the state of the union the two branches jointly govern. It has become a tradition that the president deliver the State of the Union address to a joint session of Congress in late January or early February each year. Generally the address is confined to high-sounding, optimistic reports about the economy or the nation's emergence from whatever problems it is having.

Nixon's January 30 address to Congress was extraordinary. He acknowledged the dismal state of affairs in the country at the time. The speech also was a battle cry. He talked of cooperating with the special prosecutor's office and the House Judiciary Committee and urged them both to move quickly. "One year of Watergate is enough," he said, adding he had no intention of resigning despite the recent increase in calls for him to do so.

Nixon recognized the Judiciary Committee's responsibility for impeachment, he said, but there was one limitation to his cooperation with it. "I will follow the precedent that has been followed by and defended by every president from George Washington to Lyndon B. Johnson of never doing anything that weakens the office of the President of the United States or impairs the ability of the presidents of the future to make the great decisions that are so essential to this nation and to the world."

Almost as if to answer Nixon's statement, the committee held its first formal session as an impeachment panel the next morning—to approve by voice vote the subpoena power resolution that Doar's staff had written. The only fight at the meeting was over the Republican effort to attach an April 30 cut-off date to the impeachment. It was defeated 23–14. (The GOP side was one short at the time because of the resignation of a Republican member earlier in the month.)

The members took a hard line at the meeting, which had been opened to television cameras, the public, and the press. The impact of the event was contained in the opening words of the resolution:

Resolved, that the committee on the Judiciary, acting as a whole or by any subcommittee thereof, is authorized and directed to investigate fully and completely whatever sufficient grounds exist for the House of Representatives to exercise its constitutional power to impeach Richard M. Nixon, President of the United States of America. The committee shall report to the House of Representatives such resolutions, articles of impeachment or other recommendations as it deems proper.

The resolution then empowered the committee to command the testimony or attendance of any persons, save the president when it would collide with his Fifth Amendment right against self-incrimination. And it could command the production, without limitation, of such things as

books, records, correspondence, logs, journals, memoranda, papers, documents, writings, drawings, graphs, charts, photographs, reproductions, recordings, tapes, transcripts, printouts, data compilations from which information can be obtained (translated, if necessary, through detection devices into reasonably usable form), tangible objects and other things of any kind.

During the committee debate over the resolution, Rodino established that the refusal to furnish any of the materials the resolution gave the committee the power to request would itself be grounds for impeachment. If Nixon cited executive privilege as a defense—as Nixon had suggested in his State of the Union address that he would—the House could cite him for contempt, Rodino said.

For the record, Rodino stated that the power the committee was seeking could only be delegated to it by the House and "does not depend upon any statutory provisions or require judicial enforcement." It was his formal announcement that the committee did not recognize any judicial authority over impeachment.

Asked later if the resolution meant that he planned to call Nixon himself to testify, Rodino said, "If it became necessary for the completion of the inquiry, that certainly would be a possibility—especially to assure a fair judgment.''

Jack Brooks said he still wasn't satisfied with the language of the subpoena and thought the committee need do no more than say, ''We have full subpoena authority and, by God, let's exercise it.''

The committee clearly was feeling its power, taking its cue from the tired, but more confident Peter Rodino. His earlier qualms about bringing up the touchy subject of the subpoena power had subsided. When the resolution was taken to the House floor the following week, he was confident he would win.

So in the committee's first formal action on impeachment, it had been unanimous in its support of having absolute authority to conduct its impeachment inquiry. Further resistance by Nixon, then, could only erode his support on the committee. Until then, Nixon had the unfaltering support of every Republican on the committee, and possibly the three southern Democrats, meaning that he not only could deny the committee a bipartisan vote in favor of impeachment, he also could deny a majority for it.

Although he was confident of winning, Rodino still had to face the entire House with the matter. He didn't relish forcing his colleagues to cast a vote on the impeachment matter. There were staunch Nixon loyalists in the House who didn't believe the committee should be even remotely involved in impeachment activity and they could cause trouble. He had no idea how strong their numbers might be.

Between the committee meeting and the following Wednesday, February 6, Rodino did some in-House politicking. He met with the Democratic leadership to line up its backing for the resolution and talked to the Republican leader, John Rhodes of Arizona, to get his support. He pointed out that the resolution would allow Ed Hutchinson and him jointly or separately to issue subpoenas. If one of them chose to, he could refer the matter to the full committee for a vote.

The day before the vote, he fortified the members of his committee with a closed briefing on the progress of the inquiry staff, what it had, where it planned to go and who it planned to go with. Doar told them the staff numbered ninety persons, including thirty-nine attorneys, twenty-seven chosen by the Democratic side and twelve by the GOP.

Sensitive to political problems, he noted that the attorneys came from fourteen states and the District of Columbia. They were selected from more than five hundred prospects, he said, and all had undergone the same grilling to which he had submitted.

By the time the staff was completed a few weeks later, it would number 104, with 43 attorneys, a staff bigger than either that of the special prosecutor or Senate Watergate Committee. The age range was from twenty-five to sixty-six, salaries ranged from $14,000 to $36,000. Four staff members were black and three were women. Doar had avoided the criticism leveled at Archibald Cox, the first special prosecutor, for choosing mostly young liberal lawyers from Harvard Law School.

Doar also outlined the investigation going on in the six categories he had established. Under the category of "domestic surveillance activities conducted by or at the direction of the White House" were allegations concerning: illegal wiretaps in 1969; a plan to coordinate widespread domestic surveillance, concocted by a White House aide, Tom Huston; the activities of John Caulfield and Tony Ulasewicz, who were doing private detective work for the White House; activities of the "White House plumbers," formally known as the Special Investigative Unit; and the activities surrounding the Daniel Ellsberg trial.

The second category covered "allegations concerning intelligence activities conducted by or at the direction of the White House for the purposes of the presidential election of 1972," and included: White House "dirty tricks" in the 1972 campaign; intelligence activities of the Committee to Re-Elect the President; the falsified cables alleging a White House–ordered assassination of South Vietnamese President Ngo Dinh Diem during the Kennedy administration; the plan to burglarize and firebomb the Brookings Institution in Washington; and "Operation Sandwedge," Caulfield's code name for the campaign intelligence plan that preceded "Operation Gemstone."

Category three was the Watergate break-in itself and its alleged cover-up. It included allegations concerning: G. Gordon Liddy's widespread campaign intelligence plan; the destruction of files, documents, and other evidence in the days immediately following discovery of the break-in; payments to the Watergate defendants; the relationship between the CIA and the Watergate investigation; offers of executive clemency to the defendants; the role of John Dean in the investigation; the firing of Archibald Cox and the "Saturday Night Massacre"; and the subject of the presidential tapes.

Under the heading of the president's personal finances, the allegations included: tax deductions taken for the gift of Nixon's vice-presidential papers; deductions and expenditures on his private homes in San Clemente and Key Biscayne; the sale of his New York apartment; tax deductions he took on his home in Whittier; the sale of some lots in Florida; the possibility that Nixon's personal use of government facilities and services ought to be counted as taxable income; and government improvements to his two homes unrelated to security. Doar pointed out that since the Joint Committee on Taxation was reviewing Nixon's income tax returns, the inquiry staff was not going to duplicate that investigation and wasn't equipped to do so.

The fifth category concerned use of government agencies for political purposes and alleged White House involvement with illegal campaign contributions. They included: allegations of links between dairy industry contributions and dairy import quotas and price supports; allegations about the compilation of an "enemies" list and action taken with various agencies, particularly the Internal Revenue Service, to punish persons on the list; allegations that the Antitrust Division of the Justice Department had been ordered to give International Telephone and Telegraph favorable treatment because of a campaign contribution; and the allegation there was a connection between the White House and alleged attempts by Nixon aides to interfere with a government case against financier Robert Vesco, who had secretly contributed $200,000 to Nixon.

The final category was the catch-all one, concerning the secret bombing of Cambodia and the impoundment of congressional appropriations.

Doar described the complex filing system and the extensive library the staff already had compiled and the duties of each supervisory member of the staff, right down to Benjamin Marshall—a retired Air Force colonel who had specialized in security and who was the sergeant-at-arms for the inquiry staff—who would be named to deliver the subpoenas to the president.

A task force, composed of both majority- and minority-hired staff attorneys, was assigned to each category, and a seventh was assigned the duty of making "constitutional and legal analyses."

As soon as the subpoena power was granted by the House the next day, Doar told the committee members, the staff would be ready to sift the material already on hand, and armed with the new subpoena power resolution clarifying the committee's standing, ask Jaworski for the Nixon material he had. The inquiry staff then would decide what else it would need, and make its requests by the end of the month.

Doar's litany was an impressive first report to the members.

And Doar had taken Rodino's caution to heart. Several times during his presentation, he said he wanted to emphasize "that these are mere allegations. The fact that an inquiry is being or will be made should not be taken to mean that we think there was necessarily wrongdoing there, nor should it be taken to mean that there has been any prejudgment whatsoever."

Doar was almost consumed by the need to appear impartial. He was careful to keep his voice neutral when he said anything about the allegations or the material that had been collected. The members could construe the material as evidence if they wished, but he would not characterize it as such.

The meeting was encouraging. It was conducted entirely in a nonpartisan manner, with Democrats and Republicans asking similar questions and raising the same concerns. Tom Railsback suggested the committee introduce a separate resolution, setting up a court procedure for enforcing the subpoenas the panel might issue. Both Bob McClory and George Danielson (D-Calif.) opposed the idea of the legislative branch asking the judicial branch for help in a matter assigned solely to the legislative.

After listening for nearly an hour without speaking, Ed Hutchinson voiced the opinion he would hold throughout impeachment:

"I think this committee should avoid confrontations, either with the president or with the court, and I am still of the frame of mind that I cannot believe that the White House wants to face a confrontation with this committee, because it has been my observation that the White House has been losing these confrontations right and left. . . . If we subpoena somebody and they simply are contemptuous of us, that is one thing.

"But, I am talking about subpoenas to the White House or to Mr.

Jaworski. I would think that once armed with the subpoena power, that subpoena power ought to be used as a matter of last resort and not the first resort, because I still hope that we can get what we need through negotiations because these are reasonable men.''

The members also were told that the committee had received 350,000 pieces of mail expressing opinions on impeachment. The mail was running more than twelve to one in favor of impeachment, but down from the thirty to one ratio shortly after the ''Saturday Night Massacre.''

When the session broke up after two hours, the doors were opened and reporters poured in to hear essentially the same report from Rodino and Doar. Rodino also expressed his concern that the public might not have the proper perception of what impeachment meant.

''I hope the public soon learns the impeachment process is to determine whether there is probable cause'' to believe the president may be guilty of impeachable offenses and to recommend to the House that it impeach him if it does determine there is cause. The House can send the case to the Senate for trial if it chooses and the Senate can convict him and remove him from office if it chooses, Rodino added.

Hutchinson, who also stayed for the press conference, struck the only negative note of the day: ''If the committee doesn't have firm, solid evidence against the president personally by the end of April, there would be no justification for the inquiry to proceed further.''

Although the GOP members of the committee already had failed during the January 31 committee meeting to attach the April 30 cut-off to the investigation, they planned, led by McClory, to try to attach the cut-off date on the House floor the next day when the subpoena power resolution, H. Res. 803, was brought up for a House vote.

Under House procedure, a bill must pass through the Rules Committee, which passes its own resolution determining how the bill will be handled on the floor. In the case of the subpoena resolution, it already had passed a ''closed rule,'' one that would allow no amendments to the resolution and thus preclude the McClory amendment. But the rules' resolution itself can be changed if the members vote to defeat the ''previous question.'' That would make the Rules Committee resolution the pending business and it could be changed to allow amendments to the subpoena power resolution.

The next morning, before the vote, John Rhodes gathered the GOP leadership and committee Republicans in his office to discuss the handling of the subpoena power resolution. Rhodes urged the committee Republicans to forget plans for defeating the ''previous question'' in order to try to add the cut-off date. He was convinced, he said, that the Democrats could easily win such a vote. He said he was afraid the vote would be interpreted as one against the president and a reflection of the sentiment for impeachment in the House. Unanimity by members of both parties on the subpoena power resolution would make the vote meaningless as a measure of impeachment sentiment, he said.

McClory argued that the American people, regardless of party affiliation, were more interested in an end to the impeachment than any expression of sentiment at that point. He said he thought not only the Republicans, but several Democrats, especially the pro-Nixon conservatives from the South, would join committee Republicans.

The rest of the House Republican leadership supported Rhodes and said they were confident they could control the other Republicans. Rhodes added that the White House and Vice-President Ford supported his position.

All sides held firm on the issue later that afternoon and McClory was defeated, 342–70, in his effort. The subpoena power resolution itself was then overwhelmingly approved, as expected, 410–4.

The four congressmen casting negative votes were all Republicans, including Carlos J. Moorhead of California, a member of the committee. The other three were David Treen of Louisiana, Ben Blackburn of Georgia, and Earl Landgrebe of Indiana.

Moorhead had filed minority views stating his position in the committee report accompanying the resolution. ''I cannot concur with this overly broad grant of the subpoena power,'' he said. ''There is no limitation placed in the rsolution to restrict materials subpoenaed to matters which are relevant to the inquiry. This can only precipitate a constitutional confrontation and further divide the people of our country. This will delay rather than expedite the present proceedings.''

The following day the Republican leadership, without getting his consent, chose Representative Delbert Latta (R-Ohio) to replace William Keating, also Ohio Republican, on the Judiciary Committee. Latta was one of the more senior House Republicans, very conservative and a strong Nixon supporter.

On Sunday, Rodino opened a public campaign to force cooperation by Jaworski and the White House with the impeachment probe. In a nationally televised interview, he said, ''I don't want to contend with Mr. Jaworski, but now that we have the subpoena authority, I think that this is a different matter. . . .

''The power that the House has now vested in the Judiciary Committee is such that all of those documents should be turned over that are necessary to this inquiry,'' he said. ''We believe that the right to inquiry under the power of impeachment is such that it can go as far as the secret recesses of the presidency, as President Polk once said.''

Still Jaworski resisted. He said he needed one more thing—assurances that what he turned over would be kept confidential.

John Doar and Bert Jenner had heard the same argument from James St. Clair in their first meeting with the president's special counsel on Monday, February 11, the same meeting at which St. Clair had raised the question of the president's right to have counsel present at impeachment proceedings and to cross-examine witnesses.

St. Clair had taken over as Nixon's special counsel on January 2 and was assigned to defend him on three fronts—the Senate Watergate Committee, the special prosecutor's office, and the House Judiciary Committee. The Senate panel soon ended its deliberations, but St. Clair would be spread dangerously thin dealing with the other two.

As soon as he sat down in his office in the Old Executive Office Building next door to the White House, St. Clair was confronted with the question then before the courts—What caused the eighteen-minute gap in the June 20, 1972, tape?

Soon after, he was immersed in issues on several fronts and built his staff up to a total of seven lawyers, most of them recruited from the Justice Department. It wasn't nearly as big as the staffs of any of his adversaries, but he thought it was sufficient.

His first contact with the Judiciary Committee was a letter to Rodino on February 5 announcing his availability. The following week, after the House had vested its broad subpoena power in the committee, St. Clair and two of his lawyers, Malcolm Howard and John McCahill, took a White House limousine to the impeachment inquiry's headquarters.

Their initial conversations with Doar and Jenner were exploratory, but they did raise the thorny issues that Doar reported to the committee session later that week.

St. Clair was immediately surprised in the meeting, however, by Jenner's attitude. He had been selected as Republican counsel, but he didn't appear to reflect the defense of the president that St. Clair had anticipated when Jenner's appointment was announced the week following his own. As St. Clair described it later on the way back to the White House, "He seemed very anxious to outdo Mr. Doar in his enthusiasm for the prosecution."

St. Clair had taken the job with the idea that the impeachment process was a political one "in the highest sense of the word." The people making the initial judgment had a great deal of responsibility to their constituents and to the public as a whole and always had to be conscious of the impact of their actions on the American public. That's what politics was about, St. Clair felt, responsibility to the public and not to a judge, jury, or any government body. He couldn't think of anything more political.

The president's counsel had expected, then, some adversary relationship between Doar and Jenner, since one was majority counsel and the other minority counsel. "I found none," he said. "We will have to become counsel to the minority, in effect. Someone has to defend the cause and obviously he isn't." His opinion didn't change in subsequent meetings.

Sam Garrison felt that way, too. He was saddened by the selection of Jenner over himself, but had no reason to doubt Jenner would work for the minority.

Some Republican members had doubts about it, though. At one of their caucuses, Jenner was forced to back away from the interview he had given in Chicago in mid-January stating that he thought a president could be impeached for the crimes of his subordinates. That and the revelation that Jenner had contributed to the campaign coffers of a Democratic senator had invited heavy GOP criticism. Jenner explained that the senator's family and his were old friends. Jenner kept his job.

By late February, Garrison was angry with Jenner. He didn't feel comfortable with the stuffy attitude of Hutchinson, so he decided to go to McClory with his complaints. In an hour-long talk, he told McClory the differences between him and Jenner went right down to the basics. Jenner felt, he said, that there must be complete agreement among the impeachment inquiry staff on every issue. His fear, he said, was that the Democrats would prevail on every issue, since Jenner would not express a difference of opinion with Doar on any major question. There were differing views held by the minority staff on several questions, he said, but Jenner was not expressing them and Jenner was the only one with direct entree to Doar. Much of his information of the progress of the inquiry came to him indirectly, Garrison said.

McClory said he felt Jenner's relationship with Doar was important to the Republicans because without it, the Republican staff members would be left to work independent of the majority staff and would be left ignorant of much of the conduct of the inquiry. As it was, he was satisfied that Jenner was keeping him abreast of the progress in almost daily telephone conversations. Nonetheless, McClory was unhappy that Jenner was failing to represent the minority position.

After Rodino assigned Doar the task of compiling a report on what impeachable offenses might comprise, the Republicans, led by Hutchinson, McClory, Wiggins, David Dennis of Indiana, Wiley Mayne of Iowa, and Larry Hogan of Maryland, told Jenner his minority staff should compile one for the Republicans.

Jenner didn't order it. Two GOP lawyers, William Weld and John Davidson, whom Garrison had hired before Jenner joined the staff, split off from their regular inquiry staff work to do it themselves.

Jenner was upset about their work and, a week before Garrison had complained to McClory about Jenner, Jenner complained to McClory about Garrison. He said Garrison had not been loyal to him and had written a note to Hutchinson advising of the preparation of a minority memorandum bolstering Hutchinson's view that impeachable offenses were confined to criminality. Weld and Davidson had worked in a third-floor office on their minority report without even reporting to Jenner about it, he complained.

The matter of defining "impeachable offenses" was not an easy one. Constitutional scholars were all over the field on what that might mean, ranging from the interpretation that a federal officer could be impeached only for violations of felony statutes to the opinion expressed by Gerald

Ford when he was pressing for the impeachment of Justice Douglas in 1970—''An impeachable offense is whatever a majority of the House of Representatives considers it to be in any given moment in history.''

Doar presented the broad view of impeachment to the committee Democrats on February 20 and to the full committee the following day. The Republicans, with the help of Weld and Davidson, countered with their own, narrow view. Soon after, the Justice Department offered its narrow interpretation and later St. Clair offered his for the president.

The broad view was ''solidly approved by the staff,'' Rodino said when describing the document. Robert Drinan said it was blander than it otherwise would have been if Doar hadn't made an effort to get Jenner's endorsement of it.

Doar's report taking the broad view anticipated the argument that a president could be impeached only for violations of criminal statutes. It said that if the framers of the Constitution had meant to limit the meaning they easily could have confined the language to ''treason, bribery or other crimes.'' They did not do so, the report said, because the framers borrowed on the impeachment provisions in ancient English law that were not confined to criminality.

The emphasis, the report said, traditionally has been on ''the significant effects of the conduct.'' It added, ''where the issue is presidential compliance with the constitutional requirements and limitations on the presidency, the crucial factor is not the intrinsic quality of behavior but the significance of its effects upon our constitutional system or the functioning of our government.''

St. Clair's brief, released a week later, said Doar missed the point. The English impeachment practice, St. Clair said, was divided into two distinct types, one ''a well-established criminal process for reaching great offenses committed against the government by men of high station—who today would occupy a high government office. The other type of impeachment used this well-established criminal process in the 17th and early 18th Century for the political purpose of achieving the absolute political supremacy of Parliament over the executive.''

St. Clair's brief said the framers of the Constitution rejected political impeachments and ''narrowly defined the grounds for impeachment'' by including elsewhere in the Constitution requirements for due process and procedural safeguards. The phrase "high crimes and mis-demeanors," had a unitary meaning to the framers, the brief said, like "bread and butter issues." Therefore, it said, "there is no evidence to attribute anything but a criminal meaning to the unitary phrase 'other high crimes and misdemeanors.' " It said, "Not only do the words inherently require a criminal offense, but one of a very serious nature committed in one's governmental capacity."

Very few of the committee members subscribed totally to any of the views offered. Even Charles Wiggins, one of Nixon's strongest de-fenders on the committee, rejected St. Clair's narrow view of impeach-ment.

Perhaps the best definition of impeachable offenses was offered by Ray Thornton (D-Ark.). He said he saw impeachment as a "safety valve to eliminate any forces which would tend to overthrow or destroy the structure of government itself. It is not a punishment for crime." He viewed "high crimes and misdemeanors" as meaning, in impeachment, "not something which the criminal laws or other laws can take care of." To Thornton, the word "high" modified both "crimes" and "misdemeanors" and therefore the phrase meant that a felony charge wasn't necessary, it could be a misdemeanor that threatened the system of government. In that case a felony might not be enough. If the presi-dent committed murder, it might not be impeachable unless that particu-lar murder threatened the system of government. He could stand trial for the murder after he left office, Thornton believed. But if the president sought to cover up that murder by using the powers of his office, such as the FBI and the CIA, then that would be a threat to the system of gov-ernment and the act would have risen to the height of impeachable of-fense.

Within hours of Doar's presentation of the "broad view" report to the committee, Jaworski's office delivered to the impeachment inquiry headquarters a detailed list of all seven hundred items, including tapes, that he had received from the White House since the special pros-ecutor's investigation began under Archibald Cox nine months earlier. St. Clair had given his permission to Jaworski to release the list. But St. Clair would not give his approval for Jaworski to give the committee the list of the material he had sought from the White House but not received. By that time, however, the committee had been furnished with all the relevant material from the Senate Watergate Committee.

In a closed session the previous week, the committee had affirmed informal plans by Doar and Jenner for maintaining the confidentiality of any secret material they might obtain. The system established allowed only Rodino, Hutchinson, Doar, and Jenner to have access to the confidential material collected until it was presented in the evidentiary hearings still months away. Other members could inspect the culled material at the inquiry headquarters after that, however.

Following St. Clair's statement that he would not object, the confidentiality plans apparently were enough to satisfy Jaworski and he released the index of material received.

Drawing on Senate Watergate testimony, grand jury trasncripts and suggestions from Jaworski, Doar's staff had prepared a list of items it would request of the White House. The index they received from Jaworski helped fill in a few gaps. A five-page letter was drafted during the weekend and presented to Rodino and Hutchinson the following Monday, February 25. They approved it and it was delivered by hand to James St. Clair at the White House. Attached was an explanation of each item requested.

Since it was the committee's initial request for material from the White House, it was considered good politics to keep the request simple and noncontroversial. It asked for

all tapes, dictabelts or other electronic recordings, transcripts, memoranda, notes or other writings or things relating to the particular conversations . . . between the President and Mr. Haldeman or Mr. Ehrlichman or Mr. Dean in February, March and April, 1973, as follows:

(a) Conversations between the President and Mr. Haldeman on or about Feb. 20, 1973, that concern the possible appointment of Mr. Magruder to a government position;

(b) Conversations between the President, Mr. Haldeman and Mr. Ehrlichman on or about Feb. 27, 1973, that concern the assignment of Mr. Dean to work directly with the President on Watergate and Watergate-related matters;

(c) Conversations between the President and Mr. Dean on March 17, 1973, from 1:25 to 2:10 P.M., and March 20, 1973 from 7:29 to 7:43 P.M.;

(d) Conversations between the President and Mr. Ehrlichman on March 27, 1973, from 11:10 A.M. to 1:30 P.M., and on March 30, 1973, from 12:02 to 12:18 P.M.; and

(e) All conversations between the President and Mr. Haldeman and the President and Mr. Ehrlichman during the period April 14 through 17, 1973, inclusive.

The sixth item requested was "all conversations between the President and Mr. Kleindienst and the President and Mr. Petersen during the period from April 15 through 18, 1973, inclusive."

The Watergate story had been in progress for twenty months by that time. As generally happens with a complex subject, in the public mind, attention on the Watergate scandal had been reduced to the most easily understood, lowest common denominator—criminality.

The special prosecutor's office already was known to be focusing on the period surrounding March 1973, since John Dean had testified to the Senate Watergate Committee and the special prosecutor's office that during that period Nixon authorized clemency and blackmail payments to the Watergate defendants and was otherwise heavily involved in the Watergate cover-up. To the special prosecutor and to the grand jury, it was the key to Nixon's criminality.

Nixon had said in a news conference the previous May that it was on March 21, 1973, that he first learned that White House employees might have been involved in the cover-up and that he had given orders then for it to end. Investigators then could most easily focus on any evidence that would prove that Nixon knew of the Watergate cover-up before that time and, thus, had been a participant in the conspiracy surrounding it.

Since the March 21 tape was on the list of material that Jaworski's office had received in December, it was not included in the February 25 Judiciary request. Doar and Jaworski had been negotiating the question of getting all the material the special prosecutor's office had assembled and Doar was optimistic about getting it. There was no need to duplicate it. Anyhow, Doar told Rodino, he didn't expect the White House to comply with the Judiciary Committee's request.

And the inquiry staff's assignment was not as simple as the special prosecutor's. The special prosecutor could only deal with violations of criminal statutes. The impeachment assignment was more ephemeral than that, as indicated in the "broad view" of impeachment that the staff had reported to the committee. Criminality not only might not be necessary for impeachment, it also might not be enough. It all depended on the case. Impeachment was emerging as a case pointed towards not just a Watergate offense, but the pattern of presidential activity. For that, the staff would need much more evidence than just whether Nixon was proved as of March 21, 1973, to be engaged in criminal activity.

The request, then, for taped conversations immediately preceding and following that date, would help establish whether there was a pattern of involvement on the part of the president in the matters of the cover-up and blackmail.

The relevance of those tapes was established in testimony the previous summer before the Senate committee and through logs of the meetings Nixon held with certain staff members, also furnished to the Senate panel.

The following day, February 26, Rodino sent a letter to Nixon advising him that Doar had asked St. Clair for the material. He asked for Nixon's cooperation "without difficulty or delay."

As part of the plan for keeping White House material confidential, only Rodino, Hutchinson, Doar, and Jenner knew what was in the request. That stood for nearly two weeks while the White House and the committee engaged in a public relations battle, the White House through a televised news conference by Nixon and through his new communications man and point man in the offensive, Ken Clawson. White House news briefings also were used in the offensive; the committee got its point across through responses to those statements.

Doar had said before the request was made, and just after Jaworski had given him the list of materials he received, that "it wouldn't take very long (for the White House) to assemble the material. It's not a matter of weeks, it's a matter of a day or two." Doar said the plan was to give the administration a reasonable amount of time to respond, however, before any decision would be made on whether to issue a subpoena.

After a week passed without a response, Republicans began pressing the White House to give the committee what it sought. Bob McClory said, "If there's any evidence of a delay or stalling or refusal I don't think there's any question'' that a subpoena would be issued. Tom Railsback sent a letter to Nixon urging him to comply. And Ed Hutchinson said the request had been reasonable.

Rodino also joined the campaign, saying ''in my judgment it's been a reasonable time. It's been eight days.'' The next day, he threatened a subpoena.

Unfortunately, the letter requesting the White House material had announced the intention to ask for much more material and included a paragraph asking how the White House files, presidential papers, conversations and memoranda, and files of certain former employees were indexed. ''If we could work out a way whereby members of the inquiry staff may examine these files for the purpose of selecting materials which, in our opinion, are necessary for the investigation, I believe that the inquiry would be expedited,'' said the committee's letter over Doar's name.

The White House offensive seized on that paragraph and accused the committee of seeking unlimited access to the White House files. St. Clair sent Doar a letter on March 6 saying the White House would give the committee the seven hundred documents and nineteen tapes it had given the special prosecutor and those would be ''more than sufficient to afford the Judiciary Committee with the entire Watergate story.''

In a news conference, Nixon said the committee wanted the White House ''to cart everything that is in the White House down to a committee and have them paw through it on a fishing expedition.''

The committee members found themselves in the embarrassing position of defending a request they knew existed but did not know the contents of. One member, Elizabeth Holtzman, had gone to inquiry headquarters to see the letter and had been denied a look.

The day after St. Clair's letter and Nixon's news conference, the committee held a briefing, open to the press, on just what had been requested. Doar read all of the February 25 letter to them except for the specific tapes that he had requested. He said the letter listed ''six separate items, some dealing with a particular conversation, some dealing with conversations, all conversations between particular people on particular days.''

Robert Drinan said he had heard enough and moved that the committee issue a subpoena for the material. Rodino, with the backing of most of the other members, talked Drinan out of it, saying they should give Nixon another week or two just in case St. Clair didn't understand the request.

Doar's choice of words enumerating the requested tapes was unfortunate. Members left that meeting armed with what they thought was the ammunition to counter the White House offensive. They chided Nixon for his obstinacy in not giving up a mere six tapes. News stories about the growing confrontation between the committee and the president emphasized the dispute was over "six tapes." A few committee members from both parties went on nationally televised interview programs the following Sunday to press their defense against the White House campaign.

Holtzman's experience at the inquiry headquarters notwithstanding, some members of the committee were able to find out during that period what was in the request. At the same time, so did Ken Clawson, from St. Clair.

A reporter covering impeachment discovered while talking to some of the members on March 11 that the six tape items requested actually were groups of tapes and by talking to several other members, established there were forty-one to forty-three segments of taped conversations involved in those six categories. Almost simultaneously, Clawson leaked to selected White House reporters the contents of the February 25 request, hitting on the fact the committee really was asking for forty-two tapes and not just six, and accusing the panel of trying to hoodwink the public.

The issue exploded into the committee's first credibility problem. Committee members were as angry with Rodino as they were with Nixon. Their public reaction lambasted the White House for violating the rules of confidentiality by releasing the contents of the letter the committee had succeeded in keeping secret. Privately, they were furious with Rodino for keeping the matter such a secret that many members had to find out from the White House what the letter included.

With the revelation spread across that morning's papers, the committee gathered behind closed doors for a session unrelated to impeachment. But the opening fifteen minutes consisted of Rodino's confirming to the members what the newspapers had said. Copies of the February 25 letter would be released to the press, he said. But he offered no details of the request or what was behind it. Several members made pointed remarks about being kept in the dark, until Rodino cut off further discussion of impeachment and returned to the matter on the agenda, action on a bill dealing with pocket vetoes by the president.

The more radical committee Democrats—who became known as "bomb-throwers" by reporters and committee members alike—weren't mollified. John Conyers of Michigan called a rump meeting of the angriest Democrats in his office. They agreed that Rodino had been pussyfooting around long enough, and it was about time they stopped letting the White House call the shots and push the committee around, making members look like a bunch of weak fools. It was ridiculous to continue sitting back like that when the panel could easily issue subpoenas and cite Nixon for contempt if he refused them. They also could move for an immediate vote on impeachment. In either case, they were ready to bring about the confrontation the White House undoubtedly was seeking.

The rump group sent a delegation to Rodino. He argued that perhaps their reaction was just what the White House wanted. Did they honestly think, he asked, that they would win any confrontation at that time? What if the House did take an immediate impeachment vote? The president probably would win on a precipitous move like that by a 2–1 majority. That probably was just what Nixon wanted, he said.

But Rodino got nowhere. The delegation left as angry as it had entered. A Democratic committee caucus had been set for 3:30 that afternoon. It had been called to discuss the long-festering problem of whether to grant the president's counsel a role in the impeachment proceedings. Instead, the caucus bogged down on the issue of the confrontation with the White House. Several members sniped at Doar for his failure to level with them on the request.

Rodino called another caucus for the next morning and spent the rest of the evening trying to figure out how to salvage the situation.

At 8:30 A.M., Rodino, Doar, O'Brien, and Zeifman met in Rodino's office to decide what to do to get the committee back in line. They agreed that the only thing left was to lay all of the strategy out to the members and let them in on it in the future, despite the increased chances for leaks. It would be better to take the brickbats for occasional leaks than to put the members in the embarrassing position of boxing shadows.

That day was March 13, the 106th anniversary of the day the House voted to impeach Andrew Johnson in 1868.

After they had a night to sleep on it, it was easier for the "bomb-throwers" among the committee Democrats to understand Rodino's caution. He told them, "We are dealing with Mr. St. Clair" and not the president's press spokesmen. He advised them to pay attention only to what St. Clair said, and no one else. The White House campaign, he said, was trying to make the committee look irresponsible and if the panel did something precipitous, like pushing an immediate vote to hold Nixon in contempt, the committee would be irresponsible. Nixon also was "trying to set up the method of operation, the method by which the impeachment will be conducted, on his terms." But it will be the committee that decides how it will be conducted, Rodino said. If the president continues to refuse the requested material, then of course the committee would have to vote subpoenas. But they should not be pushed into voting them.

Ed Hutchinson, the ranking Republican, had agreed to join Rodino in a press conference that afternoon. Hutchinson offered his endorsement to the committee's February 25 letter, calling it reasonable and proper.

At the press conference, Rodino displayed uncharacteristic toughness. He said that if Nixon continued to refuse the committee's request, the committee would "utilize the power we have and that is the power of the subpoena."

What Nixon and his aides had been saying about the committee wanting "to back a truck up to the White House and cart off boxes of records for examination by the impeachment inquiry staff" was not true, he said. He then released copies of the February 25 request.

When the Watergate grand jury returned indictments against seven former White House or reelection committee aides on March 1, it also handed Judge John Sirica a sealed report and two locked briefcases. A covering letter told the judge the jury wished the material sent to the House Judiciary Committee because it related to impeachment.

Court matters are not handled that simply, however, and the judge invited comments. The committee stood by its contention that it must not submit to the jurisdiction of the courts, but did authorize Rodino to send a formal letter to Sirica requesting the material for its impeachment investigation.

Sirica decided to give the material to the committee, but had to allow the seven indicted men to appeal his decision. The deadline for appeals of Sirica's decision expired on March 25.

The next day, John Doar and Bert Jenner, accompanied by a Capitol policeman, went down to the district courthouse and took possession of the sealed report and two locked briefcases. The contents were revealed in Judge Sirica's locked chambers so they could be checked against a list to be sure everything was there. Two hours later, Doar, Jenner, and the policeman were on their way back to impeachment inquiry headquarters.

They opened the envelope and the two briefcases. The envelope contained the report that said that the grand jury had named Nixon an unindicted co-conspirator and felt that the evidence in the accompanying two suitcases should be transferred to the committee for its impeachment inquiry. The report was free of any accusations or judgments.

The rest of the report was a dry recitation of the evidence that had led to the decision to name Nixon as part of the conspiracy to cover up White House involvement in the Watergate break-in. The report pieced together the events leading up to the March 21, 1973, conversations in which Nixon instructed his aides to pay "hush money" to the Watergate break-in defendants.

The chronology established that throughout the day on March 21, conversations were held among various White House aides, including Nixon, to discuss blackmail demands being made on the White House and to discuss the possible involvement of several aides and former aides, including former Attorney General John Mitchell.

The report—its design was adopted by Doar in presenting the evidence to the committee members—included a paragraph of facts similar to one later presented by the inquiry staff:

On March 21, 1973 at 12:30 P.M. H. R. Haldeman spoke by telephone to John Mitchell, who was in New York City. In addition to reflecting the 12:30

P.M. call, Haldeman's telephone log for that day also shows a conversation with John Mitchell's office at 4:06 P.M. with a marginal notation "car—9:30 A.M. (word illegible) Nat'l—Amer 520." Haldeman has testified that he does not recall asking Mitchell on March 21 whether Mitchell was going to take care of Hunt's demand for money.

After that paragraph, the report referred to Haldeman's telephone log, his testimony to the grand jury on January 30 and Dean's testimony to the grand jury on February 14.

The next paragraphs then noted other conversations, including a twenty-minute one in which Nixon spoke of a possible pardon or clemency for E. Howard Hunt, who had been making the demand for money, questions about what was being done about Hunt's demand and Mitchell's involvement. Another paragraph related the events of the evening of March 21, stating that nearly $75,000 was delivered to Hunt's lawyer and mentioning testimony implicating Mitchell in the orders to pay it. More logs and testimony were referred to.

All the material for which references were given was contained in the briefcases, along with the tapes of the conversations that the special prosecutor's office had obtained from the White House. One of them was the by then celebrated twenty-minute tape of the March 21, 1973, conversation between Nixon, Haldeman, Ehrlichman, and Dean.

Also in the briefcases were restaurant checks, hotel bills, and other data the grand jury used to fix times, dates, and places where persons might have been at particular times. Thus, it had Mitchell's hotel bills for that period and his receipt for the American Airlines ticket for the flight from New York to Washington on the morning of March 22.

At 11:00 A.M., another paragraph in the report stated, Mitchell and others met in Haldeman's office where Mitchell reported that E. Howard Hunt was no longer a problem, according to one of the participants.

The staff work that Richard Cates had done earlier had reached the same conclusion, but without the specific evidence that the grand jury report and briefcases pinned down.

Beyond that, the material was significant to the committee because it was the product of twenty-three grand jurors who represented average citizens. They felt they had information that was relevant to the impeachment of their president. That knowledge certainly would help dispel the White House characterization of the House Judiciary Committee and the news media as engaged in a witch hunt.

Doar and Jenner assigned three other staffers—and no more—to carefully record the material in the briefcases and put them in a vault to which only Doar and Jenner had keys.

The next day, a Wednesday, Rodino and Hutchinson visited the inquiry headquarters where, for four hours, they listened to the tapes and studied the evidence the grand jury had offered. Hutchinson returned the next day for a more thorough review, but told reporters later that he had heard nothing on the tapes that would implicate Nixon in any crime.

Although Hutchinson maintained a stolid defense of the president in public, he told a few of his colleagues at the same time that there could only be one reason why Nixon would refuse to give up the tapes the committee had requested—because they would prove what the March 21 statement had failed to establish, that Nixon approved of the "hush money" payment to Hunt.

While attention swirled around speculation about what evidence the grand jury had sent, the White House had been quietly completing its delivery to the impeachment inquiry headquarters of the nineteen tapes and documents that it previously had given to the special prosecutor.

But the White House remained adamant in refusing to yield the forty-two tapes the committee had asked for on February 25. Rodino had held off the "bomb-throwers" in March, but when April began it became obvious the committee would have to take some positive action. Perhaps the time had come to issue a subpoena.

CHAPTER VI

Impressions

At the beginning of April 1974, the committee could see no end to its torturous impeachment procedure. Rodino had long ago let his reluctant target date slip to April 30 and then to midsummer. For six months the committee staff had been working to determine whether to try to impeach President Nixon, and yet hadn't even decided who it would call as witnesses the following month. It had no idea how or even whether proposed articles of impeachment would be presented and hadn't decided what role, if any, the president's lawyer would have in the proceedings. The complaints continued from all sides.

Rodino was worried. Had he been thrust onto the world stage only to bungle one of the biggest jobs a member of Congress had ever been given? Had he dallied too long, been too careful, too naive in thinking his committee could ever come up with a bipartisan vote for or against impeachment?

Ever since he received the impeachment charge, Rodino had attempted to convince the public the impeachment inquiry was a bipartisan effort. His attempt was predicated on the belief that recommending articles of impeachment would be fruitless if the vote were twenty-one Democrats for and seventeen Republicans against. Rarely had a committee chairman been so concerned about the feelings of his minority members.

The inquiry had begun with one purpose—to determine whether the facts supported any of the impeachment charges. It was not to uncover and publicize the Watergate scandal as the Senate Watergate Committee had done, and its purpose was not to determine whether criminal charges should be brought against anyone besides the president, as Jaworski was doing at the foot of Capitol Hill. After the facts were laid before the committee, members were to decide individually whether they thought the facts presented justified an article of impeachment.

The public and much of the press had lost that conception, however. They had been numbed the previous spring and summer with revelations and they expected more. Polls showed Nixon's support dropping slowly as the impeachment process dragged on. The White House joined the fray, putting Dean Burch, Bryce Harlow, Ron Ziegler, Ken Clawson, and Fred Buzhardt out front along with James St. Clair to denounce each tiny step the committee was taking, move to delay any advancement it made and then respond with charges it was dragging its feet.

Republicans on the committee took up the administration cudgels in the fight against impeachment. They discounted the need for evidence at the same time they demanded proof a crime had been committed. Acrimony was present even among Republicans. There were those who felt that the longer the impeachment proceedings dragged on, the more Republicans would be hurt in the approaching election. There were also those who felt that the sooner the House voted, the closer the vote would be against Nixon; conversely, the longer the vote was delayed, the more responsive the congressmen would be to the constituents they felt did not want Nixon out of office.

Committee members had said all along that none of the outside pressure was having any effect on them, that not even their constituents' sentiments on impeachment—which many had tested during previous recesses—would influence their vote. They would consider only the facts in the case as lawyers, they said. In reality, they were still politicians and they wanted to see where their constituents stood.

Jaworski was still balking at giving his evidence to the committee. Rodino had said repeatedly that he didn't want to duplicate Jaworski's investigative effort. "If we start from scratch it could go on from now to God knows when," Rodino said once.

The impeachment inquiry staff had grown so large and taken so long that it was running out of money. Rodino was embarrassed that he was going to have to return to the full House and ask for another one million dollars to continue the inquiry.

And the mail was still pouring in. There were vituperative letters on both sides, but most were against Nixon. There were hundreds of thousands of letters and they could not be ignored. And there were continuing pressures on Nixon to resign and on the committee to grant immunity if he would agree to do so.

By early April, Rodino could not ignore the committee's chief frustration—its ineffectual demand for the evidence it had asked Nixon for back on February 25. All he did, however, was to keep saying the committee could wait no longer. The president was making him look weak and stupid.

The argument between Nixon and Rodino boiled down to which was the greater right, that of the president's executive privilege to maintain the confidence of his private conversations or the panel's right to access to all evidence upon which to make the initial impeachment decision?

The committee had been urged by Judge Sirica to delay its inquiry until the Watergate cover-up trials were over. As it turned out, that would have meant more than a year's delay. The committee's Republicans and Democrats, plus the White House, found one thing they could agree on, however, and rejected Sirica's appeal out of hand.

The two parties of the committee were brought closer when they became lodged in a common defense against an increasingly vituperative White House campaign against the committee. Even Nixon's lawyer, James St. Clair, tried to cool the White House campaign, but without success. It wasn't helping his case at all.

Through all of this, Rodino had shown utmost patience. He would shout, rant, and rave at Francis O'Brien when they were alone, but he refused to disclose publicly he was rattled by any of the events which swirled about him. But there had to come a point beyond which even Rodino would not be pushed.

The comity that had developed between Democrats and Republicans in March as they found themselves engaged in a mutual defense of the committee's credibility began eroding by the end of the month, when they turned increasing attention to the question of what role, if any, the president's counsel, James St. Clair, would have in the impeachment proceedings. It was to be the most important decision the committee had to make, one on which the credibility of the impeachment rested, and Rodino almost blew it.

St. Clair said he should be allowed to cross-examine witnesses during the proceedings, which he said would have the nature of a trial. Impeachment Counsels John Doar and Albert Jenner contended there was no role for a defense counsel in a grand jury proceeding, thus there would be none in its impeachment counterpart. If the House voted to impeach Nixon, there would be a trial in the Senate. That's where St. Clair's role would begin, they contended. Rodino agreed.

Jerry Zeifman and Frank Polk, the two chief counsels for the regular House Judiciary Committee work, had done their own research on the issue. Both had been on the Judiciary Committee staff in 1970 when the panel had to determine whether William O. Douglas would be impeached. At that time, the full committee assigned the task to a subcommittee, which held hearings on the charges against Douglas. Present throughout the hearings was Douglas's counsel, Simon Rifkind. The subcommittee later voted against the impeachment of Douglas and the matter was dropped, but a precedent for the attendance of defense counsel had been set. Otherwise, precedents fell on both sides of the question.

Tom Railsback took the matter of counsels one step further in one closed briefing for the committee: "I do not think they have any right" to be present at impeachment proceedings, "but I think it has been done as a matter of legislative grace."

St. Clair sent letter after letter to Doar demanding he be granted the right to be present at the taking of depositions or affidavits from witnesses, that he be allowed to cross-examine committee witnesses, allowed to call his own witnesses and even have the right to issue his own subpoenas to compel testimony before the committee. In other words, he said, he wanted full and formal rights to be a participant.

By that time, Doar, Rodino, and O'Brien had formed an unofficial triumvirate that met practically every night, sometimes until long after midnight. O'Brien, practically as green as Doar in congressional matters, offered Doar his full support on not allowing St. Clair a role. Together they convinced Rodino.

Rodino was fortified in that view every morning when he participated in a ritual of having coffee with Doar and Bert Jenner at 8:15 or 8:30 in the inquiry headquarters.

Zeifman and Polk, however, took up St. Clair's cause. They were more attuned to the political aspects of the impeachment case and both had done the research the previous year that led to the first impeachment publication by the committee.

Zeifman was becoming very disturbed by the hard line the triumvirate was taking against participation by St. Clair. He considered it politically dangerous to exclude St. Clair. Zeifman wanted the panel to vote for impeachment, but feared some of the borderline members would use the right-to-counsel issue as a fallback position and vote against impeachment if Nixon were denied a legal defense at that stage.

Zeifman lobbied Rodino heavily. Rodino admitted the precedents lay on both sides. But he also agreed with Doar that the committee should exercise its rightful role as a panel collecting evidence. He also feared, he said, that if St. Clair were let in the door he could disrupt the proceedings and perhaps, given his reputation as a skilled trial lawyer, win the case in the face of overwhelming impeachment evidence. That wasn't the way the impeachment of a president should be decided, he said.

But Rodino also agreed that the political realities of the case argued that the president have a counsel at the proceedings. He knew the committee faced charges of a kangaroo court if St. Clair were not allowed to sit in.

So Rodino faced another dilemma.

As he did when he faced an argument on the definition of impeachable offenses, he tried to resolve it by suggesting the committee hold hearings and have experts testify. Just as in February when members on both sides of his committee voiced overwhelming oppositions to the hearings on impeachable offenses and forced him to drop the idea, they also opposed hearings on the right of counsel and forced Rodino to back down.

A caucus of Democrats, however, endorsed the Rodino/Doar position on denial of right to counsel, while Republicans held their own caucus and reached a unanimous conclusion the president should be represented.

The dispute came to a head on March 21, when the committee devoted more than an hour to arguments on the issue. Tom Railsback summed up the GOP position when he said to Rodino, "I think the only way you are going to have a successful inquiry is to see that this respondent is treated as other respondents have been, particularly in recent cases." The meeting broke up without a resolution of the issue, but Rodino at least knew the committee was becoming polarized again along party lines.

It had been nearly a month since the committee had asked Nixon for forty-two taped conversations. The committee had to take some action but Rodino couldn't very well have a vote on a subpoena, for which he wanted bipartisan support, while the panel was as divided as it was on the right-to-counsel issue.

Unable to impress his viewpoint on the Rodino-Doar-O'Brien triumvirate, Zeifman began meeting with individual Democrats on the committee, lobbying them to give in on the right-of-counsel issue to avoid tearing the committee apart and sinking the chances for impeachment. Even if the president had no legal right to have counsel present during the proceedings, he argued, the committee should follow the precedents that granted the defense counsel a role. Politically it was the only realistic choice for the committee.

His efforts picked up trickles of support. If some Democrats were not exactly joining the Republican position, their opposition was softened when the committee held another briefing session on April 4. By that time, Doar, under Rodino's instructions, backed off a bit from his intransigence against the presence of counsel. He came to the briefing armed with a twenty-five–page report on the procedures for handling the rest of the inquiry, including allowing St. Clair to receive the evidence the same time as the committee members. It skirted the issue of St. Clair's actually being present in the same room as the committee members.

Rodino thought he had given in enough when he allowed St. Clair that much.

Rodino opened the meeting by reading what was for him a strongly worded statement. In the matter of the president's refusal to comply with the committee's request for material, he said,

We have been respectfully patient. The courts were patient, the House has been patient. The people have been patient for a long, long time.

The patience of this committee is now wearing thin. We have a constitutional responsibility in this inquiry. When we made our request, we made it not out of curiosity, not because we were prosecutors, but because it is our responsibility. We have tried to pursue it in a spirit of accommodation with this President.

Yet there comes a time when patience and accommodation can begin to undermine the process in which we are engaged. Feb. 25, the committee made a specific request to the counsel of the President for specific evidence of specific facts of specific relevance to our inquiry.

That request so far has not been honored.

The staff had composed a memo on the participation of the president's counsel, he said, and at a subsequent meeting the committee could resolve that issue. "However, we are going forward. We have asked for evidence. . . . We shall not be thwarted by inappropriate legalisms or by narrow obstacles to our inquiry."

Rodino instructed Doar to read a letter to St. Clair that was being sent out that day, telling St. Clair to "reply by Tuesday, April 9, at the latest, with respect to whether or not the conversations referred to in our letter of Feb. 25 will be delivered to the committee." Ed Hutchinson supported Rodino's statement.

The Republicans then returned to the counsel issue, making it clear they were still unhappy with the staff work on the right of counsel to be present. They wanted him in the room and they wanted his subsequent role in cross-examining witnesses and presenting exculpatory evidence decided before the committee began hearing the evidence. Republican staff members had prepared a counterproposal to allow the counsel full participation in the proceedings and St. Clair had sent one of his own.

Debate on the issue continued unabated through the weekend. Sam Garrison, acting now as the Republican's unofficial special counsel on the inquiry, drew up a secret proposal that would have the Republicans act, en bloc, on the House floor to press for an immediate vote on impeachment, sending the matter on to the Senate for trial. Their excuse would be that if the House would not grant Nixon the right of counsel, then the case should go directly to the body where he could be represented.

Zeifman continued pressing Rodino and others on the need for St. Clair's participation. In a meeting in Rodino's office, Doar, O'Brien, Zeifman, and Rodino argued heatedly. Zeifman said that if the president didn't have his own counsel present, then the Republicans would feel compelled to defend Nixon themselves.

Doar and O'Brien said the Republicans were pushing for the right of counsel because they were puppets of the White House. They should be ignored. Rodino said he also thought the matter was part of the White House strategy to either divide the committee on the issue or, if the Democrats gave in, to obstruct the proceedings. Zeifman countered that the Republicans were not puppets of the White House and it certainly wasn't the position of the committee Republicans to obstruct the proceedings. Rodino answered that Zeifman had miscalculated the situation entirely.

Zeifman followed Rodino to the House floor and tried to impress upon him the notion "that some of the Republicans might want to vote 'yes,' on impeachment and would find it more difficult to do so if the president is not represented by counsel." Rodino again rejected Zeifman's arguments, and Zeifman threatened to resign if St. Clair were not allowed to participate. He didn't want to be any part of the inquiry in that case, he said.

The next morning Zeifman had breakfast with Don Edwards, a California Democrat who by that time was emerging as a leader on the committee. Edwards, although viewed in some quarters as a radical liberal, was thought nonetheless to be a reasoned one who bent over backwards to be fair. Many members paid attention to Edwards because of that perception, but so far Edwards had not taken advantage of that following to guide the proceedings. Edwards told Zeifman he was beginnning to agree with Zeifman, that perhaps the issue was too great to insist upon excluding St. Clair. But Edwards remained silent the next Monday when the committee held another stormy session on the issue. The two sides were still sharply divided.

The Republicans, led by Bob McClory of Illinois, had developed the strategy earlier in the year of taking their case to the public via the floor of the House when they felt they were being treated unfairly by the Democratic majority on the committee. McClory felt that the president's right to counsel was such a case, and reserved some special time at the end of that day's House session. Seven other committee Republicans joined McClory in a wide-ranging criticism of the conduct of the inquiry, centering on the counsel question.

To McClory's surprise, Edwards joined in the discussion and sided with the Republicans on the counsel question. The next day, Jerome Waldie, one of the committee's Democratic ''bomb-throwers,'' also let it be known he would side with the Republicans if the issue came to a vote.

Just before a Democratic caucus the next day, Rodino stormed around his office and shouted to O'Brien, who also served as a vote-counter for Rodino, to ''find me some votes.'' O'Brien replied, ''There aren't any.''

At the caucus, Rodino threw in the towel and agreed to let St. Clair participate in the impeachment proceedings when the evidentiary phase began the following month. Rodino told Doar after the caucus to prepare him a statement in favor of granting the right to counsel.

Later that day, April 9, St. Clair sent Doar the reply the committee had demanded. He said the White House was in the process of reviewing the material that the committee was seeking. ''We expect that the review can be completed by the end of the Easter recess, and that additional materials furnished at that time will permit the committee to complete its inquiry promptly.''

The letter added, ''Regarding an important related issue, I hope that the committee will decide my role in its proceedings before the upcoming recess,'' which was scheduled to begin at the close of business on April 11 and last until April 22.

St. Clair's timing couldn't have been worse for the president's case. It was another nonresponse to the request for material and another indication that St. Clair intended to continue stalling the committee and attempting to direct the conduct of the committee's impeachment inquiry.

Even Ed Hutchinson, a stalwart defender of Nixon on most of the issues confronting the committee, was stunned by it. He freely told reporters, "I think it was offensive to the House, I'm sorry to say." The letter said, in effect, "We're going to decide what you need and you damn well better be happy with what you get." Nonetheless, Hutchinson added that he opposed a subpoena and "ultimately we're going to have to make do with what we have."

Other Republicans called the St. Clair letter "a stall," and House GOP Leader John Rhodes telephoned St. Clair to try to work out a compromise to forestall the subpoena, which it was widely feared by almost everyone involved would bring about a constitutional confrontation.

Adding to the negative reaction was the knowledge the letter came on the heels of a Nixon trip to Paris for the funeral of French President Georges Pompidou and a meeting with the other world leaders there to pay their respects. Nixon also had worked in a campaign swing through Michigan before arrival of St. Clair's reply.

That night, Rodino, Doar, and Zeifman discussed St. Clair's participation. Doar had not provided the proparticipation statement Rodino had requested, so Zeifman wrote one and handed it to Rodino.

Doar, normally stoic and expressionless, then spoke emotionally to Rodino, trying to dissuade the chairman from reversing his position and delivering the statement. He said he couldn't disagree more with Zeifman's position. Not only did the subject of an impeachment have no right to take part in the inquiry stage of impeachment proceedings, he said, inclusion of St. Clair would lead to interferences and stalls and the committee never would be able to complete its work.

"I'm concerned about our personal dignity and the self-respect and dignity of the members of the committee," Doar said to Rodino. "To make such a statement at this time making those kinds of concessions to St. Clair would detract from the dignity of the committee."

Zeifman said that to the contrary, a reversal "would not be a sign of weakness. It would be a sign of strength, especially if we are going to issue a subpoena to the President at about the same time the statement will be made."

Late the following night, Zeifman met again with Rodino to review the scenario of a Thursday morning committee meeting called to vote on the subpoena. They discovered that despite Rodino's instruction to Doar that afternoon, the inquiry staff had not produced the subpoena the committee would be voting on. Zeifman called Joseph Woods, the staff member in charge of administrative functions, and Woods said Doar had not even talked to him about it. Zeifman went over to the inquiry headquarters, and he and Woods worked past midnight writing the subpoena and making copies for the members.

Crowds gathered for the commitee session the next day, to be present when the panel voted to issue the first congressional subpoena ever served on a president.

At 9:45, Rodino and Doar were in the chairman's tiny office at the rear of the committee room going over last-minute details, when St. Clair called. He told Doar he would have all of the specific conversations requested of the president within the next day or two, but could not supply the two general requests "for all conversations between the President" and aides April 14 through 18, 1973. But St. Clair said he would not deliver the first part without the second unless the committee agreed to withhold the subpoena. Doar replied that he could not speak for the committee.

Doar glanced at Rodino, smiled, and knowing he had the upper hand, pressed St. Clair. As St. Clair responded, Doar reached deep into the huge, brown, battered briefcase he carried everywhere. He extracted a single sheet of paper, squinted at it and cited that portion of St. Clair's letter of the previous day that said he and Nixon expected that the material that would be furnished by the end of the month "will permit the committee to complete its inquiry promptly." That seemed to suggest, Doar said, that the forty-two tapes that would be subpoenaed would be all the material the commitee would request.

Not so, Doar said. In fact, he said, the staff already had prepared a request for more tapes and documents dealing with the Watergate cover-up and some dealing with the ITT and dairy cases. And even more might follow those, he said. Doar hung up, and he and Rodino went into the commiteee room prepared for the showdown.

Rodino smoothed the way with an opening statement that said St.

Clair would be afforded the privilege of sitting in on the impeachment proceedings, requesting witnesses and cross-examining them, and making his own presentation to the commitee. The participation would be embodied in a set of rules of procedures the panel would vote on after the recess in preparation for the evidentiary phase of the inquiry set to begin in May, he said. Because the House was scheduled to depart early that afternoon for its Easter recess, and out of a fit of pique that he had been forced to publicly reverse himself on the president's right-to-counsel issue, Rodino had arranged to limit the debate on the subpoena to thirty minutes, far less than the normal time. Republicans protested loudly, but Rodino would not back down. A roll call vote was forced and Rodino won, but on a strict party-line vote of 21–17.

Larry Hogan (R-Md.), who had been shouting "parliamentary inquiry" all morning, outshouted his colleagues with the same demand after another party-line vote on a procedural matter and said, "I would like to say, Mr. Chairman, that I resent the way the debate was cut off" on the previous amendment.

Rodino, usually the model of decorum while in the chairman's seat, responded, "The chair recognized the gentleman for parliamentary inquiry and not for one of his harangues."

Insults like that were rarely spoken in the club that was Congress and certainly not by Rodino. The wear and tear, the approach of an Easter rest and the division over impeachment issues was telling.

After nearly ninety minutes of wrangling over the issues, Delbert Latta (R-Ohio) sought to offer a simple amendment to make the request for the last two items in the six-item February 25 letter to the White House more specific. Rodino snapped that since Latta hadn't prepared the amendment in advance, it wouldn't be considered.

Republicans maneuvered to get a ninety-minute recess of the committee to give Latta time to prepare his amendment. Latta told Rodino during the break that he and other Republicans would be willing to vote for the subpoena but they would insist on his amendment. Otherwise, he said, Rodino might end up with a partisan vote on the panel's first impeachment subpoena. Rodino had cooled by that point. Since he still wanted a bipartisan vote on the subpoena, he agreed to accept Latta's amendment if he offered it. Bob McClory, meanwhile, took advantage of the break to call the White House with a last-minute plea to avoid the subpoena. He lost.

When the session resumed, Rodino endorsed the Latta amendment. It passed by voice vote and the committee then voted, 33–3, to issue the subpoena to President Nixon. Latta and thirteen other Republicans joined with the majority Democrats.

Technically, the subpoena instructed Benjamin Marshall, the inquiry's chief of security, "or his duly authorized representative," to march down the hill to the White House, subpoena in hand and "summon Richard M. Nixon, President of the United States, or any subordinate officer, official or employee with custody or control of the things described in the attached schedule" to appear with the material, before the committee "on or before April 25,1974, at the hour of 10 A.M."

Obviously, no one envisioned a committee's security chief, perhaps with House mace in hand, trooping by the White House guards and into the Oval Office and slapping the subpoena into the president's outstretched and quivering hand.

The subpoena would be delivered, but the committee knew it had no way to enforce it if Nixon chose to ignore it. And most members expected the president to refuse to comply with the committee's subpoena just as he had refused to comply with subpoenas other Watergate investigators had issued.

But the committee had options. As lawyers, the committee members appreciated the principles of evidentiary law. One principle, as old as the common law of England, held that if a person withheld evidence from the court, the evidence could be presumed to be evidence that would have been adverse to the person who withheld it. It was called "inference of guilt" and was widely accepted by U.S. courts. A judge could instruct a jury that if evidence that could prove or disprove a point was withheld by a defendant, "you may infer it may be adverse to him."

The subpoena had a much-needed salutary effect on the inquiry. Committee members finally had been able to cast a vote on a major impeachment issue, right before Easter and their return home for constituent sampling. It would make them appear not to be wasting their constituents' time. The manifestations of this new feeling of power were felt almost immediately. Not every member of Congress was on his or her way home on Friday. Republicans all over Congress used the opportunity to apply a little muscle they hadn't felt they had in the past.

Nixon's only response to the subpoena vote was sent through his press secretary, Ron Ziegler, who said the president would provide "additional material." Ziegler refused to say Nixon would comply in full.

The committee's staff had prepared the membership for the possibility that Nixon would not comply at all. In a legal memo, it said, "If the President refuses to comply, the practical difficulties of enforcing the subpoena may well be insurmountable," but it added pointedly, "noncompliance by itself may be a ground for impeachment."

David Dennis (R-Ind.) delayed his trip home to make some statements that expressed better than anyone else the GOP feeling in Congress on the issue. He said he would use the Easter recess to convey to Nixon the message that six Senate GOP leaders had conveyed earlier that week—that his own best interests dictated that he comply with the subpoena.

But Dennis also offered an out for Nixon. Visualizing the possibility Nixon would ignore the subpoena, he said, "Even if the president is held in contempt of Congress, standing by itself that's not enough to impeach him. The country will want some positive proof of real wrongdoing by the president. A legal hassle between Congress and the president just won't do."

The position was clear. Republicans believed Nixon innocent of any impeachable crime, but sincerely wished he would comply with the subpoena and produce the tapes.

But the most satisfied person on Capitol Hill at the beginning of that recess period was Peter Rodino. Although a vote to subpoena evidence that almost everyone agreed should be supplied was something less than a vote to impeach the president of the United States, it had the effect of a steam locomotive beginning to move away from the station platform. It wasn't moving very fast, but it finally was chugging in some direction. The vote appeared to unite both sides in a similar, high-minded cause. Its effect would be felt for many weeks to come. Almost immediately the tide had begun to turn.

And if Rodino was glad to see that locomotive chugging after a standstill of four months, others also were aware for the first time there was a distinct possibility a president would be impeached not only in their lifetime, but by the end of the summer. The overwhelming vote for a subpoena appeared to prove to many doubters that the impeachment committee meant what it said, and would not accept any longer what it had accepted for nearly two months.

For his part, Nixon continued to stonewall it during the Easter recess. He was planning a trip to Moscow in late June, and although the brief trip to Paris had provided no comforting relief from impeachment, there was still hope in the White House the nation would think twice before calling for the removal of the great peacemaker on the eve of his return from another trip to ''arch-foe'' Russia.

But even as he planned, there was renewed talk that perhaps the newly created Twenty-fifth Amendment ought to be put into effect—the president should step down and let the vice-president serve as president until the impeachment issue was resolved. The reasoning was that with the cloud of impeachment hanging over Nixon, he could not be an effective president, especially in fields of foreign policy where he insisted on roaming.

The White House also appeared to be playing games with the House Republicans. In late March, before the subpoena vote, House GOP Leader John Rhodes had suggested to McClory over lunch that if the committee would agree to the presence of St. Clair or someone else designated by the White House, the White House probably would agree to allow Rodino, Hutchinson, Doar, and Jenner to listen to the tapes and screen out irrelevant and national security matters. McClory assumed Rhodes was making a proposal for the White House and suggested the compromise to Hutchinson and Rodino. Both agreed to it, although Rodino wanted it kept informal, between counsel. Jenner told McClory he thought the inquiry staff would jump at such a compromise.

When he got no response from the White House, McClory realized the offer was part of a tactic to put out a feeler so the White House could announce an attempt at compromise if the committee refused the offer, and deny the compromise had been offered if the committee accepted it. His suspicions were confirmed in mid-April when a series of leaks suggested Nixon would give the committee verbatim transcripts of the tapes it had requested. But there still was no hint of full compliance. Rodino, who stayed in Washington during the recess to review the next tapes request the committee would make and to work on other impeachment matters, issued a rare public statement insisting on the tapes, not transcripts.

In a television interview, Rodino said, "We have to indicate quite strongly that we mean business and that the House has given us this authority and therefore this [offer by Nixon] would be a refusal not only to comply with the request of the committee but with the House of Representatives as the sole power to inquire in impeachment proceedings."

Rodino added that unless Nixon complied fully, "it is going to be considered by the committee as a refusal on the part of the White House and could be considered as a possible crime of impeachment." Full compliance was "the only way that the committee inquiry can be satisfied."

Rodino had reason to be confident. A recent Harris Poll had shown for the first time that a majority of Americans favored Nixon's impeachment.

The next day, April 19, Doar sent a letter to St. Clair requesting more tapes. The previous request included tapes from as early as November 15, 1972, and went through March, 1973, a period when Nixon discussed blackmail and other things many believed signaled the beginning of the cover-up. It may have been fishing a bit, but the new request asked for conversations two months before the June 17 break-in and tapes of conversations on June 20 and June 23, the dates Cates originally had selected as key to the cover-up. The letter laid out in detail the reason for the requests.

The panel needed the material, the letter said, so it would know

whether any of the conversations in any way bear upon the knowledge or lack of knowledge of, or action or inaction by the President and/or any of his senior administration officials with respect to, the investigation of the Watergate break-in by the Department of Justice, the Senate Select Committee, or any other legislative, judicial, executive or administration body, including members of the White House staff.

The letter also asked for Nixon's daily diaries for the period of April through July 1972, February through April 1973, July 12 through July 31, 1973, and October 1973, an indication the panel intended to look into the decisions behind the "Saturday Night Massacre." In all, the request included seventy-five more tapes the staff wanted for its cover-up investigation. But the panel also included requests for forty-six tapes dealing with illegal campaign contributions and possible related favors to the milk industry, and twenty tapes involving possibilities of a convention donation by ITT in return for dropping a government antitrust suit against the corporation.

The response had been anticipated. Ken Clawson, Nixon's communications director, said, "The demands of the House Judiciary Committee are the same excesses that led to the demise of the Senate Watergate Committee."

Hutchinson, Rodino, Doar, and Jenner had been spending many hours that week working on the additional request for materials and listening to the nineteen tapes that St. Clair had allowed the special prosecutor to give to the committee. Predictably, Hutchinson said he had, as a result of listening to the tapes, "no reason to believe" Nixon guilty of any major criminal acts. Based upon what he had heard so far, he said, he would vote against impeachment. Rodino would make no comment.

Members of the committee filtered back to Washington after the Easter recess and brought with them reports that showed Nixon faced a greater danger of being impeached than he had before Easter. Members generally reported constituent attitudes hardening against the president.

The members said their decision on whether to recommend articles of impeachment to the full House would not depend on constituent sentiment, that they would base their vote on the evidence. But, as Walter Flowers (D-Ala.) said, "We are all cognizant of the public's attitude. All of our actions are influenced by constituents."

On April 22, Congress's first day back, St. Clair called Doar and asked for a five-day extension of the April 25 deadline for complying with the subpoena issued on April 11. St. Clair said he was having difficulty getting the material together and that Nixon hadn't reviewed it. Doar told St. Clair he couldn't answer for the committee but would get Rodino's reaction and call back.

After conferring with Hutchinson, Rodino wanted to know why St. Clair couldn't supply at least some of the material. Doar relayed the question, and St. Clair said Nixon wanted to review all of the material at one time. Doar reported back to Rodino, and the two leaders of the committee agreed to a five-day extension. The request was kept secret until the White House leaked it the next day. Rodino called an afternoon news conference and announced the committee would have to vote on the request. The vote was set for April 25, the day the subpoenaed material was due.

The following day the inquiry staff circulated to the committee members a status report on its work, recommending that the fifty-five allegations against Nixon be reduced to thirty-seven. The staff had recommended that the allegations involving the secret bombing in Cambodia, dismantlement of the Office of Economic Opportunity, and impoundment of funds appropriated by Congress—all charges in Robert Drinan's original impeachment resolution—be dropped from further investigation.

Rodino and Doar agreed to leave these allegations in the status report, however, to placate Drinan, John Conyers, and Elizabeth Holtzman, Democratic "bomb-throwers" who strongly favored these charges. Rodino feared he would lose if he tried to face the issue head-on with them. He wanted the status report to please everyone. And he slipped the word to the Republicans that these three Drinan charges would be dropped.

Narrowing the charges left the staff to concentrate its energies on the Watergate cover-up, ITT, the dairy contribution, and Nixon's personal taxes.

When the committee met on April 25 to consider St. Clair's request for an extension of the subpoena deadline, it approved the request by a vote of 34–4, but not before several members vented their anger at

Nixon's delay. Holtzman, one of the four who opposed the extension, said, "We have leaned over so far backwards that I am afraid some of us have fallen over."

The reaction to Nixon's delay in furnishing the material the inquiry had subpoenaed was mild, however, compared with the response his next tactic would receive.

Nixon appeared on national television the following Monday evening, April 29, to report to the people on Watergate and impeachment. With a touch of drama, Nixon turned from the television cameras to some blue-bound books on the table behind him, saying, "In these folders that you see over here on my left, are more than twelve hundred pages of transcripts of private conversations I participated in" during the period covered by the tapes the Judiciary Committee had subpoenaed, plus "transcripts of other conversations which were not subpoenaed. . . ."

The transcripts covered portions of forty-six tapes, including eight of the nineteen the committee already had received via the special prosecutor's office.

The bomb as far as the committee was concerned followed: "I shall invite Chairman Rodino and the committee's ranking minority member, Congressman Hutchinson, of Michigan, to come to the White House and listen to the actual, full tapes of these conversations" to assure them the transcripts were accurate. Nixon said he would meet with them personally if there was any disagreement over the contents.

"The task of Chairman Rodino and Congressman Hutchinson will be made simpler than was mine by the fact that the work in preparing the transcripts has been completed, all they will need to do is satisfy themselves of their authenticity and their completeness."

What Nixon didn't tell his television viewers was that Rodino already had warned Nixon his panel would "accept no less" than the tapes themselves. And Nixon's compromise offer pointedly omitted Doar and Jenner from the list of those who could check the veracity of the transcripts, even though it was made clear following the White House feeler of a month earlier that Rodino and Hutchinson would not go to the White House to listen to tapes without their special counsels. The counsels were the persons familiar with the nuances of the evidence, they said.

Rodino and Hutchinson also knew that the written word couldn't provide the inflections and nuances of the spoken word. There would be no way to check for tampering without the tapes themselves. And Rodino and Hutchinson had found listening to the nineteen tapes they already had time-consuming and difficult because of poor tape quality.

The committee also had demanded tapes in its subpoena and not transcripts. "The subpoena was for the tapes and we got no tapes," Rodino said in response.

The White House explained to the Republican House members that the counsels were omitted because Jenner was making too many speeches and suggested the committee Republicans put a muzzle on him.

The transcripts, which the White House had completed only the previous Friday and which Nixon had taken with him to Camp David the previous weekend, arrived at the impeachment inquiry headquarters early the next morning, April 30.

It was the anniversary of the day Nixon had accepted the resignations of his two chief aides and his attorney general and had fired John Dean.

A loaded station wagon with half a dozen White House aides following in another car, pulled up the curved driveway to the hotel entrance one-half hour before the 10:00 A.M. deadline for compliance with the committee's subpoena. A cart was wheeled out, and the transcripts, bound into two beige cardboard folders for each of the thirty-eight committee members, were loaded on the cart and hauled to the elevator and up to the second floor. There an armed, intent guard watched carefully, lest any unauthorized person slip by. In black satchels, for Rodino, were the copies that were behind Nixon during his TV appearance.

The delivery did not include any of the hundreds of other documents or tapes the panel had subpoenaed.

Elsewhere on the Hill, members' offices began to receive the first of what was to become a flood of telegrams from irate constituents demanding that something be done about Nixon's production of transcripts instead of tapes. Most also urged impeachment.

Committee Democrats knew they were mighty angry with the Nixon response, but they didn't know what to do about it. Rodino and Doar knew it wasn't what they wanted nor what they could accept, but they knew they had to head off any precipitous action.

Rodino called a Democratic caucus later that afternoon. Committee Republicans also called one. Rodino rejected an offer of network television time to respond to Nixon's address.

Rodino and Hutchinson spent the day between delivery of the transcripts and the afternoon caucuses at the inquiry headquarters reading the transcripts and discussing ways to resolve the conflict and avoid a showdown with the White House. Before they parted, they agreed the showdown was sure to come.

Minority Leader John Rhodes, who had joined the Republican caucus, told reporters later that most of the members in the room considered Nixon "in substantial compliance with the subpoena" by turning over transcripts instead of the tapes. But three Republicans quickly separated themselves from Rhodes's remark. Tom Railsback, Bill Cohen, and Hamilton Fish all said they were not satisfied with the response.

Much of the attention that day centered not on a response to Nixon's refusal to comply with the subpoena, but on the transcripts themselves. Word of their content quickly spread among all the members in the Capitol, and most who read sections of them concluded they not only were inadequate, they showed the shabbiness of the man sitting in the White House as their president.

The transcripts were loaded with omissions labeled "inaudible," or "unintelligible," or "expletive deleted," phrases people would remember longer than the rest of the words on the pages. Readers tended to fill in for the "expletive deleted" words far more obscene than the ones Nixon actually spoke.

There were just too many holes to allow the transcripts any credibility. All thirty-eight Judiciary Committee members were lawyers and as lawyers they felt they were entitled to the best available evidence. In that case it was the tapes, not the transcripts.

Also by that time, the committee already had three different transcripts of some of the tape recordings they had received in the two briefcases delivered by the special prosecutor's office. One transcript had been made by that office, another by the Senate Watergate Committee, and the third by the impeachment inquiry staff. The new White House transcripts provided the fourth copies of eight of the nineteen tapes the committee had.

Before the end of the day, the word had been passed among most of the committee members that the White House versions were the worst of the lot. In some cases they were even erroneous, ascribing quotes to the wrong person and citing completely fictitious quotes.

Rodino scheduled a committee session Wednesday evening to decide on a response to Nixon's refusal to deliver the subpoenaed tapes.

The Democratic members caucused Tuesday evening to agree on their response. John Conyers of Michigan and Jerry Waldie of California were outraged and opened the meeting with a demand the committee move as quickly as possible to have Nixon held in contempt of the House and to make that an article of impeachment. They got no support, however. Others thought the committee might have to abandon its position against court action on impeachment-related issues and get the court to uphold its subpoena. Most wanted to stick with their previous stance, however.

There weren't many other options. Congress had no army, so it couldn't physically force compliance with its subpoenas. The best recourse appeared to do nothing, or next to nothing.

Members already had the staff brief that was circulated when the committee voted to issue the subpoena. It said the strongest recourse would be to assume adverse inference and make each count of refusal part of an article of impeachment. But many Democrats still wanted to respond in some way, take some official action expressing the committee's dissatisfaction with Nixon's failure to comply. They decided a simple letter would suffice.

The next day the Republican committee members got wind of what the Democrats were up to and held another caucus with the GOP House leadership in the assistant minority leader's office. Ed Hutchinson had told the same group the day before that the committee's Democrats were in a bind on the issue and that the Republicans shouldn't do anything that would make the situation any easier for the opposition. Following his lead, there was near unanimity against sending a letter to Nixon accusing him of any deliberate or apparent attempt to mislead the committee or to flout its demand for information.

St. Clair hadn't helped the GOP caucus any that morning when he told reporters that the committee had all it was going to get from the White House. There would be nothing else.

Bill Cohen was in a particular bind. He agreed with the Democrats that Nixon had failed to comply with the subpoena and should be told that, but at that point Cohen did not want to buck his party's position.

The Democrats were preparing a brief letter stating that the president was "in noncompliance." Cohen thought his position would be easier if he could get the committee to accept a letter that was more constructive, that explained why the committee felt the president had not "complied fully" with the subpoena and explained why the committee believed it should have the things it asked for.

He called Rodino and suggested to him that the committee abandon the short-letter approach and adopt a longer one explaining the situation. That would make the committee appear to be the more reasonable participant in the fight, he said.

Rodino invited Cohen up to his office. He told Cohen the Democrats were irate over what they considered a slap in the face by Nixon. They were highly insulted that he would offer inadequate transcripts as the best evidence and not even mention the rest of the material subpoenaed. Rodino took extra time with Cohen. Waldie and Conyers already had declared they would oppose a response to Nixon that consisted of no more than a letter and Rodino was aware the Republicans had agreed to oppose the letter. Unless he got a Republican to bolt, the motion to send the letter would lose on a tie vote. Rodino tried to convince Cohen that the committee needed to flex some muscle on the impeachment issue. The White House was still trying to push the committee around, he said, and its effort to influence the committee was becoming very effective.

Cohen practically pleaded with Rodino to support his longer, conciliatory letter, which he already had prepared and shown to Rodino. Heating up the confrontation would be futile, Cohen argued. When Cohen left Rodino's office little more than an hour before the committee's evening session was scheduled to begin, there had been no agreement.

Doar led off the session recounting the events that had led the committee up to that point. He propped up a chart to illustrate graphically how many tapes had been requested and how many had been supplied indirectly. The April 30 response with transcripts of many, but not all of the tapes originally requested, and the committee's other requests for more tapes had confused the issue in the minds of many members.

Even the chart, relatively innocuous, sparked haggling. The haggling made it appear the Republicans were grasping at straws for a defense they felt they owed Nixon, but that Nixon was undermining their defense on the major issues.

Late in the evening, as orchestrated, Harold Donohue (D-Mass.) was recognized to lay before the committee the proposed letter to Nixon.

Then ensued the debate on the motion to send it. Waldie said he wanted a vote holding Nixon in contempt of the Congress. Cohen said he wanted a longer letter, one reexplaining the need for the tapes and declaring only that Nixon was "not in technical or full compliance."

Rodino listened to both. Then he gave a speech himself, something unusual for the chairman, who wanted to act more as a moderator between opposing forces than as the man in control of everything. Rodino accused Nixon of delaying the impeachment proceedings: "We did not subpoena a presidential interpretation of what is necessary or relevant for our inquiry. And we did not subpoena a lawyer's argument presented before we have heard any of the evidence."

It was harsh language for the soft-spoken Rodino to use in public. The proceedings must "be absolutely straightforward and not equivocal, in any way," he said. But without the tapes, the events and actions the committee was considering couldn't be explained to the American people. "It would only raise questions about the committee's inquiry."

He said the committee intended to move ahead as planned and revealed that he had instructed Doar to equip the committee room so that each committee member could listen on headphones to Oval Office tapes, whether they were the nineteen supplied by the special prosecutor's office or more.

Rodino also had said he wouldn't accept Nixon's invitation to go down to the White House to listen to tapes unless Doar and Jenner were allowed to go. Hutchinson followed Rodino with a speech of his own, stating he was willing to go, but wouldn't without Rodino. Since the White House had confined the invitation to only the two congressmen, the upshot was that nobody was going to the White House to listen to tapes. John Seiberling (D-Ohio) moved to cut off discussion at 11:15 P.M. His motion was adopted by voice vote.

Brooks, who still thought the letter of response was too namby-pamby, offered a motion to change the language in the letter from ''are in noncompliance'' to ''have failed to comply'' and it was accepted by Donohue, who sat between Rodino and Brooks. Cohen moved to get acceptance of his version and was defeated by a 27–11 vote.

Then the simple, four-line letter as altered by Brooks was voted on. Delbert Latta introduced a motion to kill the letter idea altogether, but it lost and the vote occurred shortly before 11:30.

Conyers and Waldie voted against the motion because they wanted Nixon held in contempt. Cohen felt his substitute had been given a fair chance and thought some sort of noncompliance letter should be sent, so he voted for it. As it turned out, his vote in favor saved the letter from defeat on a tie vote. The result was a 20–18, vote in favor of the four-line letter, a dangerously partisan vote on a major issue.

Conyers then tried his contempt citation and lost on a 32–5 vote with one abstention, that of Drinan. Supporting Conyers were Bob Kastenmeier, Waldie, Charles Rangel, and Elizabeth Holtzman. The committee had made its decision and adjourned at 11:40 P.M.

The letter was delivered to the White House by messenger the next day:

Dear Mr. President:

The Committee on the Judiciary has directed me to advise you that it finds that as of 10:00 A.M., April 30, you have failed to comply with the Committee's subpoena of April 11, 1974.

> Sincerely,
> Peter W. Rodino, Jr.
> Chairman

The next day the White House announced that the president rejected the letter the committee had spent three hours fashioning and that he would supply no more material. That sparked another round of heavy criticism.

Rodino already had decided the evidence the inquiry staff had compiled would be presented behind closed doors beginning the following Tuesday, May 7. The evidence was gathered into black-bound notebooks, laying out in paragraph form all the information the inquiry staff had collected from the White House, the grand jury, federal agencies, the Senate Watergate Committee, and any investigations the staff had conducted on its own.

Rodino intended to push ahead. Things would be looking bad again for the inquiry if Nixon's actions the past few days hadn't weakened his position as much, if not more, than the committee's partisan vote on the letter had weakened the inquiry.

One Republican expressed the fears of many, that Nixon might interpret the vote on the letter as a signal that he need not comply with the committee's second request for tapes.

But what the public, the White House, and even some of the members didn't fully appreciate was the peace of mind a decision to use Nixon's refusal as "adverse inference" had brought to the committee members.

On May 2, the committee formally approved the rules of procedures it would follow to a decision on impeachment. They would give St. Clair permission to question witnesses, suggest additional witnesses, address the committee, and raise objections to questions posed by others, including committee members. But Rodino would retain the power to overrule St. Clair and to shut him up, in effect, whenever he pleased.

On the morning of May 9, the *Chicago Tribune* printed an editorial calling for Nixon to resign. The fact that a conservative, pro-Nixon newspaper like the *Tribune* would urge resignation was more than symptomatic of the erosion of Nixon's support across the country. Its effect was almost absolution for Tom Railsback and Bob McClory, both Illinois Republicans whose districts were influenced by the *Tribune*.

And it was on that day that the product of more than six months of impeachment work would get its first airing for the members—two days late because the staff members couldn't prepare all the material in time. The first congressional hearings in a century to consider the impeachment of a president began.

Charleen Treffinger, twenty-five, of Joppa, Maryland, was first in line for the historic session that was scheduled to begin at 1:00 P.M. She had been in the hallway next to the committee hearing room since shortly after 9:00 A.M.

The Capitol Hill police gathered in force, kept spectators and press behind red velvet ropes at the end of the hall leading past Room 2141.

A few members of the public, more than a hundred reporters, and the thirty-eight members were present when Rodino rapped the gavel several times and announced, "The meeting will come to order."

He reviewed the activity that had brought the committee to that point and announced the forthcoming schedule. Hutchinson gave his own brief speech and Rodino recognized Donohue for a motion to close the hearing to the public and the press. Donohue made it, Conyers tried to get a discussion of it, failed, and demanded a roll-call vote. A few others who objected to closing the hearing tried to get a discussion of it, but Rodino was adamant. The roll call was taken and the 31–6 vote to close the session recorded. (Walter Flowers was absent.)

The television lights were turned out, the press and public filed out of the room, and at 1:40 the doors of the ornate room—now equipped with strange-looking dials and headphones at each seat on the two-tiered dais—were closed and locked.

That was the beginning of what would be ten full weeks of closed-door meetings to hear the evidence for impeaching Nixon, decide what it meant and what to do with it.

CHAPTER VII

✦

Worried

If John Doar fit any stereotype, it was that of a meticulous, compulsive librarian.

Every minute piece of information in the impeachment inquiry headquarters was carefully organized. All of it had been recorded on three-by-five index cards and filed in chronological order within each of Doar's six categories.

The early months of 1974 were spent fitting all of the material that Richard Cates had collected and all of the Senate Watergate Committee information into the system Doar had established.

When the carefully organized pair of briefcases were received from the Watergate grand jury, Doar had their contents broken apart and organized according to his system.

But Doar was struck by the organization of the grand jury material into what lawyers knew from law school as a "trial book." A trial book generally had a paragraph of information that the lawyer might want to present, followed by citations of the source for each statement of information made. In that manner, the lawyer would not be caught making a statement in court that he was unable to back up with evidence.

By the middle of April, the inquiry staff had compiled and filed all of the material it had received relevant to the impeachment investigation. More material had been sought from the White House, but was not relinquished. More subpoenas would follow in an attempt to secure those materials.

But the committee couldn't wait to see if they would be produced. The pressure on the committee to complete the impeachment inquiry had been building for the past several weeks. All of the House and one-third of the Senate faced reelection that fall, and neither the Democrats nor the Republicans wanted the cloud of impeachment hanging over their campaigns.

Soundings already had been taken around the Capitol and there was widespread agreement that there were enough votes in the House for impeachment. The White House also had counted the votes and had aimed much of its anti-impeachment campaign towards the Senate, assuming that a trial there was inevitable.

The beginning of the evidentiary hearings was set for May 9. The proceedings would have to be interrupted for committee votes to subpoena other information, but in general, the panel was ready to buckle down for six weeks to receive evidence. The evidence would be presented behind closed doors, since some of it had been produced by still-secret grand jury proceedings.

When the members arrived on Thursday, May 9, for the first hearing of the evidence, they found two thick, black, loose-leaf notebooks at their seats. One contained an index of all the impeachment material the staff had compiled and divided into sections. The other contained an arrangement similar to the trial book organization in the two briefcases forwarded by the grand jury.

At a long table facing the two-tiered dais sat Doar, flanked by nine other lawyers. Each had a large briefcase by his chair. At a shorter table adjacent sat the president's counsel, James St. Clair, and an assistant, John McCahill.

As soon as the room was cleared of spectators and cameras and the doors were locked, Rodino noted the presence of counsel for the president and reminded everyone in the room that all were subject to the rules of confidentiality the committee had imposed upon itself. Turning to St. Clair, Rodino said, "I would hope that Mr. St. Clair recognizes that he will be requested and will be expected to comply with the rules of confidentiality insofar as these material are concerned."

It was St. Clair's first appearance before the committee and he was nervous. "I do, your honor. Mr. Chairman, excuse me," St. Clair replied, red-faced. St. Clair and the inquiry staff were then introduced to the committee members. Rodino choked off statements some of the members tried to make and ordered Doar to proceed.

Doar outlined the organization of the two notebooks the members had received and explained how the evidentiary phase would proceed for the next six weeks. Then he lapsed into the tone he would use to the committee members for the next six weeks—devoid of inflection, free of emotional words or phrases. No one was going to be able to accuse him of presenting the evidence in a prejudicial manner. The evidence was referred to as "statements of information," a deliberate choice of a neutral phrase.

But it was boring to listen to. Many complaints would be made about Doar's presentation and some members, plus St. Clair, would even fall asleep while he read.

An easel had been set up and on it was a large chart showing the organization of White House personnel. Doar began with a memorandum, "Background Information":

On Jan. 20, 1969, Richard Nixon was inaugurated as the 37th President of the United States. On that day, 81 persons were sworn in as members of his staff. H. R. Haldeman was appointed as assistant to the President. John D. Ehrlichman was appointed counsel. From that day until May 19, Mr. Haldeman, who worked with President Nixon since 1956 in the political campaigns, acted as President Nixon's chief of staff. He was in charge of the White House operation. He worked directly for the President in implementing his decisions and directions. He directed the activities of the appointments secretary, the White House staff secretary. He received copies of memorandums [sic] and letters written by senior staff assistants to the President. He established and approved, subject to the final approval of the President, of course, the White House budget. He had no independent schedule. His schedule was that of the President.

Most members didn't realize it at the time, but with that opening paragraph, Doar had set the tone of the proceedings. It was the first thread in a web designed to ensnare the president of the United States. It was the first thread of Nixon's "patterns of conduct." Until that point, the purpose of all of the evidence gathered by other agencies was to prove participation by others in criminal acts. For the first time, the evidence was being presented in a manner to prove that the president also was involved.

Haldeman and Ehrlichman had been indicted on April 1, charged with conspiracy to cover up the Watergate break-in. The effect of Doar's opening paragraph was to tie Haldeman so closely to the president that he could have been seen as the president's shadow. The statement, "His schedule was that of the President," conveyed the image that what the president knew, Haldeman knew, and vice versa.

Doar continued, mapping the rest of the personnel structure close to the president in the White House. The meticulous Doar must have felt a flash of empathy when he read the next paragraph:

President Nixon is a very disciplined President. He likes order and his system of management of the White House clearly reflects that. That will be apparent, members of the committee, as you go through these hearings.

Doar described the president's automatic tape-recording set-up, and then described the personnel on the Committee to Re-Elect the President:

The information that we will furnish to you during the course of these hearings will establish that the White House staff was active in the formation and operation of these organizations. I will say more about that as we go into the proceedings today. And there were other people operating and supervising and directing, especially Mr. Haldeman, CRP's campaign activities. That, I believe, summarizes the background information that I wanted the committee to have. . . .

Again Doar returned to the streamlined White House operation:

It was very tight, a military staff organization, directed by Mr. Haldeman under the President's direction. I think the information that we will develop will show that the President spent most of his free time with Mr. Haldeman. We do not have all of President Nixon's appointment calendars, but I think there will come strong evidence that that was the fact. Mr. Haldeman, as I say, was the implementer of the presidential decisions of President Nixon. It was President

Nixon's habit to get to work at a regular time in the morning, to meet with his staff before 10 o'clock, to have appointments from 10 until 1 o'clock and then to have lunch and take a nap. And then to start with appointments about 3 o'clock until 6:30. And then he would go either to the White House (Oval Office) or over to the Executive Office Building for dinner where he would work in his suite. . . .

He flipped over pages on the easel as he spoke, showing diagrams of the White House and the president's EOB suites. For three hours Doar, spelled only briefly by other staff members, droned on, explaining a "statement of information," reading from a memorandum or a portion of a transcript, and referring to sections of the members' notebooks.

During a ten-minute recess in the middle of his presentation, he was asked to slow down, he was speaking too rapidly for some members to comprehend.

The first day's presentation carried the members from December 2, 1971, when Gordon Strachan, Haldeman's assistant, outlined political intelligence plans in a memorandum, up to "tab 20" in the members' index which read:

On June 17, 1972, at approximately 2:00 A.M., McCord, Barker, Sturgis, Gonzalez and Martinez were arrested for burglary in the Watergate offices of the DNC.

When he arrived shortly before 1:00 P.M., for the opening of the first evidentiary hearing, St. Clair told waiting reporters that, "I predict the president will not be impeached."

After the first three-hour presentation was completed, members emerged to tell reporters they had heard nothing new in the presentation but were impressed by the organizational structure at the White House and how closely tuned Nixon was to everything that went on there. The structure raised questions, one member said, about whether Nixon really was in the dark about the pre-Watergate planning. Other members suggested the committee would like to subpoena tapes of some conversations Nixon held with H. R. Haldeman before the Watergate break-in to determine if he did have prior knowledge.

Some members said they were convinced, more than they had been before, of the relevance of the tapes requested from the White House for the impeachment inquiry.

That first day's evidence comprised Book I.

The following Tuesday, the committee reconvened at 9:30 A.M., and was promptly told it would be listening to its first tape-recorded White House conversations. An extra table with machinery and two operators to run the tapes had been placed in the room.

The day's litany began with Evan Davis, a wheelchair-bound lawyer on the inquiry staff, reading "tab 1" of Book II:

On June 17, 1972, shortly after 2 A.M., five persons, including James McCord, a security consultant for the Committee for the Re-election of the President, were arrested in the Watergate headquarters of the Democratic National Committee. Immediately after the arrest, Howard Hunt and Gordon Liddy left the Watergate Hotel. Hunt took with him a briefcase belonging to McCord that contained electronic equipment . . . Hunt went to his office in the Executive Office Building and withdrew from his safe $10,000 previously provided to him by Liddy for use in case there was a mishap. Hunt placed McCord's briefcase in the safe. In the early morning hours he delivered the money to an attorney on behalf of the five persons arrested at the DNC headquarters.

Doar then said, "Tab 1.1 is the testimony of one of the law enforcement officials who was at the scene. At page one hundred and five of that testimony he describes the actual arrest in the office of the Democratic National Committee, the materials, equipment that was seized at that time and the arrest. On 1.6 the location of the arrest with respect to the location of the office of the chairman in the Democratic party, Mr. Lawrence O'Brien. It also indicates that the men gave names that were proved later to be false."

Doar and Davis continued, with Davis reading the information and Doar explaining the evidence supporting it.

The pair then recounted how the District of Columbia police department notified the Secret Service that one of the men arrested carried a document referring to a Howard Hunt, White House employee; that the Secret Service notified John Ehrlichman; Ehrlichman called the president's press secretary, Ron Ziegler, who was with Nixon in Florida; and that Ehrlichman also telephoned Charles Colson, Nixon's special counsel. Doar and Davis also noted that later that evening, Assistant Attorney General Henry Petersen notified Attorney General Richard Kleindienst of the document tying the burglars to the White House.

On the following day, June 18, 1972—according to the Davis and Doar litany—Haldeman telephoned Jeb Magruder in California and ordered Magruder to return to Washington. He was to meet with John Dean, Gordon Strachan, and the treasurer of the reelection committee, Hugh Sloan, to determine what had happened and find out the source of the money the burglars had. Ehrlichman and Haldeman discussed the break-in in another phone call.

On June 19, 1972, Kleindienst telephoned acting FBI Director L. Patrick Gray in Palm Springs and asked to be briefed about the agency's investigation of the break-in because Nixon wanted to talk to him about it that day or the next. Nixon, still in Florida, spoke with Colson on the telephone for one hour that day about the break-in. Hunt went to his office in the Old Executive Office Building, inspected the contents of his safe, and told Colson's secretary that it contained sensitive materials. The materials pertained to the campaign intelligence activities. That same afternoon, Ehrlichman, Colson, Dean, Haldeman staff assistant Bruce Kehrli, and Deputy Communications Director Ken Clawson discussed Hunt's White House status. Ehrlichman instructed that Hunt's safe be broken open, and Dean told Liddy to advise Hunt that he should leave the country. Dean, who had his instruction from Ehrlichman, shortly retracted the suggestion to Hunt. That evening, John Mitchell met in his Washington apartment with Dean, Magruder, Robert Mardian, and Fred LaRue and discussed the break-in. Ziegler, in Florida with Nixon, described the break-in as a "third-rate burglary."

On June 20, 1972, Doar and Davis continued, Haldeman, Ehrlichman, and Mitchell discussed the break-in, and Dean and Kleindienst joined the group later. Less than ninety minutes later, Haldeman met with Nixon, who had returned to the White House. The subjects they discussed included the break-in. They discussed a public relations offensive and how they should "be on the attack—for diversion." A tape recording of that conversation contained an 18½-minute buzzing sound that obliterated the section of the conversation reconstructed from Haldeman's notes. Strachan showed Haldeman a copy of a political intelligence memo, and Haldeman ordered him to destroy it. Strachan shredded it and told Haldeman and Dean that he had done so.

On that day or the next, the Davis-Doar team read, Mardian and LaRue met with Liddy, who related the plans for the break-in and other campaign intelligence activities. Mardian and LaRue described the meeting to Mitchell. All White House telephone lists bearing Hunt's name were recalled and reissued later with Hunt's name deleted.

Later on June 20, Mitchell issued a press release denying any CRP involvement in the break-in. At 6:08 P.M., Nixon spoke by telephone with Mitchell, and Nixon said on his dictabelt later that Mitchell had expressed regret he hadn't kept better control over the CRP people. (The Judiciary Committee members then heard their first tape, a playing of the dictabelt referred to.)

On June 21, Ehrlichman told Gray he was to coordinate the FBI investigation of the break-in with Dean. Dean met with Gray and said he would sit in on FBI interviews of White House staff members. Doar then noted conflicting testimony about whether Ehrlichman told Dean to "deep six" the contents of Hunt's safe. Dean said Ehrlichman did; Ehrlichman said he didn't.

On June 22, the two narrators continued, the FBI interviewed Colson in Dean's presence and asked about the contents of Hunt's safe. Gray reported to Dean that the FBI had traced some of the burglars' money through Mexico City to a U.S. businessman and offered the theory that the break-in was a covert CIA operation. Dean reported that to Haldeman. At a news conference, Nixon was asked whether there was a White House connection to the break-in; he denied it.

Davis read,

Tab 31, on June 23, 1972: H. R. Haldeman met with the President and informed the President of the communication John Dean had received from Acting FBI Director Gray. The President directed Haldeman to meet with CIA Director Richard Helms, Deputy CIA Director Vernon Walters, and John Ehrlichman. Haldeman has testified that the President told him to ascertain whether there had been any CIA involvement in the Watergate affair and whether the relationship between some of the Watergate participants and the [abortive 1961] Bay of Pigs [invasion of Cuba] was a matter of concern to the CIA. The President directed Haldeman to discuss White House concern regarding possible disclosure of covert CIA operations and operations of the White House Special Investigations Unit—the Plumbers—not related to Watergate, that had been undertaken previously by some of the Watergate principals.

The President directed Haldeman to ask Walters to meet with Gray to express these concerns and to coordinate with the FBI, so that the FBI investigation would not be expanded into unrelated matters that could lead to disclosure of the earlier activities of the Watergate principals.

Doar said the staff didn't have Nixon's log of that day, but that Haldeman's log showed three meetings, two of them with Ziegler present. "We have asked Mr. St. Clair if the president would produce those recorded conversations. Mr. St. Clair has advised us on the president's behalf, that the president declines to make those conversations available. We will be asking the committee tomorrow at its meeting that it consider the issuance of a subpoena for those three recorded conversations."

During the afternoon of June 23, Davis continued, Mitchell met with Maurice Stans, CRP finance chairman, in Mitchell's office. There Stans identified the check written by Kenneth Dahlberg, a Minnesota businessman and Nixon campaign contributor, as one that Sloan had given to Liddy to convert to cash. Doar said the check was the one traced by the FBI through Mexico to the burglars. It had been a campaign contribution that had been made three days after the April 7, 1972, cut-off date for unreported contributions.

Then Davis read tab 33:

At approximately 1:30 P.M., on June 23 1972, pursuant to the President's prior directions, H. R. Haldeman, John Ehrlichman, CIA Director Helms, and Deputy CIA Director Walters met in Ehrlichman's office.

Helms assured Haldeman and Ehrlichman that there was no CIA involvement in the Watergate, and that he had no concern from the CIA's viewpoint regarding any possible connection of Watergate personnel with the Bay of Pigs operation. Helms told Haldeman and Ehrlichman that he had given this assurance directly to the Acting FBI Director Gray. Haldeman stated that the Watergate affair was creating a lot of noise, that the investigation could lead to important people, and that this could get worse. Haldeman expressed concern that an FBI investigation in Mexico might uncover CIA activities or assets. Haldeman stated that it was the President's wish that Walters call on Gray and suggest to him that it was not advantageous to push the inquiry, especially into Mexico. According to Ehrlichman, the Mexican money or the Florida bank account was discussed as a specific example of the kind of thing the President was evidently concerned about. Following this meeting, Ehrlichman advised Walters that John Dean was following the Watergate matter on behalf of the White House.

All of the evidence backing up tab 33 had been known to Dick Cates at the time he put the case together in November 1973, and concluded that Nixon had ordered the CIA to call off the FBI investigation of the White House involvement in the break-in.

At 1:35 P.M., on June 23, Davis read, Dean telephoned Gray to tell him Walters would be visiting that afternoon. Walters cautioned Gray that because of possible CIA activity that might be endangered, he should limit the FBI investigation to the five burglars arrested. The FBI had not located Dahlberg, who already had been asked by Stans to fly into Washington for a meeting.

Davis and Doar traced the cover-up activities through June 28 and then threw the session open to questions from the members. There were only a few and the committee recessed at 5:20 P.M. until the next morning.

Before the hearing of evidence resumed, however, the committee voted to issue five more subpoenas. The key subpoena sought tapes that were recorded before the Watergate break-in, the six Nixon conversations with Colson and Haldeman on June 20, and his three conversations with Haldeman on June 23. That subpoena was voted with only Ed Hutchinson dissenting. The votes for the other four subpoenas, all for various periods of Nixon's diaries, were cast by margins ranging from 36–2 to 29–9.

The subpoena votes were cast in the face of St. Clair's announcement the previous week that Nixon would comply with no further subpoenas, even if that meant a constitutional confrontation with Congress. But the votes also came after two days of evidentiary hearings that impressed upon the members the need for the subpoenaed tapes. St. Clair had tried to give the panel the previous evening a memorandum protesting the upcoming subpoenas on grounds that "if the special staff had utilized all of the evidence available to it, no evidentiary gap would exist."

St. Clair had sat among the spectators while the votes were being taken. The evidentiary hearing was supposed to continue immediately after the vote, but because the voting session had run to close to noon, the committee decided to return after lunch, at 2:00 P.M.

After the doors were closed and locked that afternoon, Davis and Doar picked up where they had left off on Tuesday. The committee recessed in the evening and continued the next day, Wednesday, May 15.

Doar and Davis resumed their story, recounting that on September 15, 1972, the five Watergate burglars, plus Hunt and Liddy, were indicted in U.S. District Court in Washington. The committee members already had heard the evidence stemming from the break-in up to that date and knew of John Dean's close connection with the cover-up.

Late in the afternoon of May 15, Doar and his staff played the damning White House tape from September 15. On the tape, Nixon, Dean and Haldeman discussed the indictments and the fact the White House had emerged relatively unscathed. The date of the recording was less than two months before the November election. It provided some good insight into the thinking of Richard Nixon.

Nixon, Dean, and Haldeman had been discussing "all of those that have tried to do us in."

PRESIDENT: They didn't have to do it. I mean, if the thing had been a clo—, uh, they had a very close election, everybody on the other side would understand this game. But now they are doing this quite deliberately and they are asking for it and they are going to get it. And this, this—. We, we have not used the power in this first four years, as you know.

DEAN: That's right.

PRESIDENT: We have never used it. We haven't used the Bureau and we haven't used the Justice Department, but things are going to change now. And they're going to change, and, and they're going to get it right . . .

DEAN: That's an exciting prospect.

PRESIDENT: It's got to be done. It's the only thing to do.

HALDEMAN: We've got to.

PRESIDENT: Oh, oh, well, we've just been, we've just been just goddamn fools. For us to come into this election campaign and not do anything with regard to the Democratic senators who are running, and so forth. [Characterizations deleted] That'd be ridiculous. Absolutely ridiculous. It's not going, going to be that way any more, and, uh . . .

The three discussed the problem of containing further investigations into Watergate and turned their attention to the *Washington Post,* which had been revealing all of the Watergate connections up to that point.

PRESIDENT: That's right. Right. The main thing is that the *Post* is going to have damnable, damnable problems out of this one. They have a television station

DEAN: That's right, they do.

PRESIDENT: and they're going to have to get it renewed.

HALDEMAN: They've got a radio station, too.

PRESIDENT: Does that come up, too? The point is, when does it come up?

DEAN: I don't know. But the practice of nonlicensees filing on top of licensees has certainly gotten more

PRESIDENT: That's right.

DEAN: more active in the, in the area.

PRESIDENT: And it's going to be goddamn active here. Dean laughs.

PRESIDENT: Well, the game has to be played awfully rough. . . .

When the staff played the September 15, 1972, tape conversation between Nixon, Dean, and Haldeman, the tape did not contain all of the discussion. Dean had testified that Nixon talked about using the Internal Revenue Service to get at his enemies by harassing them with income tax audits. The tape had been turned over to Judge Sirica for use in the special prosecutor's case, but Sirica had judged that portion of the tape to be irrelevant to the grand jury's considerations. Since he judged himself to be only a custodian of the tapes, Sirica deferred to the White House a decision on whether to hand over the rest of the tape, which Doar had requested, to the House Judiciary Committee.

After the committee meeting, one of the members leaked a copy of the transcript that contained the references to the *Post* to a reporter from the newspaper and it appeared in the next day's edition. The White House and St. Clair launched a public campaign to have the hearings opened on grounds the leakers only revealed evidence adverse to the president.

That incident and other less significant leaks led eventually to a committee-imposed rule that each transcript would be identified by the name of the member or staffer who received it and all would be returned at the end of the day's proceedings.

The first evidentiary hearings had a devastating effect on the committee members. For nineteen hours during the first four days, they had heard a litany of evidence against the president. What they had heard was a report of conduct not easy to accept. By the end of that week, several members began to have their first doubts about Nixon's innocence of impeachable offenses.

Some attributed the effect to hearing Nixon's own voice say the things that until then had appeared only on paper. Somehow the words appeared more damaging when they heard him speak them himself. Tom Railsback told a reporter, "It made the conversations come alive. We got the emphasis, the voice inflections and the tone of the conversations."

Adding to the devastating effect of the voices were other revelations the members discovered when they went to inquiry headquarters to listen to portions of the tapes that had been censored by Rodino and Hutchinson, who had decided to omit ethnic slurs and statements defamatory to certain persons. The members were struck by the vituperative attitude Nixon displayed in his conversations and the near-paranoia he expressed toward friends when they did something he didn't agree with.

Railsback, and Bill Cohen had felt themselves slipping farther and farther from Nixon's side as he refused to cooperate. Bob McClory, the other Illinois Republican, already had been considering whether a president could be impeached for refusing to comply with an impeachment panel's subpoenas. Alabama Democrat Walter Flowers also had found himself leaning away from Nixon, as the president became more adamant about giving up information.

Those who were inclined to vote in favor of impeachment before the evidentiary hearings even started, readily admitted to the great effect the accumulation of facts had on them. Most of the information had been public for nearly a year, but never before had it all been presented in one package aimed at the president's possible participation.

Nixon's defenders conceded privately that the cumulative presentation of all the information was overwhelmingly impressive. Most cited Doar's outlining in minute detail of the organizational structure of the White House staff in the winter and spring of 1972, including "who reports to whom" and the physical layout of the mansion and connecting offices. One member said, "There was a strong impression of extremely tight control in the White House," noting that everything went to Nixon's chief of staff, H. R. Haldeman, and then to the president. Another said the inference was overwhelming that Nixon not only knew of, but approved at least indirectly, every directive that emanated from the White House and that he could hardly have been ignorant of much, if any, White House–connected activity.

Some members seriously believed that Nixon had prior knowledge of the Watergate break-in. They cited Nixon's and Haldeman's logs showing the two had many discussions daily, many of them following closely upon Haldeman's conversations with others known to have played a role in some aspect of the break-in or of its subsequent cover-up. One member said that if Haldeman had a conversation with someone who was putting together the intelligence operation and then went in to talk to the president, "there must be an inference." And the members were impressed with the frenzied activity of the White House immediately after the June 17 break-in. Such activity, they surmised, was not likely to occur on the heels of "a third-rate burglary."

When the committee resumed the following week, on Tuesday, May 21, it reached another key point in the inquiry staff's case against Richard Nixon. The two briefcases from the Watergate grand jury included a tape of a conversation Nixon had with Dean from 10:12 to 11:55 A.M. on March 21, 1973. Haldeman joined them at 11:15.

The tape was the most damning evidence yet presented against Nixon. The White House had given transcripts of that conversation to the committee and the public but, like its other transcripts, they were almost unreadable. The transcripts had entire speeches marked "unintelligible" and "expletive deleted." The special prosecutor's office had had a greater dedication than the White House staff in preparing transcripts of the tape recording and did so. But the impeachment inquiry staff had had the greatest dedication. It had purchased superior equipment that enhanced what already was on the tapes. With the machinery and close attention to every nuance and detail on the tapes—transcribed by staff lawyers, not secretaries—the staff had come up with a near-perfect transcript of the key March 21 tape, received from the Watergate grand jury.

That date in the Watergate chronology had been fixed by the White House and the special prosecutor as the key to the case against Nixon. The White House contended the tape was inconclusive, that persons who were trying to fix the president's criminality were just reading things into the tape that weren't there. But as the committee members listened for nearly two hours to the tape, they were impressed with the manner in which Dean recapped the entire Watergate chronology, of which he thought Nixon was unaware, and Nixon's acceptance of Dean's report in a matter-of-fact manner.

Nixon and Dean discussed the "hush money" and clemency demands that Hunt was making of the White House in return for Hunt's silence about the Ellsberg break-in. They discussed the possibility of keeping Hunt quiet until after the November 1974 congressional elections. When Dean suggested it might take a million dollars to keep Hunt quiet, Nixon said that there was no problem with raising that much money. They discussed using John Mitchell as a conduit for the money. Mitchell had resigned from the reelection committee two weeks after the burglary and returned to his home in New York. Haldeman joined the pair and expressed no surprise at what they were discussing. Nixon suggested at one point that the White House people being called to testify under oath "stonewall" the juries and just say they couldn't recall the facts they were asked for.

Near the end of their lengthy conversation, Dean said of some of the people appearing before grand juries: "They, they're going to stonewall it, uh, as it now stands. Except for Hunt. That's why, that's the leverage in his threat."

HALDEMAN: This is Hunt's opportunity.

DEAN: This is Hunt's opportunity.

PRESIDENT: That's why, that's why,

HALDEMAN: God, if he can lay this—

PRESIDENT: That's why your, for your immediate thing you've got no choice with Hunt, but the hundred and twenty or whatever it is. Right?

DEAN: That's right.

PRESIDENT: Would you agree that that's a buy-time thing, you better damn well get that done, but fast?

DEAN: I think he ought to be given some signal, anyway, to, to—

PRESIDENT: Yes.

DEAN: Yeah—You know.

PRESIDENT: Well for Christ's sakes get it in a, in a way that, uh—Who's going to talk to him? Colson? He's the one who's supposed to know him.

Dean said Colson didn't have the money, that Mitchell apparently had talked to Tom Pappas, who was the cochairman of Nixon's finance committee and a big Nixon contributor: "Apparently, Mitchell has talked to Pappas, and I called him las—John asked me to call him last night after our discussion and after you'd met with John to see where that was. And I, I said, 'Have you talked to, to Pappas?' He was at home, and Martha picked up the phone so it was all in code. 'Did you talk to the Greek?' And he said, uh, 'Yes, I have.' And I said, 'Is the Greek bearing gifts?' He said, 'Well, I want to call you tomorrow on that.' "

Nixon then asked how Dean would relay the money. Dean explained the money had to be laundered and that Mitchell would know how to do that. The talk then turned to possible maneuvering to get a new grand jury called to conduct a Watergate investigation. That initiative would have the effect of making it appear the White House was cooperating while enabling the president to try to stall the Senate Watergate Committee's investigation on grounds the matter was before a grand jury. The meeting ended with a decision to get Mitchell down to Washington as soon as he could come.

Half an hour later, according to the next insert in the committee members' notebooks, Haldeman called Mitchell and noted that Mitchell was scheduled to arrive the next day.

The White House version of the key conversation was much briefer and less damaging. It had Dean saying: ''They're going to stonewall it, as it now stands. Excepting Hunt. That's why his threat.''

H: It's Hunt's opportunity.

P: That's why for your immediate things you have no choice but to come up with the $120,000, or whatever it is. Right?

D: That's right.

P: Would you agree that that's the prime thing that you damn well better get that done?

D: Obviously he ought to be given some signal anyway.

P: [Expletive deleted], get it. In a way that—who is going to talk to him? Colson? He is the one who is supposed to know him?

The Nixon version agreed with the committee's transcript on Dean's account of the ''Greeks bearing gifts'' story.

Other evidence introduced by the inquiry staff before and after the members listened to the March 21 tape established that the $120,000 had been requested by Hunt and that on the evening after the discussion in Nixon's office, $75,000 of the $120,000 was relayed to Hunt.

The initial phase of presentation of Watergate evidence was completed on May 29, and the committee used the rest of the week to decide what it would do about Nixon's refusal to comply with its latest subpoenas.

The previous week Nixon had written a three-page letter to Rodino stating that he not only would not comply with the subpoenas the committee had voted on May 15, he didn't intend to produce any tapes or documents at any time.

So at the end of the month, the committee emerged from behind closed doors long enough to send a subpoena for forty-five more tapes and a strongly worded letter that Nixon faced impeachment for his refusal to comply with the previous subpoenas. The letter was approved, 28–10.

In two days of votes, the committee also rejected, by a 29–9 margin, a resolution by John Conyers, that Nixon be held in contempt of Congress for his refusal. Another designed to summon Nixon before the House to show cause why he should not be held in contempt, lost by a 27–11 vote. And the panel voted, 32–6, against a move by Tom Railsback to ask the courts to uphold the committee's subpoenas. It also voted, 23–15, to keep the rest of the hearings closed.

For the next three weeks the committee reviewed the evidence presented in relation to allegations Nixon offered government favors to ITT and the dairy industry, authorized illegal domestic surveillance, and tried to get the IRS to harass his supposed enemies. It reviewed the events leading to the firing of former Special Prosecutor Archibald Cox, the 18½-minute gap in the June 20, 1972, tape, and the charges about the president's tax returns.

But the Democrats had been complaining to Rodino since late May that the way the evidence was being presented was too fragmentary. They couldn't get their hands on a solid piece of evidence, "the smoking gun" that would allow them to construct a simple sentence to say why Nixon was guilty of an impeachable offense. One Democrat likened it to "grabbing for a handful of smoke." If the presentation of evidence continued that way, they complained, they faced the likelihood of going into an impeachment vote unable to explain to their constituents exactly why it was they were voting to impeach. The constituents hadn't been inside that room. How could they be made to understand? The members would be voting naked, they said.

Several of the concerned Democratic members—including Bob Kastenmeier, Don Edwards, Bill Hungate, and John Conyers, decided they would have two of the regular committee staff members—Bill Dixon and Arden Schell—interpret the evidence for them. They were to come right out and say what the evidence meant.

Dixon had been one of the first Judiciary Committee staff members assigned to the inquiry the previous fall. He left the inquiry, however, in a dispute with Doar over the special counsel's work style. Dixon had done much of the initial work on ITT allegations against Nixon. Dixon and Schell prepared the memos that the Democrats had sought, primarily side-by-side comparisons of the differences in the tapes that the committee had heard and the Nixon transcripts of the same tapes, released on April 30.

Their first memo, over Dixon's name, was a five-page summary of the case, involving Nixon's statement that he had instructed John Dean on March 21, 1973, to go to the presidential retreat at Camp David to put together a report for him on the facts of the Watergate case. Nixon had said that day was the first time he had known about White House involvement in the cover-up. Dean denied these were Nixon's orders.

Dixon's memo, dated June 4, 1974, quoted six pieces of conversation from some of the transcripts and concluded the conversations

may be interpreted to support the assumption that the President never asked Dean to write a report for the purpose of giving him additional facts, but merely so it could be relied on as an excuse in the event things came "unstuck" and the President needed justification for his inaction.

Near the end, Dixon had typed a parenthetical paragraph:

(NOTE: None of the above six statements appears in the publicly released version of the tapes. Nor does any portion of the following general discussion between Mitchell and the President regarding what had happened up to March 22, 1973, what will happen in the future, and Nixon's advice [as the Nation's chief law enforcement officer] to Mitchell.)

Dixon then quoted only Nixon's statements, picking out his order to his people to "stonewall it" when testifying, and to plead the Fifth Amendment "to save the plan" of containment.

Dixon wrote fourteen memos like that and many were leaked to the press. The news media also were getting oral reports from several members on what they were hearing each day. The leaks got international attention when Secretary of State Henry Kissinger held a news conference in Austria and threatened to resign over a leak from the committee connecting him with orders to wiretap reporters' phones before he became secretary.

Many members were becoming alarmed over the incidents. So was Rodino. At one hearing, he said he wanted the leaks from the panel to stop immediately. He began snapping at the members during some of the sessions and called Democratic caucuses to discuss the possibility of making all the evidence public as one way of defending the committee from charges of leaking. He feared that continued leaks would demean the committee, or at least cause it to lose the public's confidence. During those weeks of wrangling over leaks, he turned sixty-five, most people's retirement age.

The Democrats decided to have a full committee vote on the proposal to make the evidence public after the evidentiary phase was completed and to keep cool until then.

The evidentiary hearings were completed on June 24. That afternoon, the committee voted to issue more subpoenas, and to allow St. Clair to present his defense later that week.

The next day, the panel voted, 22–16, to release the material that had been presented as evidence in the hearings. Then it took up the thorny question of calling witnesses. St. Clair had campaigned for the right to call his own witnesses to offer exculpatory testimony, and to call persons whose testimony in other forums, without cross-examination, was being used as evidence in the impeachment inquiry. The committee Republicans strongly supported St. Clair's request and campaigned to allow him all he wanted.

By the beginning of June, St. Clair had held several meetings with the House Republican leadership. Although the committee Republicans kept St. Clair at arm's length because they feared the appearance of impropriety—since they, too, were supposed to be jurors in the impeachment case—St. Clair had made few requests of them. What requests he made were relayed through the GOP leadership. At one meeting between the House GOP leaders and the Republican committee members in May, the leadership relayed St. Clair's request that he be allowed to cross-examine some witnesses. But he didn't specify whom.

On May 22, Ed Hutchinson entered the hospital for a gall-bladder operation, leaving the second-ranking Republican, Bob McClory, to take his place.

Rodino called McClory on June 3 to discuss some of the inquiry matters with him, and McClory mentioned the possibility of calling witnesses. St. Clair had expressed a desire—and the Republicans acting in caucus had concurred—to question Charles Colson, H. R. Haldeman, John Ehrlichman, and John Dean.

St. Clair had been aching to get Dean on the stand ever since the evidentiary proceedings began. He still firmly believed that Nixon had been telling the truth about Watergate and that Dean was lying. Although the evidence tended to corroborate most of what Dean had said and to contradict Nixon's public statements, St. Clair didn't accept his testimony. "I can't wait to get to him," St. Clair said to an aide after one of the committee hearings.

Although St. Clair already had written off the committee as ready to vote for impeachment, he rejected the likelihood of a House vote for impeachment, and was certain that even if the case got to the Senate, where he could become a trial lawyer once again, he could win.

Colson had successfully plea bargained with the special prosecutor's office to get several serious charges against him dropped, in exchange for his guilty plea to a lesser charge of obstruction of justice. He also offered to cooperate with the House Judiciary Committee. His plea was entered in court the morning that Rodino called McClory, so McClory mentioned Colson as an example of the witnesses he would like to hear.

Rodino objected to calling witnesses. He said that if the committee got into interviewing witnesses, the inquiry would be drawn out even longer and would become confused. "I feel that would be going over the same ground, quite frankly," Rodino said.

Although he didn't mention it to McClory, Rodino also had detected during May a majority of the committee members in favor of impeachment, including some Republicans he badly wanted on any impeachment vote. But he deemed the Republicans to be "soft votes." A few more weeks of evidence presented in the same slow, cumulative manner in which the evidence had been presented during May should solidify their votes and add some more, he thought. Rodino already had decided he would vote for impeachment if a bipartisan majority voted that way.

The only danger Rodino saw was St. Clair. He had a formidable reputation as a cunning trial attorney. Rodino preferred not to see how effective he really was. Until then, St. Clair's role in the impeachment inquiry had been silent. He hadn't spoken a word during the evidentiary phase. The committee had voted to allow him to make a presentation and to cross-examine witnesses—if there were any. Rodino didn't want to call any and was angry with McClory for raising the question again.

After hearing evidence concerning Nixon's alleged misuse of the Justice Department and trickery with his income tax returns, McClory told Bert Jenner in mid-June that he would like to call, in addition to Colson, Henry Petersen, head of the Criminal Division at Justice, and Herbert Kalmbach, Nixon's personal attorney who had raised campaign funds and helped work out some of Nixon's tax deductions.

On June 24, St. Clair sent a letter to Rodino asking that six witnesses be called: Dean; John Mitchell; Haldeman; Howard Hunt's attorney, William Bittman; Fred LaRue, Mitchell's aide on the reelection committee; and Paul O'Brien, a reelection committee attorney. All six were connected in various ways to the tale of the $75,000 hush money to Hunt.

St. Clair had decided by then that except for the events of March 21, 1973, the committee's case had not proved anything damaging. The special prosecutor's office had thought March 21 the key to the case against Nixon and the White House had based its defense against the Watergate charges on the events of that day. So would St. Clair.

Although St. Clair considered impeachment essentially a political undertaking, it was an undertaking that had to rest on a bedrock of evidence. Circumstantial evidence that might be sufficient in an ordinary criminal prosecution was not enough to justify a member of Congress's vote for impeachment, he felt.

The March 21 story was dangerous to St. Clair's defense strategy. He still felt that Dean was lying and that all he had to do was face him in the witness chair.

During the previous two weeks there had been a steady call for the committee to summon witnesses. The requests came from those Republicans whom Rodino had thought to favor impeachment. His fellow Democrats also were beginning to make statements in favor of witnesses, so Rodino decided to fall back on the advisory group, a panel he hadn't used since the beginning of the year.

The group advised him that it would, indeed, be wise to call witnesses. After a lengthy discussion, the eight senior Democrats and seven senior Republicans on the committee reached a consensus in favor of calling eight witnesses, dropping Mitchell and Haldeman from St. Clair's list, adding the three that McClory had mentioned, plus Alexander Butterfield, the former Nixon aide who had blown the whistle on Nixon's taping system the previous year. The group decided those eight men should be able to furnish whatever the committee required, and that to call Haldeman and Mitchell would only duplicate evidence already presented. The group also felt that Haldeman and Mitchell would decline to appear, even under subpoena, since both were under indictment on Watergate-related charges. And Ed Hutchinson already had convinced the group that no immunity from prosecution should be granted any witnesses.

The fifteen senior committee members also decided on the groundwork for the testimony, limiting it to questions by staff counsel and St. Clair, who would ask questions for the members only if they were presented in writing. But that part of the plan required the committee to obtain an exemption from House rules, which required that all committee members be allowed to question witnesses. So a resolution for the exemption was formally adopted.

Over the next two days, the advisory group agreement fell apart. Several junior members from both parties had their own preferences for witnesses and the proposed list was changed several times. The one presented at the committee session on June 26 was different from any of those previously agreed upon.

Ray Thornton (D-Ark.) introduced the motion to call witnesses. It would have the committee call Butterfield, Kalmbach, Petersen, Dean, and LaRue and instruct the staff to interview Colson, Mitchell, Haldeman, O'Brien, and Bittman so Rodino and Hutchinson could decide whether to call them as witnesses.

Rodino was still adamant against allowing St. Clair too much margin in the evidence he could present, but as votes were taken on various amendments to add and subtract names, move names around on the list, he could see the Republicans gaining a majority for their position. Finally, an amendment by Maryland Republican Larry Hogan was adopted by a 21–17 vote. As Hogan said in offering it, the amendment had the effect of giving St. Clair the witnesses he asked for.

Rodino had lost. He called an unusual, half-hour recess of the committee and talked to Don Edwards, Walter Flowers, Jim Mann, and Wayne Owens, all of whom had voted with the solid Republican bloc in favor of Hogan's amendment.

Hogan's amendment was made to a motion offered by New Jersey

Republican Charles Sandman, which would have added still other names to the original motion Ray Thornton had introduced for Rodino. Edwards had withheld his vote until he saw that it wouldn't affect the outcome. Edwards, widely recognized for his overriding sense of fairness, felt that the Republicans and St. Clair should be permitted to call whatever witnesses they wanted, but he also was a member of the Democratic party and wanted to side with the Democrats where it counted.

Rodino persuaded him to change his vote on the Sandman amendment, which would be the pending motion when the recess ended. He also got Mann to change his vote, but couldn't budge Flowers or Owens. But two was enough. When the votes were cast on the Sandman amendment, it was 19–19, a tie. Ties fail and the original Thornton motion survived and was passed, 33–5.

But in getting his way, Rodino was dangerously close to alienating not only all seventeen committee Republicans, some of whom had been leaning his way on impeachment, but two of the southern Democratic members, Flowers and Mann, whose support was still viewed as soft.

Republicans labeled Rodino's actions that day as "high-handed tactics," and there was widespread fear among them that Rodino was toughening and would bully his way through the impeachment inquiry, denying a fair hearing for the president in the process.

Rodino later backed a move to force all of the witnesses' testimony to be taken behind closed doors. If there had to be witnesses, Rodino didn't want to allow St. Clair to put on what he feared would be a grandstand performance in public, possibly destroying the proimpeachment sentiment that had been building for the previous several months. The motion to close the sessions was killed, however, on a 25–12 vote.

The day before the vote on witnesses, the Democrats had prevailed on a 22–16 vote to release all of the evidence to the public before the impeachment vote—set for a month later—was taken. That, too, rankled the Republicans and smacked of a steamroller. Even if some Republicans wanted to vote for impeachment at that point, they didn't want to do so amid accusations the president didn't get a fair shake.

The committee also voted, 31–6, to seek permission from the House for the committee to ignore the House rule requiring that each member be allowed five minutes to question witnesses. The committee would consume more than three hours on each of the eight witnesses if all thirty-eight committee members were allowed to question each witness for five minutes.

Rodino certainly didn't want the impeachment inquiry to be dragged out by questioning witnesses. He said he would have the matter brought up on the floor of the House the following Monday under expedited procedures that would require a two-thirds majority for approval. The committee didn't have the time to allow the resolution to follow the normal, more time-consuming procedures for getting a measure to the floor.

On Thursday, June 27, St. Clair began two days of counterarguments to the inquiry staff's evidence. He based them almost entirely on the March 21, 1973, events and argued that Nixon did not order hush money paid to Hunt on that day, that even Dean had said in previous testimony that it wasn't ordered, and that the matter was "left hanging." St. Clair was often criticized by members during the session for offering biased conclusions on evidence he was supposed to present in a neutral manner.

At 1:30 P.M. the committee took a one-hour lunch break. As was his custom, Rodino returned to his office to have lunch at his desk. While he waited for a staff member to fetch it he wandered into Francis O'Brien's office. Three reporters following impeachment were sitting in O'Brien's office. One of them asked Rodino if he had any idea what the vote on impeachment would be.

Rodino was uncomfortable around the people he didn't know well. His extemporaneous speech was rarely quoted at length, because the more uncomfortable he was in his surroundings, the more garbled his syntax became. His sentences—like mountain roads—often started out with a definite direction, only to change course in the middle, double back, go off on a tangent, and then end suddenly without his thought having been completed.

His answer that day took one of those circuitous routes. He began, "If St. Clair keeps this up"—a reference to his stalling on answering subpoenas and then that day's characterization of his evidence. The sentence rambled through several twists and turns and returned to, "then all twenty-one Democrats are going to vote for impeachment." He was asked how many Republicans he thought would favor impeachment, and he listed five as most likely—Bill Cohen of Maine, Henry Smith of New York, M. Caldwell Butler of Virginia, and Tom Railsback and Bob McClory of Illinois.

A story appeared in print the next morning quoting Rodino as saying that Democrats were united behind impeachment and that he thought it would take the votes of those five Republicans to send a strong bill of impeachment to the House floor.

Rodino turned pale when he arrived at the office and O'Brien showed him a copy of the story. When Rodino got to the committee room shortly after ten o'clock for the second day of St. Clair's presentation, photocopies of the newspaper report were being circulated among the members and several asked him if he had really said that. Democrat Walter Flowers of Alabama was incensed. He was catching a plane that afternoon to return for a weekend of politicking in Alabama and would have to face angry constituents who would think he had made up his mind.

House Speaker Carl Albert called Rodino out of the hearing room shortly after the session began and advised him to make a strong public denial of the report. Criticism of Rodino's injudicious remarks already was reverberating about Washington, and the White House's Ken Clawson had attacked the statement with a charge that ''Rodino's partisanship and the bias of other Democrats on the House Judiciary Committee was confirmed today out of Mr. Rodino's own mouth.'' Rodino should be replaced as chairman, Clawson said.

Rodino missed most of that day's presentation by St. Clair, while he and O'Brien worked on a denial speech for him to deliver before the television cameras and on the House floor. He also worked to soothe Flowers's anger.

Rodino's statement said, ''I want to state unequivocally and categorically that this [news report] is not true. There is no basis in fact for it, none whatsoever.'' He said that none of the members had discussed a vote with him and ''were it otherwise, I want to assure the House, that I would not be sitting as chairman of the committee: I would withdraw myself from that capacity.''

But the controversy did not die. Some House Republicans joined in the attack on Rodino and it became clear that he might fail to get enough support the following Monday when the resolution denying the members the right to question witnesses was scheduled for consideration.

On Monday morning, July 1, Rodino decided he would have to regain some of the Republican support he had lost, so he called Mc-Clory and said he was making a big concession to the Republicans. He would, he said, issue subpoenas to all of the witnesses that had been requested by the staff and by St. Clair.

McClory supported Rodino later that day on the floor vote on the resolution, but it fell twenty-five votes short of the two-thirds necessary to carry, although it won a majority. The vote was partisan, 207–140, Democrats over Republicans with many Democrats absent. It was a strong rebuff of Rodino. That meant that each committee member would be allowed to question the witnesses and it also meant that Rodino's wishes for a bipartisan impeachment were in great jeopardy.

Even though the committee had voted earlier against closing the hearings when witnesses were questioned, Rodino still wanted the testimony taken behind closed doors. The Republicans had decided in a caucus earlier that day that they were unanimously in favor of keeping the doors open. Rodino faced a widening of the partisan rift later in the day when the committee voted again on whether to close the proceedings when it questioned witnesses. The debate on the motion that afternoon showed that the partisanship had not abated. Democrats decided to follow their chairman's wishes. The final vote was 23–15 in favor of closing the hearings, with all of those Republicans Rodino had listed as possible proimpeachment votes the previous week joining the staunch Nixon Republicans.

It was a bad, partisan beginning for July, the month that was to climax the impeachment inquiry. But something else was happening at the same time that was going to be of immense help.

The Dixon memos, for all of the stir and criticism they caused, hadn't been much help to those who requested them. Since Dixon and Schell were on the Judiciary Committee staff, neither had been totally immersed in the evidence being gathered and organized on the second floor of the Congressional Hotel and couldn't be as familiar with it as regular members of the inquiry staff. The group of Democrats who earlier had asked for someone to help them interpret and pull together the evidence, really wanted Dick Cates to help them. But Cates had left town.

Doar had been instructed to lay out the evidence against Nixon in a nonpartisan, neutral manner, make no conclusions and avoid judging the credibility of the evidence being presented. Cates was not diplomatic, so when he was asked for a conclusion, he gave one. Doar felt that was undermining his work and the friction between the two men grew.

Cates had spent much of his time since Doar's arrival teaching the case to new arrivals on the staff. In March he began conducting interviews of prospective witnesses, traveling to the various prisons where many of the former administration officials were being held. These interviews had been completed by the end of May, and Cates decided it was time for him to leave. The evidence was being presented to the committee and he had no real part in it. His farm in Wisconsin needed attention and he originally had signed on only for six months. He decided to return home, at least for a month, until the committee began voting and getting ready for a presentation to the House.

Jack Brooks and John Conyers discovered Cates was leaving and tried to dissuade him. The committee needed an advocate, they said. Doar's manner of presenting the evidence wasn't making the case. Cates insisted he had to leave, but would return. He left just before Memorial Day. He returned during a mid-June weekend to pay his rent and talk with Doar about a definite date for his return to the staff. They settled on July 1.

But after Cates returned to Madison, the Democrats held a caucus at which they laid out their complaints about Doar's presentation. Brooks made a motion that they bring Cates back as a Democratic advisor. Doar said Cates would come back only as an inquiry staff member. Kastenmeier and Edwards, who also had talked to Cates before he left, confirmed Doar's judgment, but the consensus of the group was that when Cates returned, he would return as an advocate even if he was still on the inquiry staff.

CHAPTER VIII

Undecided

July, the month in which the members of the House Judiciary Committee would be called upon to cast their votes for or against impeachment, began with the committee in disarray.

For the committee members, the impeachment inquiry had moved from the "Saturday Night Massacre" that shocked the nation and set the impeachment process in motion, to watching from a distance as the evidence was compiled, to listening day after day to a monotonous, droning voice slowly reading them each piece of evidence and its source. The members had listened to tape recordings and read transcripts. But the case against Nixon still was incomplete and many members were still uncertain.

Then on July 2, a Tuesday, Alexander Porter Butterfield, the man who disclosed a year earlier that he had been keeper of tape recordings Nixon had made surreptitiously of his conversations and telephone calls, walked into the committee room at 9:55 A.M. There, protected from the public by security officers and locked doors, he raised his right hand and swore to tell the truth to the committee. Butterfield had occupied the office next to the president's as secretary to the Cabinet and aide to H. R. Haldeman. He was aware of the day-to-day movements in and out of the Oval Office.

For nearly ten hours, Butterfield answered questions put to him by Doar; by Doar's Republican counterpart, Jenner; by St. Clair; and by nearly all the thirty-eight members of the panel. Butterfield painted a picture of a president closely tuned in to all the events of the White House and actions of its personnel.

Although many Democrats and Republicans disagreed on the importance or even the meaning of the testimony of Butterfield and the eight men who followed him to the witness table during the next two weeks, the members generally agreed that it was very helpful to have faces and voices presenting evidence about the conversations and events they had only heard Doar describe to them or listened to on tapes.

The witnesses also provided first-hand knowledge of some of the events and actions that made up the Watergate scandal. Sitting before the members, the witnesses corroborated much of the evidence the inquiry staff had collected and, in some cases, such as John Dean's, were able to testify clearly on events that had not been made clear during the Senate Watergate Committee hearings. The members also were impressed by St. Clair's inability to shake the testimony of key witnesses like Dean.

Even before the witnesses arrived, many House Republicans were viewing impeachment as inevitable. They discussed in June a compromise to avoid impeachment by having a House vote to censure Nixon, a move that would show dissatisfaction with the president's actions, while at the same time taking the steam out of impeachment. Other Republicans talked of the possibility of moving for an immediate and hopefully unanimous impeachment vote on the floor in order to send the matter to the Senate for a trial, thus taking the members off the hook about their own stands on impeachment.

The views of committee Republicans were becoming solidified, however. Ed Hutchinson had taken advantage of his operation late in May to give up his leadership role on the committee. By July he rarely even participated in GOP caucuses. His view of impeachment hadn't changed. He often had told his fellow Republicans on the panel that he couldn't conceive of a Republican voting to impeach a Republican president.

Bob McClory, who had moved in to fill the leadership void, already had determined that he could support a move on the House floor to hold Nixon in contempt for his refusal to comply with committee subpoenas. He could even vote for an article of impeachment embodying that complaint. His leadership of the committee Republicans, then, was not the "defense-at-any-costs" attitude of Hutchinson.

Tom Railsback was awed by the massive amount of evidence against Nixon presented during the six weeks of evidentiary hearings just ended. He was teetering on the brink of deciding for impeachment. He was beginning to think in terms of his survivability as a congressman if he voted to impeach.

Hamilton Fish also was a possibility as July began. One Saturday, instead of returning to his district for politicking, he visited the Congressional Hotel impeachment headquarters to listen again to some of the tapes that had been played for members. As he listened, staff members sat around the table ready to explain the significance of certain passages. Fish was particularly interested in the tapes of conversations referring to the "hush money" for E. Howard Hunt. Although he would waver several times during July, Fish realized that Saturday that he could justify a vote for impeachment.

Bill Cohen was a good friend of Railsback's, but they hadn't discussed their respective views on impeachment. Each knew the other was a possible vote for impeachment, however, judging from the questions both had asked during the evidentiary hearings.

The three southern Democrats on the committee—Walter Flowers, Jim Mann, and Ray Thornton—had particular problems. Their southern districts generally had given Nixon more support in 1972 than the districts many Republican committee members represented. If the southerners voted for impeachment they were going to have to be able to justify it convincingly. They agreed with other Democrats on the committee when they complained about the lack of bite in Doar's presentation.

Dick Cates, who had put the case together to his own satisfaction seven months earlier, arrived back in Washington on July 1.

Doar, via Rodino, had been receiving complaints from the members that the presentation of evidence had been inadequate and they weren't sure that hearing from the witnesses was going to be enough to prepare them to vote. Rodino had set a target date of late July for the first vote on impeachment. He had counted five Republicans he thought he could rely on for impeachment votes—and was sure he had the three southerners. But his mistake in revealing his estimate, and the White House attack on it, had endangered all of those votes. Doar had told Rodino before about his conflicts with Cates, that he had had to hold Cates in check because he was becoming too much of an advocate of Nixon's alleged guilt. Knowledge of his advocacy position had spread among the Democratic members, some Republicans were aware of it and it wouldn't be long before the public became aware of how strongly Cates felt. Cates's month-long leave from the inquiry staff had helped to relieve the problem for a while, but now he was back. Doar, with Rodino's permission, decided "to unleash him," allow him to begin laying out for any member who wanted to listen, the case in favor of impeachment.

Doar was well aware of Cates's popularity with some of the Democrats on the committee. Bill Hungate, Don Edwards, and Bob Kastenmeier, who knew Cates was scheduled to arrive back in town on Monday, had told Doar they wanted to meet with Cates to have him conduct "night school" for them. When Cates arrived at the impeachment inquiry headquarters, Doar told him, "I want you to meet with anyone who wants to meet tonight and tell them the case." Word was spread among the Democrats that Cates was available that evening.

A dozen members, primarily the more liberal members, showed up in a small hearing room across from Kastenmeier's office above the Judiciary Committee offices. The only "soft vote" in the group was that of Ray Thornton, who impressed Cates with his grasp of the importance of the circumstantial evidence that had been compiled.

The rest of that week Cates spent most of his waking hours either in the committee room while the witnesses were being questioned, or in meetings with one, two, half a dozen, or a dozen members. They met either at breakfast or dinner, in meeting rooms or in the offices of Waldie, Hungate, or Paul Sarbanes (D-Md.). By the end of the week, all of the Democrats had sat in on at least one of Cates's "night schools."

Cates didn't have to bone up on the subject. It was essentially the same scenario he had outlined to the inquiry staff in November and December. It had been augmented, however, by additional evidence from the two briefcases turned over by the grand jury in the spring, some of the tapes the White House had given the special prosecutor, and additional grand jury information turned over during previous months.

In his matter-of-fact way, Cates led the members step-by-step, date-by-date, from the July 17, 1972, Watergate break-in chronologically through the cover-up. It wasn't necessary, he said, for example, to trace the money from the campaign contributor to the burglars who entered the Democratic National Committee headquarters: "The question that you are facing is 'What did the president say on June twenty-third to Haldeman?' That is the decision that you folks have to make. Did the president tell Haldeman, did he give him instructions to interfere with the FBI's investigation for purposes of hiding the fact that that investigation would uncover CREEP money in Mexico? That is really what this is all about."

In considering their own decisions about whether the president did or did not order interference with the FBI investigation on June 23, he said, "You have got to look at facts which, in my judgment, are in this record and have been established beyond question."

He then went through the same facts that had been presented during the evidentiary hearings, but connected them in a way that hadn't been done for the members before. And Cates inserted his own logic and reasoning.

If the FBI had been permitted to continue its investigation, Cates said, it would find the link between the contribution to Nixon's reelection committee and the Mexican bank through which the money was laundered. "I think you must examine the significance of that link. You have got to ask yourself, 'If they found that out, what would really be the complexion of the investigation at that time?' There would be an immediate realization that there was a relationship between CREEP and the burglaries that would no longer be hidden.

"Second, they would have found out that [G. Gordon] Liddy was involved in this, because he was the man who had given the money to Barker [Bernard Barker, one of the five arrested inside Watergate], so that Liddy would have been exposed. And third, as it relates to this Liddy plan and the financing of it, you see, inquiry into the Mexican money leads you into an understanding of how CREEP was able to raise cash to finance matters that they did not want traceable. As Haldeman explains in the transcript in April, the use of cash that came to the White House, the three-hundred-and-fifty-thousand-dollar fund, was for money to spend that was not traceable. Well, if you are going to spend money that is not traceable, you have to raise it in a way that is not traceable. And so what I am trying to say to you is that that was something that would have been exposed, a method of washing money, laundering money.''

Cates took the members up to June 23, 1972, six days after the break-in, and said, ''When you are required to decide what were the president's instructions on June twenty-third, logic compels me to look at things that may have been of consideration to him and that is really what I am purporting to do for you, to explain those things that I think rational men must look at to decide, if they can, what it was that was said on that date.''

If there were questions, he would lay the scenario out in greater detail, taking his listeners step by step in describing who talked to whom and what was likely to have been said in relation to what had been said before and what had been done afterwards.

''I guess all that we are really concluding is the fact that reasonable men examining all these circumstances and the significance of these circumstances, have a basis to conclude that the president of the United States may well have directed Haldeman to deliver this message to Helms to interfere with the investigation to keep the CREEP money from being exposed.

''What I am saying . . . the only rational, conceivable explanation that would deter someone from coming to that conclusion is going to be found in the transcript or in the tape. We have asked for the taped conversations and the president has not given them.

''I guess basically, as I see it, the understanding of the money really is just a set of facts that has to be understood [to realize] what the president intended to accomplish when he directed Haldeman to speak to Helms.''

In the same fashion, Cates also laid out the case for Nixon's order to pay hush money to Howard Hunt on March 21, 1973, and Nixon's abuse of powers of his office by ordering misuse of the Justice Department and the Internal Revenue Service. Or he laid out the case for any other subject on which the members sought information. It was a powerful presentation.

As July progressed, other factors were at work. Standing alone, the other factors weren't of paramount importance to an impeachment decision, but they had the cumulative effect of dripping water on a rock, eating away doubts about Nixon's guilt.

Jaworski confirmed what had only been guessed in public to that point—that Nixon had been named as an unindicted coconspirator in the Watergate cover-up. And Jaworski filed a bill of particulars in court, outlining the reasons for the cover-up. His conclusions were nearly the same as those Cates had been presenting that week.

Herbert Kalmbach, Nixon's attorney, entered a minimum security prison in suburban Maryland after being convicted for illegal campaign fund raising.

On Monday, July 8, the Supreme Court heard oral arguments in Jaworski's suit to force Nixon to turn over sixty-four tape recordings of Watergate-related conversations. St. Clair had to be in court to represent the president that day, so the Judiciary Committee's testimony from Frederick LaRue was postponed until St. Clair could be present.

Almost daily, the White House public relations men had been hammering away at the committee, accusing it of being on a witch hunt; conducting a kangaroo court; leaking selective, anti-Nixon information; and slanting its inquiry against the president. St. Clair had asked his press aide, Larry Speakes, to get the White House to call off the hounds, to explain that it was only hurting the president's case and St. Clair's ability to operate before the committee. Speakes was unsuccessful. The public relations campaign continued.

Rodino already had decided that during July his committee would have its own public relations campaign. He didn't necessarily orchestrate the timing of it, but certain ancillary activities did coincide effectively with the committee-room activities.

On July 9, the committee released a brown-bound, 218-page government-printed report of transcripts of eight White House tape-recordings. The White House had sent the committee transcripts of these tapes on April 30, but the committee already had copies of the tapes from the grand jury and had made its own transcripts. For the first time, the public was able to read the full, unexpurgated transcripts of those conversations and compare them with the president's heavily edited and altered versions, already available in paperbacks and on sale at bookstores.

The release of the transcripts—timed more to influence the Supreme Court decision on giving the special prosecutor the sixty-four tapes than to educate the public—not only began a new round of full-page newspaper reproductions of White House conversations, it also confirmed most of the leaks that had come from the committee during the evidentiary hearings. And it gave the public a better indication of the White House operation.

The next day the committee released the first eight volumes of the evidence that had been presented at the May and June hearings. Over the next several days, the public was saturated with the ''statements of information'' and the supporting evidence that the members had received. The same day, the Senate Watergate Committee, whose prime work had been done the previous year, released its own report on financial corruption in the White House, focusing on some of the things the impeachment inquiry was probing.

And the trial of John Ehrlichman and other defendants on charges they were connected with the Ellsberg break-in was continuing on the West Coast.

The White House didn't help its cause any when it answered the news reports about the committee transcripts by saying that their release was part of a ''hypoed public relations campaign'' and that the committee was trying to prejudice the public against Nixon in advance of its impeachment report. The transcripts also proved Nixon's innocence, a White House spokesman said.

Coincidentally, the committee was just releasing photocopies of a side-by-side comparison of the White House and its own version of the transcripts.

St. Clair joined the White House campaign, however, saying that he didn't view the conversations ''as sinister.'' Three different persons would listen to the tapes and produce three different versions of them, he said. Both St. Clair and White House press secretary Ron Ziegler labeled "inconsequential" the tape on which Nixon had instructed his people to "stonewall" legal efforts and to pretend to forget damaging information. The public read the transcripts and drew different conclusions.

Adding to the erosion of support for Nixon in July, Ehrlichman was found guilty in the Ellsberg break-in case and the Senate released the rest of its report—2,217 pages long—concluding the president probably was involved in the cover-up.

But the central question at the time was what effect the accumulating evidence was having on "the troubled middle," as Rodino labeled that group of Democrats and Republicans whose votes could not be prejudged, the swing votes who held the key to a bipartisan impeachment vote.

The first week of July, Cohen and Fish discovered in a casual conversation that they both were members of that group of "undecideds." Cohen had long been considered one of the Republicans most likely to vote for impeachment, but Fish had his own problems with his New York constituency and was wavering.

Staunch pro-Nixon Republicans on the committee began setting up their own task forces about that time to push the defense of Nixon. Many of those in favor of impeachment had been developing specialized knowledge of the evidence so they could present a good case in favor of impeachment, so Charles Wiggins suggested the Republicans should become equally informed in order to provide an adequate defense. Many of the House Republicans who were not on the Judiciary Committee had taken up the White House cudgels and begun denouncing the impeachment inquiry activities. Committee Republicans were caught in the middle.

The Republicans set up five task forces. On the task force on the "hush money" allegations were Bob McClory, Tom Railsback, David Dennis, and Larry Hogan. Each task force was assigned three GOP inquiry staffers knowledgable about the charges.

But when the staffers advising the Republicans on the hush money—Chris Gekas, Ben Wallis and Bill White—reviewed the March 21 evidence for the task force group, they were unable, to McClory's satisfaction, to explain away the tape-recorded evidence that Nixon ordered payment of the hush money.

On July 9, when former Attorney General John Mitchell testified before the committee (mostly refusing to answer its questions because he was under indictment), Ray Thornton was discovered to be another of the undecideds. Thornton had kept his own counsel to that point. He had attended a pair of Cates's "night schools" by that time, but had been noncommittal in his remarks. Most of the time he had just sat back and listened. By dint of his southern background, he had felt closer to Jim Mann and Walter Flowers than to others on the committee, but hadn't discussed the case with them. Thornton already considered the president's refusal to comply with the committee's subpoenas a serious offense, one which rose to the level of an impeachable offense if other impeachment charges were voted against him. Even by itself, the refusal to comply with committee subpoenas was both an obstruction of justice and an abuse of power, Thornton decided.

On July 10, when Mitchell returned for his second day of testimony before the committee, Walter Flowers and Thornton established by their questions that Mitchell had an intimate relationship with Nixon, that he could contact the president directly or be contacted by the president without the normal intercession of Haldeman.

Thornton further established in his questioning that the organizational chart that Doar had provided to the committee on the first day of the evidentiary hearings two months earlier actually worked the way it was intended to. Haldeman was an accurate conduit to and from Nixon, Mitchell testified under questioning. He was confident that Haldeman passed on any information he wished to relay to Nixon and stated, "I would have to say that in most all instances that I can recall, Mr. Haldeman's representations to me of the president's position were truthfully and fully stated." Haldeman, then, was a conveyor rather than a barrier, to the flow of information, Thornton decided. That conclusion was important to him in establishing Nixon's probable knowledge of the cover-up.

Fish told reporters during a break in the committee session that day that the committee book of transcripts that had been released the previous day "supports the circumstantial case" for impeaching Nixon.

As part of their task force duties, McClory and Railsback went to the impeachment inquiry headquarters after Mitchell's testimony that evening to listen to the tape recordings relevant to the "hush money" case.

In the course of their review, they listened to a portion of the nearly two-hour conversation Nixon had on March 22, 1973, with Mitchell, Dean, Haldeman, and Ehrlichman. The five discussed how they would handle Watergate from that point on, including citing executive privilege to protect key White House people from having to testify in public sessions of the Senate Watergate Committee.

The March 22 tape had been an especially troublesome one for the members. It had been recorded in Nixon's Executive Office Building suite and the low voices of the group caused the voice-activated tape to kick on and off, causing whirring noises on it. Even the panel's enhanced tape was of poor quality and voices were hard to pick up, even with a transcript to follow. And the White House version disputed that of the committee. The former version stated:

P: Let me ask this. This question is for John Ehrlichman and Dean. You were the two that felt the strongest on the executive privilege thing. If I am not mistaken, you thought we ought to draw a line here. Have you changed your mind now?

D: No, I think it is a terrific statement. It puts you just where you should be. There is enough flexibility in it.

P: Well, all John Mitchell is arguing then, is that now we use flexibility in order to get off the cover-up line.

E: And as I told him, I am so convinced that we are right on the statement that I have never gone beyond that. He argues that we are being hurt badly by the way it is being handled. And I told him, let's see—

The committee transcript said:

PRESIDENT: "Let me ask this. Uh, the, this question is for John Ehrlichman and, uh, John Dean. Uh, now you were the two who felt strongest, uh, on the executive privilege thing [unintelligible]. If I am not mistaken, you thought we ought to draw the line where we did [unintelligible]. Have you changed your mind now?

DEAN: No sir, I think it's a, I think it's a terrific statement. It's—It, it puts you just where you should be. It's got enough flexibility in it. It's—

PRESIDENT: But now—what—all that John Mitchell is arguing, then, is that now we, we use flexibility . . .

DEAN: That's correct.''

PRESIDENT: . . . in order to get on with the cover-up plan.

EHRLICHMAN: And, as I told him, I am, am so convinced we're right on the statement that I have never gone beyond that. He argues that we're being hurt badly by the way it's being handled. And I am willing—let's see—

Since the tapes had been played for the committee on May 22, the members had been arguing both sides of what the tape actually said. The controversy was revived when the press highlighted the differences after the committee transcripts were released July 9.

McClory and Railsback also were in disagreement. When they listened to the tape again on July 10, they had it replayed for them several times. McClory insisted he heard "Jews were to get off the cover-up." He couldn't hear either the word "plan" or "line" and told Railsback he didn't think either word existed on the tape. Railsback replied that as far as he was concerned, the committee transcript was correct, that Nixon did talk of getting on with the cover-up plan.

Sitting in on McClory's and Railsback's review of the tape were Ben Wallis, Bert Jenner, and two other staffers. After Railsback disagreed with McClory's interpretation of the tape, Wallis, a GOP staff member, interjected that it would be far more logical for the president to say that they were getting off the cover-up because a change of attitude was being expressed at the time.

Jenner interrupted Wallis and told him he had no right to interpose his view. Jenner, however, allowed the two other staff members, both Democrats, to express their view, which was that Nixon was saying he wanted to get on with the cover-up plan.

The imperfections of even the committee's transcripts had been highlighted for the public when reporters reviewing the just-released committee transcripts found later in that same March 22 conversations:

MITCHELL: All of Washington—the public interest in this thing, you know.

PRESIDENT: Isn't Nash [unintelligible] Earl Nash worries the shit out of us here in regard, regarding [unintelligible].

MITCHELL: Just in time.

PRESIDENT: But the point is that, uh, I don't—There's no need for him to testify. I have nothing but intuition, but hell, I don't know. I, but—Again you really have to protect the presidency, too. That's the point.

MITCHELL: Well this does no violence to the presidency at all, this concept—

No one in the Washington press corps had ever heard of Earl Nash and the White House version of the tape for that day had not run on that long. Reporters asked Francis O'Brien about the transcript reference and he said he didn't know who Nash was, but would have a staffer check it out.

The staff member reported that upon listening to the tape he interpreted the reference as: "Isn't nash [unintelligible] er, nash [unintelligible] worries the . . ." and guessed that Nixon was starting to say "national," as in national security.

But the point had been made. The committee members had listened to the tapes with transcripts in hand and no one had asked who "Earl Nash" was or had pointed out the possible discrepancy. It didn't speak well for their devotion to following the evidence.

The next day, July 11, the witness most of the committee members had been waiting for arrived to testify. Although St. Clair had been extremely eager to cross-examine John Dean, he appeared to be ill prepared for the confrontation. St. Clair had said he would like to have two weeks to cross-examine Dean, but lamented the fact he had only one day. "You can't save many souls in that time," he told reporters. He had told one aide on the way to the Capitol that day, "I can't wait to get to him."

St. Clair had determined by that time that several things Dean had testified to before the Senate Watergate Committee had not been supported by the tapes. One point was Dean's testimony that he had not been asked to write a report on the cover-up that he had led up to March 21, 1973. St. Clair thought the tapes clearly disclosed not only a request, but a demand that Dean write the report. St. Clair also thought Dean's previous testimony was dubious because he already had set up the machinery for payment of the hush money before it was discussed with the president on that day. And Dean did not indicate anywhere on the tape, St. Clair noted, that Dean already had made the calls setting up the hush money payments.

Doar had consumed two and a half hours of the morning portion of the session questioning Dean. After a lunch break, St. Clair got his chance; he questioned Dean for nearly three hours, followed by more than three hours by committee members.

Dean had known for more than a week that he was going to testify to the Judiciary Committee and had spent the intervening time reviewing his previous testimony and his notes. He was well prepared. Like other witnesses, he was allowed to have his lawyer present to protect his rights.

St. Clair's questioning was widely judged as the poorest of the three segments. St. Clair assumed the classic pose of a trial attorney cross-examining an unfriendly witness. His relentless questioning of Dean failed to crack Dean's previous testimony to the grand jury, to the Senate Watergate Committee, and his responses to Doar.

St. Clair's time was divided along three fronts: the special prosecutor's office, the committee, and the Supreme Court, where just three days earlier he had argued against the special prosecutor's demand for the sixty-four Oval Office tape recordings. He only had a staff of seven lawyers, compared with staffs numbering seven times that size working for each of his adversaries.

Dean's credibility, St. Clair thought, depended on his memory. At the beginning of St. Clair's questioning, Dean commented that he didn't "have a good memory" of an incident St. Clair had asked about.

St. Clair then asked Dean, "I would like to ask you a little bit about your memory. Do you have a good memory?"

Dean replied, "I would say it is a good memory, yes."

"Well, when you testified before the Senate committee, you indicated you had a very good memory, didn't you?"

"I believe I indicated I had a good memory, but it was not a tape recorder."

St. Clair continued to bore in on the fallibility of Dean's memory as he threw questions about other incidents at him in a rapid-fire manner. He attempted to challenge Dean's memory by showing that he remembered small details but forgot larger ones. St. Clair read from a transcript of the tape of March 21, 1973, in which Dean had told Nixon there were some things Nixon didn't know that he wanted to tell him about.

"And later on, at page one hundred, you said, do you recall this? 'I know, sir, it is. Well, I can just tell from our conversations that you know, these are things that you have no knowledge of.' "

Dean, without hesitation, replied, "That is a reference to pre-June seventeenth." Dean was saying the president didn't know about the pre–break-in events, not the pre–March 21 events, the cover-up.

St. Clair's line of questioning had been broken and perhaps destroyed by the mistake. He paused and said, "Well—"

Dean continued, "And I think if you read it in context, you will find it is such."

St. Clair regained his poise and said, "All right. But this was—how about the conversation? . . ."

Several times after that, Dean corrected misstatements St. Clair made, and St. Clair apologized and backed off.

At another point, Dean's lawyer objected to a question from St. Clair, and the committee members lapsed into wrangling about the conduct of the questioning.

When that ended, St. Clair was asked to repeat the question. He said, "I must apologize. May it be read? I don't recall the question."

Dean interjected, "I can save time; I recall the question and the answer I was going to give."

St. Clair was asked if that was satisfactory, and quietly responded, "Yes."

Dean said, "The questions was, 'Did Mr. Ehrlichman say there would be no problem with regard to Hunt's demand?' The answer was 'yes,' he did so respond. Mr. Mitchell responded in that manner after Mr. Ehrlichman had raised it very early on in the meeting."

St. Clair never regained the upper hand. Dean contradicted St. Clair on other points, and once St. Clair had to admit he had misread the testimony he was referring to.

St. Clair's questioning had begun in an arrogant manner. But he had failed to break Dean's previous testimony and in the process had helped to reinforce Dean's credibility in the eyes of the members. Unfortunately for St. Clair, he was not questioning the witness in front of an ordinary jury. This was a jury of thirty-eight other lawyers who had placed upon him strictures against offering conclusions about the evidence and who could judge professionally his performance as a lawyer.

When Dean's attorney objected to St. Clair's repetitious questioning and was upheld, St. Clair finally gave up and sat down, defeated.

In his questioning of Dean, McClory tried to get him to confirm his and the White House's version of the disputed March 22 cover-up discussion. Dean said he agreed with the committee version.

McClory continued the questioning and Rodino broke in to say, "I would like to state that I listened to that tape this morning."

"Well, how is your hearing?" McClory asked.

"It's good," Rodino replied. "Well, mine is too," said McClory, "and I thought it very clearly . . ." Rodino interrupted to say, "And it reads like our transcript does."

Near the beginning of his testimony, Dean had revealed that he had discussed Hunt's hush money demands with Nixon during a call Nixon had made to Dean's home the night of March 20, one day before the celebrated discussion that Nixon cited repeatedly as his first knowledge of a cover-up or of the hush-money demands.

Railsback established with his questioning of Dean that Nixon's defenders were wrong when they claimed that the question of paying the hush money was "left hanging" in the March 21 discussion. Dean said the reference to "left hanging" was to the one million dollars that Nixon had suggested could be raised to pay blackmail money.

Railsback's close and lengthy questioning on that and on the September 15, 1972, period when it was alleged Nixon authorized use of the IRS for retribution convinced Fish and Cohen that Railsback also was troubled about Nixon's innocence.

After Dean's testimony, George Danielson (D-Calif.) erased any doubts that might have existed about his vote when he told a reporter, "I think I have a clear, constitutional duty to vote for a bill of impeachment." Larry Hogan (R-Md.), on the other hand, said he had "serious doubts about Dean's credibility on the basis of his testimony." Walter

Flowers agreed, but said Dean's testimony "gave a new dimension to the inquiry in the sense it brought a little life into a sterile transcript." Henry Smith, (R-N.Y.) and Cohen agreed that Dean's testimony was damaging to the president's case, but St. Clair told reporters after the session ended that evening, "In some respects, I'm very happy" with the outcome of the Dean appearance.

Early the next morning, July 12, the committee Republicans and staff members Bert Jenner and Sam Garrison held one of their regular caucuses in McClory's office. Ed Hutchinson and three other Republicans were absent.

The Republicans talked about getting their own briefings from the inquiry staff, including from Dick Cates, whose "night schools" they had heard about by that time. Inquiry staffer Chris Gekas had spread the word that the Democrats were becoming much better informed about the case at those sessions and even if the Republicans didn't agree with Cates's advocacy, it would be helpful to sit in nonetheless.

Several of the Republicans at the caucus said it also would help them to find out what "theories of impeachment" the staff members were working on. Jenner explained that the staff was working only on theories of how the suggested articles would be grouped. For example, he said, all the allegations could be included in one article or grouped according to subject matter or by dates or several other ways. That was all the staff was working on, Jenner said. It was not drafting the articles themselves. He also assured the members that Sam Garrison was being allowed to review all of the work being done.

Hutchinson walked in near the end of the caucus as the rest of the Republicans agreed they should oppose any articles of impeachment that were proposed without specifications listing each charge against the president in detail. He was dumbfounded by the idea that the Republicans might be considering that they could possibly vote for an article of impeachment.

"It's impossible for a Republican to consider voting impeachment of a Republican president," he said. The Republicans ought to concentrate instead, he said, on getting all the information and arguments possible in opposition to any proposed articles of impeachment.

Railsback said that as far as he was concerned, Nixon had violated rules relating to grand jury secrecy by relaying information he had received from Henry Petersen, head of the Justice Department's criminal division, to Haldeman and Ehrlichman, prime subjects in the grand jury investigation. He had just reviewed the evidence because Petersen was set to testify to the committee following the GOP caucus. Railsback added that he also was considering voting for an article of impeachment charging obstruction of justice in the Watergate cover-up.

As Hutchinson listened in disbelief, McClory offered that he, too, was considering a vote for impeachment, on an article that would embody Nixon's failure to "take care that the laws be faithfully executed," as the Constitution said the president must do.

"I can't imagine any Republican voting to impeach a Republican president," Hutchinson muttered again as the members rose to go downstairs for the committee session. On the way, Fish and Cohen revealed their doubts about Nixon to Railsback and suggested the three of them get together.

Fish and Cohen had decided to accept the suggestion that the Republicans take part in Cates's "night schools." Fish asked Cates to come to Cohen's house in McLean, Virginia, on Sunday, July 14, and present his case to the two of them. For five hours at Cohen's house, with three Republican staffers present, Cates laid out his case much as he had in the sessions with the Democrats in the previous two weeks.

In the week that followed, other Republicans, even some absolutely opposed to impeachment, such as David Dennis of Indiana, joined the sessions Cates was holding. Railsback, who had spurned the Sunday meeting at Cohen's house, got one of the largest groups together at the Capitol Hill Club in Republican party headquarters. Although many of the Republicans wouldn't vote for impeachment, some said they were impressed by Cates's arguments, that he had made a very persuasive presentation in language they, and thus their constituents, could understand.

M. Caldwell Butler (R-Va.) was one of the Republicans attending Cates's sessions. Cohen, who sat next to Butler on the lower tier of the dais in the committee room, thought he had detected an increasing softening in Butler's previous resolve against impeachment. Butler's questioning of witnesses also indicated he still had an open mind on the case.

Cohen decided he would have to have some more discussions with the silent Virginian.

Jerry Zeifman, seeing the culmination of the impeachment proceedings looming, began pressuring Doar, partly at the urging of Jack Brooks. Zeifman told Doar that he should be prepared to make a hard-hitting summary no more than fifteen pages long about the significance of the case before the debate on articles of impeachment began. Zeifman wasn't sure the sessions with Cates would be enough and that members might need to hear the conclusions from Doar.

Zeifman also hadn't seen any evidence that Rodino had made any effort to help the undecided members come down on the side of impeachment. Once when he told Rodino that he should approach Walter Flowers and see what he could do to help Flowers decide, Rodino snapped, "I don't care how other people vote. I'm responsible only for my own vote."

Garrison complained to McClory that Jenner had not prepared the counter-arguments as the Republicans had instructed him. Garrison also said that articles were being drafted and that Jenner was participating.

On July 15, the Republicans held another caucus and decided unanimously that Jenner would have to be fired as their counsel. He hadn't appeared to be representing the Republican viewpoint for several months. McClory, who had sided with Jenner in the past, was selected to give Jenner the word.

The Republicans thought Jenner had been fired the day after that decision, so some were surprised to see him enter the committee room on July 17, for the questioning of Herbert Kalmbach, the president's former lawyer. The timing was excellent for Doar and Jenner, because Jenner had been scheduled to handle the financial aspects of Kalmbach's testimony, to which Jenner was better attuned than other staff members. Jenner presided throughout the questioning, serving in Doar's place.

Doar used the time to work with a task force drafting articles of impeachment and to oversee the preparation of the summary of evidence against the president, both due to be presented to the committee by the end of the week. When Republicans asked Rodino about Jenner's presence, Rodino said he was just changing Jenner's title to that of senior associate special counsel and that he would remain on the staff doing the same work. Garrison, he said, would have Jenner's old title of special minority counsel and could give the summation for the Republicans, as they had requested.

Jack Brooks, who had wanted the committee to vote for impeachment and get the business over with at the beginning of the year, had grown increasingly impatient with the timetable for the inquiry. Here it was July 17 and in one week the committee was scheduled to begin debating articles of impeachment. The inquiry staff under John Doar had not finished drafting its proposed articles. The drafts Brooks had seen, while they were being circulated secretly, he didn't like. He was a man of few, concise words and expected the articles to read that way.

In an effort to force the inquiry staff to move faster on drafting its articles, Brooks circulated seven of his own, not caring if they were made public. His articles charged obstruction of justice in the cover-up; criminal violations regarding the ITT donation; dairy industry contributions and Nixon's personal finances; abuse of the office of president; use of government agencies for personal gain; and use of the IRS to harass Nixon's foes.

Don Edwards took over the task force drafting the articles at about the same time and helped the group fashion twenty-nine different articles into five separate packages by the end of the week. Doar worked with Rodino to offer the team a package of four articles, charging in detail Nixon was impeachable for the Watergate break-in and cover-up; abuse of power, primarily in the Ellsberg break-in; refusal to comply with the committee's subpoenas; and tax fraud. Doar and Rodino knew which charges would be acceptable to a majority of the committee because they had been informed by Dick Cates on the members' reaction to his briefings. Cates was to learn later in the week, however, that the Ellsberg break-in charge wouldn't be acceptable after all, because it was action against someone the conservatives considered a traitor and Republicans weren't about to impeach the president for that, wrong as the break-in might have been.

The task force drew on articles proposed by Democrats Brooks, Conyers, Sarbanes, Seiberling, Holtzman. One article charged Nixon with obstruction of justice and listed eleven counts, naming names and dates. Another article the task force drafted said merely:

In his conduct of the office of President of the United States, Richard M. Nixon, contrary to his oath faithfully to execute the office and in violation of the trust conferred upon him by the people, has on numerous occasions willfully misled, deceived and given false information to the people of the United States and to their elected representatives in Congress.

Rodino could only guess how many votes he had. The committee was now only a week away from the beginning of debates, and Rodino realized he could not be sure of those votes from ''the troubled middle'' that he knew he must have to win a bipartisan impeachment vote—also an endorsement of his committee's work—on the floor of the House. And if he counted only the members he was absolutely certain about, they didn't even add up to a majority of the thirty-eight–member committee.

Rodino talked with Flowers and Thornton whenever he had a chance, asking them how they were leaning, if there was any problem they needed help in solving, and offering Doar's aid if they needed an explanation of anything.

All three of the southern Democrats took advantage of the offer of a special briefing from Doar that week. On instructions from Rodino, Doar took time out from his article drafting and summary writing to fortify what Cates had told them in previous briefings.

Late in the week when Rodino approached Flowers again to ask how his decision making was going, Flowers raised doubts that he would end up voting for impeachment. He said he thought Nixon was guilty of offenses, but questioned whether the punishment—impeachment and removal from office—fit the crimes.

Rodino believed Flowers was the key vote among the three southern Democrats and thought that not only could he take the other two with him, he also could pull some undecided Republicans along to whichever side he came down on. He would have to give Flowers a little more line. He impressed on Flowers the importance of his vote to the committee and offered to help him arrange the articles or the timing of them any way he could to make it easier for Flowers to explain his vote to his constituents.

Attendance was sporadic that week of July 16 when testimony was taken from Charles Colson, Nixon's former aide and confidant, and from Kalmbach. The members already had been persuaded by witnesses as much as was possible.

Doar wasn't even present during Kalmbach's testimony. Members huddled with each other, with staffers, reviewed evidence once again in impeachment inquiry headquarters or just went off by themselves to think and write. Cates was still holding sessions. Though they had decided to cast a vote for impeachment, many members still needed a thorough grounding in the evidence for the articles, so they could defend their position in the following week's debate.

The committee stayed late on Wednesday, July 17, to finish with Kalmbach's testimony. After he had left at 10:30 P.M., the committee got into a squabble over David Dennis's proposal that E. Howard Hunt be called to testify. Rodino had to use a few antiparliamentary tactics to beat back that effort and recessed the committee until the following morning, when St. Clair would begin his summation.

The case was not looking good for St. Clair. He had wanted the witnesses called, but their testimony appeared only to fuel the impeachment fire. The committee didn't act as a court of law and wouldn't look at just cold, hard facts. It could react to impressions, consider a pattern of conduct. He already had predicted publicly that he thought the committee would vote for impeachment. Now he had to sell his case to the House and he only had two hours left—before the committee on July 18.

St. Clair had refused to listen to any of the tapes in the White House, although he could have. Fred Buzhardt, whom he had replaced and who had stayed on to work more closely with Nixon, had done all the listening; St. Clair had no reason to doubt Buzhardt's characterization of the tapes. St. Clair also had convinced himself that he believed strongly in Nixon's innocence.

St. Clair had argued before the committee, the public, and the Supreme Court that, technically, the president was protected by executive privilege and that his presidency and future presidencies would be harmed if Nixon were forced to disclose conversations with persons who believed their discussions with the president would be held in confidence. And he had argued the president needed the information that he could receive only in confidence to properly conduct the affairs of the nation.

But as a practical matter, St. Clair also knew that a president should not withhold information about his conversations—in this case tape recordings—from a congressional body legally constituted to determine if he should be impeached and brought to trial. Especially with St. Clair's belief the tapes were exculpatory, he would have turned over the tapes to the committee. But he had no choice. That was Nixon's decision and Nixon decided not to give them to the committee.

But Nixon had given St. Clair a transcript of a portion of a conversation that he said St. Clair could use in buttressing Nixon's position that he did not order blackmail money paid to Hunt. All the evidence was in and all the witnesses had been heard and St. Clair still believed the case turned on the hush-money events of March 21, 1973.

During a dinner break in the Kalmbach testimony on July 17, St. Clair had one of his aides ask the White House to send him the transcript of the tape Nixon had offered. He read it while eating dinner and told one of his lawyer assistants, Mack Howard, that he was going to use it in his summation the next morning.

The transcript was from a conversation Nixon had had with Bob Haldeman on the morning of March 22, 1973, before the long conversation with John Mitchell and others. The earlier conversation had been among those tapes subpoenaed and denied to the committee.

St. Clair's aides thought it would be bad public relations to spring a subpoenaed transcript on the committee members, and St. Clair waffled, saying he would sleep on it. In the limousine going to Capitol Hill the next day, St. Clair said he had decided to use the transcript after all. He opened his summation by telling the members that Nixon might not be perfect, but that the committee had not heard any evidence that tied Nixon to a criminal act.

"An inference piled on an inference will not do, ladies and gentlemen, in these proceedings, any more than they would in any other proceeding," St. Clair said. "An inference drawn one way, where the op-

posite inference is just as logical, will not do. You know that and I
know that. The information in my view, must be clear and it must be
convincing before the major surgery that would be tantamount to a vote
to recommend an article of impeachment.''

He then attempted to refute the key charges against Nixon, including
the allegations that the president ordered or authorized payments to
Hunt. Even the proimpeachment members judged St. Clair's argument
impressive.

Later in his speech St. Clair dwelled at length on the payment to
Hunt:

It seems to me also it is clear that the evidence that we have already indicates
that he did not know even that the payment was authorized.

But the president has authorized me to distribute to and disclose to this committee a portion of a transcript of a conversation he had with Mr. Haldeman on
the morning of March 22, and I will be happy to distribute it at the close of my
argument. This is a portion of a conversation that relates to this blackmail attempt. This says, in substance—and, of course, the entire tape is available to the
chairman and the ranking member to be . . .

Several members tried to interrupt. Chairman Rodino swallowed his
anger and cut them off, telling St. Clair to proceed:

Keep in mind, now, this is the president on the morning of March 22 with
Mr. Haldeman. And he says, among other things, ''I don't mean to be black-
mailed by Hunt. That goes too far.'' Now, can a president say that on the morning of March 22 and still know of and having authorized earlier a payment that
had been effected, according to the testimony, on the evening of March 21? And
may have been effected even earlier than that?

St. Clair continued through his oration while members seethed. They
had subpoenaed that conversation and the president had withheld it. St.
Clair's presentation of it to them after the committee had spent more
than two months receiving evidence was a sharp slap in the face.

Rodino held off interruptions. St. Clair finished:

I will only say this, as I said at the beginning, that the American people, in
my view, and you will have to be the judges of this, not me, because when I will

be finished I can get up and walk out that door, but the American people are going to want to be satisfied that a president of the United States is not going to be impeached on anything less than clear evidence or justification. And I submit that does not exist in this case. Mr. Chairman, therefore, may I be excused?

Rodino reminded St. Clair of his reference to the transcript and asked him, "Are you aware that in presenting that to this committee for the first time as a transcript, that that matter was subpoenaed by this committee, that conversation from 9:11 to 10:35 A.M., and that there was a refusal on the part of the president to turn over that particular conversation?"

St. Clair replied that he was, but that Nixon had authorized the disclosure during his summation. He asked again to be excused.

The rest of the committee exploded with heavy criticism of St. Clair's surprise offer of a snippet of a transcript from a tape that had been denied the committee for months. The committee never did get the entire transcript or any of the tape.

To members, including Nixon's supporters, St. Clair had destroyed a winning argument by dumping the portion of transcript on them in that manner. St. Clair tried to explain that the committee rules allowed for introduction of evidence at any time and that that was what he did. And it proved, he said, "If the president had been in China this payment would have been made just the same" because the payment had no connection with Nixon. St. Clair was allowed to leave. His role was ended. He would never confront the impeachment panel again.

Rodino displayed more public anger than ever before when he appeared at a news conference two hours after the session. He read a statement that had been prepared in the interim to respond to St. Clair's action:

I can find no rational basis for what President Nixon has produced for the committee and has not produced. And, as a matter of fact, except for the material that he delivered to the special prosecutor after the wave of adverse public opinion following the firing of Mr. Cox, President Nixon has not produced anything and has seemed to give no consideration to what, in the judgment of the committee, was important and what is not important. I think it is fair to say that the President has not seriously attended to the question of our request for material in the quest of the impeachment proceedings. . . .

What the committee has gotten has been obtained either by sheer happenstance or forced from the President by enormous public pressure following the firing of Mr. Cox. I feel very strongly that when the President refuses to give any serious attention to this impeachment inquiry it becomes a very serious matter.

By Thursday evening, July 18, exhaustion and frustration were beginning to catch up with Rodino. The committee's internal squabbling was becoming more intense; Rodino had given a commitment that televised debates would begin the following Wednesday, July 24, and he wasn't sure he had a majority vote in favor of impeachment.

Doar had failed to complete his summary of the evidence and set of articles so Rodino could study them before the Friday session. Sam Garrison said he couldn't have his counter summary ready the coming Saturday as had been planned, and would like to wait until Monday. Democrats were still complaining that they were having difficulty getting a handle on the case, despite the coaching of Doar and Cates. Zeifman was prodding Rodino about procedures. Rodino had planned only informal briefing sessions of the committee by the inquiry staff for the next two days, July 19 and 20, but he had come to realize he might have to make them more formal and turn them into advocacy proceedings. He could only hope that Doar's summary, scheduled to be presented the next day, July 19, would be a hard-hitting and convincing case for impeachment.

Rodino's colleagues were reporting a vast lobbying campaign launched by White House aides. The aides were contacting influential Republicans and Democrats in districts represented by committee members and asking them to pressure their representative not to vote for impeachment. And the entire House was fast becoming polarized and bitter.

Following the news conference after St. Clair's summation, Rodino shuttled between the business on the House floor; his office, where he planned the committee schedule with Francis O'Brien; and the committee room where Edwards and some of the staff members, joined now and then by other committee members, were still working on drafts of articles and ''impeachment theories.'' During one of his trips to the floor he ran into Walter Flowers and suggested that things were so disjointed so close to the start of the debates that perhaps the undecided members, the swing votes, should get together and agree on what they could support. Flowers was noncommittal.

When Rodino arrived at his office early the next day for a meeting with Doar and Zeifman, Doar gave Rodino his first look at the summary of evidence and draft articles Doar had prepared. The articles took 59 pages and the summary was 306 pages long, laid out like a legal treatise, complete with a table of contents. However, it merely summarized the evidence that had been presented to the members in the closed-door sessions and in much the same chronological fashion. Together, the documents were two inches thick and weighed four pounds.

Doar's summary drew no conclusions and made no recommendations. Like a growing number of members of Congress, Rodino had become used to the staff doing most of the work and offering conclusions for the members to vote on.

Rodino exploded when he leafed through the summary. Doar had not put the case together, he said, and here it was the Friday before the Wednesday debates were to begin. He had wanted Doar to tell the members that morning in simple, everyday language the significance of the case, just why it was they were supposed to vote to impeach the president of the United States.

For seven months, Doar had been careful not to show any bias in his work. He had proceeded in a cautious, step-by-step manner and thought his job was done. He still thought it was up to the members to make up their own minds. He was merely an attorney serving another client.

Doar was reluctant to shed this nonpartisan approach. Rodino insisted he had to. They argued as they walked down the hall to the elevator and to Rodino's second office behind the committee hearing room. Rodino had given Doar a pretty free rein to that point and he was now commanding. The session was set to begin in another half-hour, at 10:00 A.M., and Doar would make an advocacy presentation as the first order of business, Rodino said. Doar stormed out of the office.

Doar had prepared notes for an hour-long speech he would give in introducing the summary of information, but like everything else he had done, it was designed to be neutral. He would have to insert into the speech the emotional language and declarative words Rodino insisted the members had to hear.

When the committee session convened, Doar began by introducing the four pounds of material the members had just been handed and ladled out the usual plaudits for the people who worked with him:

Now, what we are trying to do for you, as we understand our direction, is to assist you in finding out what has happened with President Nixon's administration as president, and why it happened so the committee can perform its inescapable constitutional responsibility in a way that is explicable now and explicable in the future to the American people.

As an individual, I have not the slightest bias against President Nixon. I would hope that I would not do him the smallest, slightest injury. But, I am not indifferent, not indifferent to the matter of presidential abuse of power, by whatever president, nor the identification and proof of that abuse of power, if I believe that it has existed.

And if, in fact, President Nixon or any president has had a central part in the planning and executing of this terrible deed of subverting the Constitution, then I shall do my part as best I can to bring him to answer before the Congress of the United States for this enormous crime on the conduct of his office.

If any president, if President Nixon or any president has committed high crimes and misdemeanors against the Constitution, then there has been manifest injury to the confidence of the nation, great prejudice to the cause of law and justice, and subversion of constitutional government.

After seven months of neutrality, Doar had managed to do it. He made a subjective statement to the committee about impeachment. He was beginning to feel the emotion of it. "Members of the committee, for me to speak like this, I can hardly believe that I am speaking as I do or thinking like I do, the awesomeness of this is so, is so tremendous."

Doar then refuted the summation St. Clair had made the previous day. He said St. Clair "has things upside down. He's had things upside down throughout these entire proceedings." St. Clair appeared to believe, Doar said, that it was all right to use the enormous power and authority of the presidency on behalf of a person who might be the subject of criminal charges.

Doar carried the members through each of the accusations against

Nixon, explaining the basis for the accusations much as Cates had explained it in his "night schools," but in a more abbreviated fashion. He summarized the evidence according to logic.

When he reached the evidence, he said,

I realize that most people would understand an effort to conceal a mistake. But this was not done by a private citizen and the people who are working for President Nixon are not private citizens.

This was the president of the United States. What he decided should be done following the Watergate break-in caused action not only by his own servants, but by the agencies of the United States, including the Department of Justice, the FBI, the CIA, and the Secret Service.

It required perjury, destruction of evidence, obstruction of justice, all crimes. But, most important, it required deliberate, contrived, continued and continuing deception of the American people.

It is that evidence, that evidence, that we want to present to you in detail and to help and reason with you, and this summary of information is the basis, or a work product, to help you.

The members were as drained as Doar was. His had been a highly emotional speech delivered with only a few notes as reference. They had never heard him speak that way and many still found it hard to believe.

Bert Jenner deferred his own summary material until Garrison presented his the following Monday. But Jenner made his own extemporaneous comments about the impeachment evidence, speaking more in the patriotic sense. He concluded with the observation that the committee members would not be "recreating the Constitution; you are preserving it; you are strengthening it . . ." by their votes on the question of whether Richard Nixon should be impeached.

The week of St. Clair's and Doar's summations was a key one in the success of impeachment.

The swing votes began coming together in groups of twos and threes, learning through long-standing friendships or casual discussions that there were several of them who probably would vote for impeachment but needed reinforcement.

Several sought out Doar and Cates to tell them again why they should vote to impeach.

By the weekend preceding the July 24 start of debates, the four Republican swing votes—Railsback, Cohen, Butler, and Fish—had met as a group and knew they were in troubled agreement.

Walter Flowers and Jim Mann had discussed their situation, but didn't know that Ray Thornton was considering a vote for impeachment. Thornton was working alone on his own drafts of articles.

Discussions by twos and threes continued through the weekend. Members discussed the drafts of articles they had seen and suggested improvements to each other.

Flowers had become concerned about how his vote for impeachment would be revealed. He wanted all of the mileage out of it he could get. After all, he reasoned, he was facing the lion by voting to impeach a president who could still claim overwhelming support in his Alabama district.

Flowers already had suggested privately that votes on any articles of impeachment be saved until the end of all the debate on them. He wanted to vote on a package of articles instead of each individually. He was concerned that if the articles were voted on one at a time, the sense of drama would be lost on every article following the first one. Rodino rejected the idea, saying it wouldn't be normal committee procedure. When the subject was broached during a committee session and Rodino again rejected it, Flowers said, "Well, that's when we will lose our audience, right there."

The four Republicans of the swing group decided in a Saturday afternoon session that they could not vote for any of the proposed articles on taxes, Cambodia bombing, or Nixon's use of federal money for improving his personal residences. Railsback left early to catch a plane back to Illinois for a day of rest. He took with him transcripts of John Dean's testimony from the previous week. Ray Thornton kept at least two members of his staff in the office to work on drafts of articles.

On Sunday, Cates held another "night school" session for Bill Cohen and Ham Fish, this time at Fish's house. The subject was abuse of powers.

On Monday, July 22, Sam Garrison gave the summation of evidence from the Republican viewpoint, arguing that the members had to decide if the "best interests of the nation warrant removal rather than retention of the officer." And then the members should weigh carefully the standard of proof they would use to decide his guilt, Garrison told the assembled committee. "It would be unfair to the president, it would be embarrassing to the House, and for both reasons equally, it would be tragic for the nation if the committee were to recommend to the House an impeachment in which, when evidence were laid out in a trial-type situation, a fully contested situation, the evidence fell short."

He said it was his opinion the evidence did fall short. And he didn't think the members should fall back on "adverse inferences" just because Nixon refused to provide more evidence.

Garrison's speech had been broken into two parts because the committee quit shortly after noon when the full House debated a resolution to allow the panel to open its debate on impeachment to television cameras. While the debate on the floor droned on, the committee Democrats caucused in a room just below the House chambers.

Jerry Zeifman and Frank Polk had been instructed by Rodino earlier in the day to prepare an outline of the procedures the committee would follow later that week. Their proposal suggested following the normal committee procedure: i.e., someone could offer a motion to impeach. Each member would be allowed five minutes to debate it. The motion would be open to amendments. The amendments would be voted on and the motion as amended would be voted on. Then the next motion to impeach would be made. The only change, because of the television coverage expected, was to allow fifteen minutes for each member to debate the first motion, that the committee vote an article of impeachment.

When the two presented their proposed procedures at the caucus, Flowers, as he had told Rodino he would, objected. He said he preferred that the committee begin debate without articles of impeachment before it. There was a coalition of swing votes forming, he said, and it would not be able to vote for impeachment unless the articles satisfied. Flowers wanted to have as much time as possible to work on the articles before presenting them to the committee in public. Two days, from that Monday to Wednesday, was not enough time, he said.

Flowers also wanted to postpone all final votes on the articles until the end of the proceedings, partially to heighten the drama. He said that voting on articles as they were proposed would put a heavy load on those who would be casting unexpected votes. If one article was voted on and the committee recessed for the weekend, as was then likely, members would have to return to their districts and face pressures or abuse from their constituents during the break. The prospect could even change some of the softer votes, he said.

Zeifman, not caring much at that point that he was a staff member taking on a congressman, argued against the Flowers approach. He said that if anything went wrong at the end of the proceedings and the package of articles wound up being voted down, there would be no chance to salvage the situation; and the committee would get bogged down in trying for fall-back articles in anticipation of just such an event.

Flowers had talked to Rodino just before the caucus and told him he had decided to vote for impeachment, but he needed some assurances on procedures for voting. Rodino assured Flowers he would allow him the latitude he wanted if it would help to ease his agony in voting for impeachment. Even though Rodino had announced the previous week there would be a series of votes, he agreed with the Flowers approach during the caucus. Zeifman got support only from Charles Rangel. After the caucus, Rodino instructed Zeifman to draw up proposed procedures Flowers's way and have them ready for a committee meeting set for the next day, July 23.

Flowers suggested to Mann that they and Thornton meet later that evening after another Democratic caucus. Flowers suggested to Railsback, "Why don't you get yours and I'll get mine and we'll meet?" They set the time for 8:00 A.M. the next day in Railsback's office. It was the first time Railsback knew that Mann and Thornton were possible votes for impeachment. Railsback had tried to get Bob McClory to join his GOP group, but McClory objected to the obstruction of justice article that Railsback felt was the key.

The committee returned behind closed doors after the House approved the television resolution, to hear the rest of Garrison's summation.

To the second caucus, Thornton and other Democrats brought proposed articles that they had prepared. As the Democrats discussed which charges would fly and which would not, several members made copies of an article Thornton proposed, encompassing charges of obstruction of justice, abuse of power, and a continuing pattern of offenses.

After that caucus, Mann asked Thornton, "Why don't you come by the office for a minute? Some of us are thinking of getting together tomorrow morning." Flowers joined them, and when they arrived at Mann's office in the Longworth Office Building, John Doar was waiting for them. They looked over Thornton's draft of the article and agreed that was the approach they would take.

The next morning the three southern Democrats met with Tom Railsback's group of Republicans in the Cannon Office Building. Seated in Railsback's office on a black leather couch and on chairs around a large coffee table in the center of the room, the seven swing votes—four Republicans and three Democrats whom Railsback dubbed "the fragile coalition"—met as a group for the first time. Also with them were two members of Railsback's staff.

Coffee was served and Railsback kicked off the discussion: "Well, we know what we're here for. What are we thinking? Where are we?" Several comments followed and the congressmen soon became aware there was no sentiment in the room for supporting any of the "lesser" articles, such as the bombing of Cambodia and Nixon's taxes or personal finances.

Flowers let the discussion bounce back and forth for a while and said, "We are talking all around the problem, but the basic issue is whether we seven here are willing to vote to impeach the president of the United States." Then the group zeroed in on the article that Thornton had proposed the previous night. The swing votes reached no conclusion at the meeting, but it was clear as they left that there was support for two articles: obstruction of justice and abuse of power. The only question was which evidence would be used to support them.

Mann was informally selected as the one who would join the task force still fashioning the articles under Edwards. The team met in a second-floor committee room following a full committee briefing later that morning. The task force at that time included Conyers, Sarbanes, and Brooks, plus up to half a dozen staff members. Rodino also had begun attending the sessions and Flowers sat in for a while.

While the seven swing votes were meeting in Railsback's office, the rest of the Republicans were holding their own opposition caucus. Zeifman had relayed the Democratic caucus position of the previous day to Polk. The Republicans agreed they would oppose the Flowers approach, although their opposition was stronger to the idea of having no article at debating time than it was to the idea of leaving all the votes until the end.

Polk relayed the opposition to Zeifman and Zeifman reported it when the Democrats caucused in his office that afternoon before a committee session to vote on procedures. But Flowers was adamant that it be done his way. His support had eroded, however, and even Mann and Thornton didn't press for the Flowers approach. Flowers said he still intended to offer his amendment in committee.

Flowers had told Butler that Flowers had the clout on the committee to insist on his approach because of his leadership among the swing votes. Butler replied that he favored the Flowers approach, but added, "Walter, if you've got that much clout, why don't you save it for something important?"

Flowers got Rodino to agree to let him offer his voting proposal first. When the session began shortly after five o'clock he offered it and the matter was debated.

Shortly before the committee session, Bob Kastenmeier had been ribbed by a reporter who said he hadn't noticed Kastenmeier doing much during the open committee sessions. After Flowers offered his resolution, Zeifman and Polk worked together during the session to fashion a compromise much like the procedures they had proposed originally. Zeifman handed it to Jack Brooks to introduce as a substitute to the Flowers motion, but Brooks handed it to Kastenmeier and he introduced it. Rodino was surprised and Flowers was angry. The Kastenmeier substitute carried, 21–16. Seven of the sixteen noes were swing votes.

Rodino saw Flowers's anger and feared the session had cost him Flowers's valuable vote. Rodino called Kastenmeier later and criticized him heavily for offering the substitute and possibly jeopardizing Flowers's vote. He also called Zeifman and told him he noted his work in getting the substitute introduced and considered Zeifman guilty of irresponsible conduct.

Also on that day, Larry Hogan, who had recently announced his candidacy for Maryland's Republican gubernatorial nomination, held a news conference to announce he was going to vote to recommend impeachment of Nixon.

Republicans were taken by surprise. Hogan was one of the most conservative members of the committee and one of the last they expected to vote that way. Railsback hadn't even thought of inviting him to join the swing votes.

Rodino asked Zeifman to prepare the opening statement that he would deliver the following day, Wednesday, July 24. Then Rodino and Doar worked on the drafting of articles and went over some suggested assignments they would give to the Democratic members to help them lay out the case during their fifteen-minute debate speeches, which would begin on live television at 7:30 P.M.

Rodino returned to his office late in the evening and fell asleep on the couch. Doar worked long into the night at inquiry headquarters.

The next morning, the Supreme Court announced that by an 8–0 vote, it had decided that Nixon had to give up the sixty-four tapes that Special Prosecutor Leon Jaworski had subpoenaed in the spring. Of the total, twenty-four had been included in Judiciary Committee subpoenas.

Bob McClory immediately began checking with his colleagues to see if there was any sentiment for a motion to postpone the debate on impeachment to give Nixon time to comply with the court order. There wasn't much.

The swing votes met in Railsback's office twice again that day, at 10:30 and at 2:30, working feverishly on an article of impeachment to be introduced at 7:30. Two buildings down the street, the Edwards drafting team worked in the Government Operations Committee hearing room because the television crews were busy in the Judiciary Committee room.

Edwards, Sarbanes, Conyers, Brooks, and now Ed Mezvinsky (D-Iowa) worked separately from the swing votes, along with Zeifman, two members of Brooks's staff, one of the inquiry staff members and two regular Judiciary Committee staffers. Jim Mann shuttled between the groups, carrying the latest product of one to the other.

At one point during the afternoon, Railsback called McClory and said he was sending over the latest draft proposal of articles—the third draft—fashioned by the swing group. He also reported to McClory on the progress he was making in drumming up impeachment support among House Republicans who didn't serve on the Judiciary Committee. Max Friedersdorff, Nixon's congressional liaison, held several meetings throughout the day with the House leadership trying to keep the Republicans in line. McClory refused to meet with the GOP leadership at one point because Friedersdorff was present.

Doar and Rodino made periodic visits to the Edwards group throughout the day. At one point, Doar criticized wording in a draft that suggested that the president had taken part in a conspiracy. A president cannot take part in a conspiracy, Doar said, because the president was the chief law enforcement officer.

The task force had a lot of difficulty in working out articles of impeachment without a presidential conspiracy being worked in. The drafting was delayed even further, finally coming into a form more in line with what had been worked out by the swing votes. They had packaged the articles into two, one on obstruction of justice, the second on abuse of powers. The second included among its charges the president's refusal to comply with committee subpoenas.

As the 7:30 P.M. debate neared, Doar visited the task force again and looked over what the group thought was its final draft, to be introduced at the coming session.

Zeifman had been proud of one of his contributions to the articles, the concluding paragraph for each. They read: "Wherefore, Richard M. Nixon, by such conduct, warrants impeachment and trial and removal from office."

Doar objected to that language, but by that time the team was tired and faced the task of getting copies made and distributed to the members in time for the debate. Doug Bellas, an inquiry staff member working on the task force, told Doar in a tired voice, "The language is simply traditional; it appeared in all articles of impeachment and after all, that is what the House is asking the Senate to do. The articles are the articles the committee is recommending that the House exhibit before the Senate.''

Doar caved in. Time was running short. Brooks picked up the copy they had just finished and hurried off to a photocopying machine where he and an aide ran off fifty copies. They were in members' hands by 7:30 P.M. when the television cameras switched on.

CHAPTER IX

Debate

A middle-aged woman named Fifi Clay, a supporter of Nixon's from Covington, Kentucky, spent the night outside the doors of the Rayburn House Office Building so she could be first in line for the handful of seats available to the general public to see the making of history.

She was a bizarre introduction to the bizarre event. She had long, stringy hair and wore huge, green-tinted sunglasses, a dress with a plunging neckline, and several pro-Nixon buttons. She wanted to be called "Princess."

Shortly before 7:30 P.M., on July 24, 1974, the Capitol police unlocked the doors of Room 2141 and released the red velvet restraining rope holding back dozens of persons lined up in the hall waiting for a chance to get inside. Fifi Clay and twenty-two others got into the two-story room before the ropes were repositioned.

Reporters, privileged members of the inquiry and committee staff, members of Congress and their families sauntered in and inspected the room. Convention-type chairs upholstered in blue were jammed as closely as possible in three separate groupings across the pale green carpeting bearing the seal of the United States in the center. Two groups of seats lined each side wall and a third filled the space from the back wall to near the two-tiered dais where the members sat. In the middle of the last group was a one-story high platform with two television cameras on top. Another camera was in the right-hand corner and a fourth was positioned four feet above the floor in what had been a window behind Peter Rodino's left shoulder.

The public, family members, broadcast and magazine reporters were seated in the group behind the two long committee staff tables. Daily press members were in the left-hand group of seats and radio and television technicians and reporters fiddled with instruments in the right-hand group. Generally, a senator or congressman can get anything he or she wants on Capitol Hill, but Senator Vance Hartke (D-Ind.) couldn't get a seat that night and had to leave.

At the committee table, opening briefcases and spreading papers were Garner "Jim" Cline, an associate counsel on the Judiciary Committee who served as its clerk during the inquiry sessions, and the five highest-ranking inquiry staff members, John Doar, Albert Jenner, Sam Garrison, Richard Cates, and Bernard Nussbaum.

The table for James St. Clair and his two aides, the president's counsels, was conspicuously absent. They had been present when the committee was hearing evidence and questioning witnesses in the previous closed-door sessions, but there was no role for them during the televised portion. John McCahill and Malcolm Howard, St. Clair's assistants, sat in two of the guest seats as spectators, courtesy of Rodino.

By 7:45, all thirty-eight committee members had taken their seats. Reporters were milling about in front of the dais trying to elicit any last-minute comments or commitments on the first impeachment vote scheduled three days hence.

Rodino picked up his gavel and rapped it. Press photographers called out for encores and Rodino rapped twice more. Strobe lights flashed despite the presence of television klieg lights suspended from the ceiling, from long poles standing behind the dais, and in all corners of the room. The jammed room was beginning to heat up beneath the lights.

While the photographers gathered their equipment and filed out, Doar and Jenner donned their glasses and shuffled papers. Garrison and Jenner smiled and talked to neighbors. After a little more bustling, the photographers were ushered out and reporters resumed their assigned seats. The stenographers, one at each end of the committee table, were poised over their tiny black machines, ready for the first words.

"The committee will come to order," Rodino announced in his already familiar raspy voice, and the history-making event was underway.

"Before I begin," he continued, looking up for eye contact while reading without emotion from a prepared text, "I hope you will allow me a personal reference. Throughout all of the painstaking proceedings of this committee, I as the chairman have been guided by a simple principle, the principle that the law must deal fairly with every man. For me, this is the oldest principle of democracy. It is the simple, but great principle which enables man to live justly and in decency in a free society."

He recalled how the founding fathers viewed justice and then said, "We have reached the moment when we are ready to debate resolutions whether or not the committee on the Judiciary should recommend that the House of Representatives adopt articles calling for the impeachment of Richard M. Nixon.

"Make no mistake about it. This is a turning point, whatever we decide. Our judgment is not concerned with an individual but with a system of constitutional government.

"For more than two years, there have been serious allegations, by people of good faith and sound intelligence, that the president, Richard M. Nixon, has committed grave and systematic violations of the Constitution," Rodino said. He recapped the history of the Nixon impeachment inquiry up to that point and the committee's duties from there on. He outlined the responsibility of the panel to decide whether Nixon was guilty of obstruction of justice and abuse of powers, the subjects of the first two proposed articles.

"Let us leave the Constitution as unimpaired for our children as our predecessors left it for us," Rodino concluded, emphasizing the last four words in a grave tone. He turned to his left and said, "I now recognize the gentleman from Michigan."

Rodino had not indicated in his opening remarks how he would vote on impeachment, although he clearly indicated there was ample justification for the inquiry having proceeded that far.

Edward Hutchinson, the reluctant ranking Republican on the committee, left no doubt that he thought the accusations against Nixon too friv-

olous to have reached that point. Reading from his own prepared remarks in a strained, though calm voice, pronoucing words in three- or
four-word bursts as if he were short of breath, he noted the Supreme
Court's momentous decision earlier that day.

"The question arises whether our committee should proceed further
until the availability of the additional evidence to the committee is determined. Many members on this side, Mr. Chairman, feel strongly that
we should not. We believe the American people will expect us to examine and weigh all available evidence before we decide the momentous
and most difficult issue before us."

Without even glancing at Rodino, Hutchinson looked toward a television camera and said he hoped the chairman would still consider postponing consideration of the articles, "until the evidence now that has
become available through the court can be made available to this committee."

Indicative of the time Congress wastes on futile debate—minds in
Congress are nearly always made up before the debating stage is ever
reached—Rodino held to his prepared script, ignoring Hutchinson's
request as if he hadn't made one. He turned to his right and said, "I recognize the gentleman from Massachusetts, Mr. Donohue."

"Thank you, Mr. Chairman," the pink-faced Harold Donohue said,
and began to read in a deep voice from the script that had been prepared
for him. He spoke in one-sentence bursts, through a mouth that seemed
too small for his round head.

"Pursuant to the procedural resolution which this committee adopted
yesterday, I move that the committee report to the House a resolution
together with articles of impeachment, impeaching Richard M. Nixon,
president of the United States."

It was necessary under the rules of order for a motion to vote impeachment to be placed before the committee before debate could
begin. Fifteen minutes were reserved for each member to speak his or
her piece on the motion, uninterrupted, before the national television
audience.

The motion that Donohue introduced, however, had little relation to
what the committee eventually would vote on. The swing votes and
other key committee members were still working on the final draft of the

first article of impeachment, aided by the inquiry staff. That work would go on all through the debating phase, until the corrected and final versions were offered as substitutes for the technical ones Donohue had introduced. The drafting task force's feverish work on the Donohue articles was to get a set of articles in the best shape as possible for introduction to kick off the debate.

His voice deeper and louder than either of the two that preceded him, Donohue then plunged into his brief statement. He, too, refrained from announcing his vote. This was television and the members were milking the event for drama.

Donohue ended his speech and Rodino, alternating by custom from Democrat to Republican in order of seniority on each side of the committee, announced the name of Robert McClory, Republican of Illinois.

McClory's fifteen-minute speech addressed the responsibilities of a Republican deciding the fate of a Republican president and the partisan differences on the committee. He spoke at twice the speed of any of the previous three members, but in a somewhat indistinct voice. At one point, Hutchinson leaned over to him and said in a stage whisper, "Go slower, you're going too fast."

McClory said he did not feel impeachment for the Watergate cover-up, or obstruction of justice, was justified. He said the case "rests upon circumstantial evidence, inferences, innuendoes and a generous measure of wishful thinking on the part of some who would indict the president even without adequate proof of wrongdoing in the Watergate affair."

Although Nixon may not have been guilty of criminal wrongdoing in McClory's mind, he added, "but there is the higher constitutional obligation to see that such criminal acts [as committed by the president's men, whom he named] are not committed or condoned, a constitutional demand to see that the laws are obeyed, particularly in the president's own house . . ."

Then McClory came to his own "cause celebre," Nixon's refusal to comply with the committee's subpoenas, an issue he called "the clearest and most convincing" before the committee, "and one which is perhaps more fundamental to our own inquiry." Nearing the end of his speech, he said that the noncompliance "threatens the integrity of the impeachment process itself." But he stopped just short of calling for impeachment because of it.

It was now 8:30 and thirty-six more speeches in the debate (Rodino's and Hutchinson's words at the beginning were merely opening remarks) were to come. In the last Democratic caucus, Rodino had urged his colleagues to use their debate time to detail the evidence for impeachment. He had received no commitments. Many members feared that announcing their decision or stating their opinions in harsh terms before the issue was debated would make them appear injudicious to constituents watching back home.

Jack Brooks of Texas, the next Democrat down the line, wasn't about to temper his enthusiasm for impeachment, even if his words were reaching millions.

He charged in: "This committee has heard evidence of governmental corruption unequaled in the history of the United States, the cover-up of crimes, obstructing the prosecution of criminals, surreptitious entries, wiretapping for political purposes, suspension of the civil liberties of every American, tax violations and personal enrichment at public expense, bribery and blackmail, flagrant misuse of the FBI, the CIA, and the IRS. Eighteen individuals have been convicted or pleaded guilty, and six have been indicted for criminal activities directly [he emphasized the word by pronouncing it díerectly] related to Mr. Nixon's reelection efforts or activities which originated within the White House.

"These individuals are not obscure government officials, but include cabinet officers, personal assistants, the closest personal advisers to Richard Nixon."

His voice became graver. "Never in our one hundred and ninety-eight years have we had evidence of such rampant corruption in government. We must decide whether this corruption attached to the president, whether there is evidence that the president by his actions, or inactions, failed in his constitutional responsibility to faithfully execute the law."

He continued through his speech and came to: "We must put to rest the argument that the corruption we have witnessed in the last five years is only an extension of what has always been done. I do not share this view or the view of those who hold that all our presidents have lied, have broken the law, have compromised the Constitution. And if

George Washington accepted bribes, it would not make bribery a virtue, nor would it be grounds for overlooking such acts by his successor.''

Brooks ended his speech by saying, ''But, we as well as the president, are on trial for how faithfully we fulfill our constitutional responsibility.''

Rodino turned to his left again and called the name of Henry P. Smith III (R-N.Y.). Smith spoke of Nixon's triumph in foreign policy.

''But, even so, if this president has also been guilty of 'treason, bribery or other high crimes and misdemeanors,' as it is stated in the Constitution, then it is the constitutional duty of the House of Representatives to impeach him and the constitutional duty of the Senate to convict him.''

He concluded: ''Except for the area of the secret bombing in Cambodia at the president's order between March 18, 1969, and May 1, 1970, where I have not yet made up my mind, I should have to vote against impeachment of the president on the state of the evidence which we have seen.''

Smith was getting the best of both worlds, playing the politician to the hilt. Here he was saying he could not vote for impeachment of Nixon on the most likely of the impeachment resolutions to be offered, but he could vote for one which scuttlebutt on the committee already had determined would never pass.

The soft-spoken Robert W. Kastenmeier began at 8:40. He opened with a defense of Rodino's decision to push on with the impeachment inquiry despite the Supreme Court's ruling earlier that day.

Then Kastenmeier became the first committee member, except for Donohue's pro forma resolution to kick off the debate, to declare straight out that he would vote for impeachment. He spoke slowly, almost inaudibly and somewhat haltingly.

''In my own case, my decision has been made. I have concluded after careful consideration of all of the evidence that President Nixon must be impeached and removed from office. . . . This decision was not reached lightly, nor was it made out of personal animus toward the president. The process of impeachment is a drastic undertaking, not only for the Congress but for the country, and cannot be taken casually.''

Kastenmeier then spoke the phrase that was to govern almost all of the decisions in favor of impeachment. Any charges to be considered, he said, "should be considered as a pattern of the whole in terms of presidential disregard for truth and for law. Mr. Chairman, it is important to draw a clear distinction between preserving the man and preserving the office. . . ."

Just as Kastenmeier began his speech, the Capitol switchboard received a long-distance telephone call from a woman who said a bomb had been planted in the committee room that day. The call was transferred to the Capitol police, who relayed the message to Ken Harding, the House sergeant at arms. Harding relayed it to Jim Cline, the clerk, and asked him to have Rodino call a recess so the room could be cleared and inspected.

Rodino waited until Kastenmeier had finished and, deciding to not frighten anyone at that moment, rapped his gavel and announced, "The chair is going to be compelled to recess for a period of time and the chair will state that the meeting will resume at the call of the chair, but it is necessary that we do recess for a period of time."

His colleagues looked puzzled as Rodino stood to leave. Reporters pressed forward for an explanation and Rodino mouthed to them the word, "bomb."

The timing had been perfect. This strange event in American history had been injected with another weird element just as a speaker had stated that he would have to vote to impeach the president of the United States.

Forty minutes later, after the room had been cleared and Capitol police with dogs trained in the art of sniffing out explosives had searched the room without finding a bomb, the doors were opened and the room filled once again.

Without referring to the reason for the recess, Rodino rapped three times with his gavel, waited for the straggling members to be seated and recognized Charles W. Sandman, Jr.

"Regardless of what is in the new tapes," Sandman said in reference to the earlier Supreme Court decision, "a majority does exist here to impeach the president for some reason or another."

He then went on to attack the committee, charging it with a breach of the confidentiality all of the members had sworn to uphold. He charged

Democrats with leaking erroneous or one-sided information from the closed sessions "every hour on the hour, some [of them] every hour on the half-hour. We have become the first forum in the history of man to release to the public every shred of information we have before a single decision was ever made. When did that ever happen before? Never. But we have done it."

Sandman punctuated his speech by constantly putting on black, half-rimmed glasses, taking them off again, pointing them at no one in particular and putting them back on again, peering over the top.

Then he began an attack on the staff, especially on Doar. The committee had progressed fairly, he said, "but things started to change three weeks ago. Three weeks ago it changed from a nonpartisan inquiry into a highly partisan prosecution if ever there was one." His reference was to the Dick Cates "night schools" and staff work on proposed articles of impeachment.

While he attacked the committee, some of his colleagues looked embarrassed for him. Others just grinned. When he turned on the staff, Doar was unsmiling. Garrison attempted to suppress a smirk.

Sandman wound up with a summary of the evidence he felt the panel did not have. His voice rose to a shout as he said, "Is there a soul here who honestly believes that sixty-seven out of a hundred senators are willing to accept this kind of evidence? I do not think so, and I think this is why we are here."

He shouted louder as he continued, "Now, maybe in the time that is remaining, someone, somehow, will point out the fact that I am only human and I am not infallible. Maybe I overlooked something. Maybe there is a tie-in with the president. All right. There's thirty-seven of you. Give me that information. Give it to two hundred and two million Americans, because up to this moment you haven't."

Reminding Don Edwards of the fifteen-minute limitation, Rodino recognized him for his speech. He took a high-road approach, providing a sharp contrast to Sandman's speech.

Edwards concluded in his reedy voice, leaning forward on his forearms, speaking quietly: "But I do believe, and this is the way I am going to vote, that the president has consciously and intentionally engaged in serious misdeeds; that he has corrupted and subverted our political and government processes to the extent that he should be impeached and the matter sent over to our sister body, the Senate, for trial to determine whether he is innocent or guilty."

Then came the turn of Tom Railsback. He listed the charges against Nixon that he could not support and said it all came down to "two serious areas of concern in respect to allegations of misconduct that have been leveled against the president."

Railsback ticked off one by one the president's actions or failures to act that bothered him. The staccato approach, via total recall and almost no notes, was devastatingly effective as Railsback used it. But his time expired before he could finish.

William Hungate shouted for recognition. Rodino called his name and Hungate yielded two of his fifteen minutes to Railsback.

Railsback ticked off a few more dates and events which bothered him and noted that certain tapes were still being denied the committee by the president.

In the folksy way of his east-central Illinois district, Railsback summed up: "I just can't help but wonder, you know, when you put all of this together in that kind of perspective, I am concerned and I am seriously concerned. I hope that the president—I wish the president could do something to absolve himself. I wish he would come forward with the information that we have subpoenaed. I just am very, very concerned."

Then a word for his constituents. Looking at the audience in the room and not at the camera, his voice became more emotional as he said he had received mail saying the country could not afford to impeach a president. Addressing his remarks to the audience, he advised that impeachment had to be considered and the truth of the issue determined as much to instill the faith of the young in the system of government as anything else.

"If we are not going to really try to get to the truth," he said, "you are going to see the most frustrated people, the most turned-off people, the most disillusioned people, and it is going to make the period of LBJ in 1968, 1967, it's going to make it look tame."

Rodino turned back to Hungate and reminded him he had only thirteen minutes remaining. Hungate picked up on Railsback's effective staccato, refined it, honed it, and delivered it as he would a speech in a convention hall.

"Should Richard M. Nixon be found guilty of obstruction of justice? Yes," he said, emphasizing the "yes."

"Should Richard M. Nixon be found guilty of abusing the powers of his office? Yes. Should Richard M. Nixon be found guilty of contempt and defiance of the Congress and the courts? Yes. And on the last charge he is a repeated offender."

Many would shrink from the duty of impeaching the president, Hungate said, because they felt the office of the presidency too awesome. So he borrowed from a letter that a man named Robert P. Weeks had written to the *Ann Arbor News* earlier in the year. Weeks drew an analogy of a mayor committing the acts Nixon had been accused of.

Hungate read the letter, which asked readers to suppose their mayor had approved illegal phone taps and mail-openings, directed phone taps and investigations of local reporters, withheld knowledge of a burglary, disobeyed a court order to produce secret tapes made in his office, tripled his wealth while serving as mayor, and committed many other acts that Nixon had been accused of committing as president.

"The citizens of your town wouldn't be complacent," Hungate said. "On this committee we are all lawyers and to become lawyers we took the same oath to uphold the Constitution which Richard M. Nixon took. If we are to be faithful to our oaths, we must find him faithless in his."

While Hungate spoke, Ken Harding relayed another message to Rodino. Another bomb threat. When Hungate had finished at 10:40 P.M., Rodino rapped the session to a close and announced the debate phase would resume at 10:00 A.M. the next day, Thursday, July 25.

The debate had proceeded slowly the first day. It was apparent that every member would take his full fifteen minutes. It wasn't often that a member of Congress had that much uninterrupted time to be seen and heard coast to coast. Only nine debate speeches had been heard during the first three hours of the debates. Thursday, then, would be a full day. The first vote on impeachment would be delayed and the committee's consideration of impeachment would not be completed until the following week.

Rodino was unhappy that the members had not utilized their time to spell out the evidence, but he was pleased with the quality of the speeches.

At 10:10 Thursday morning, all had resumed their places—a different twenty-three persons were in the seats reserved for the public—and Rodino rapped the gavel twice for order. He waited several minutes for the shuffling about to cease, rapped once more when it had and announced the first speaker.

It was Charles Wiggins, the leader of the president's supporters. The interruptions of the previous evening had caused the most important defender of Nixon to be relegated to daytime television, and a poor daytime hour at that.

His graying, blond hair providing a stark contrast to his dark tan, Wiggins began with a disavowal of his ascribed position as that of the president's chief defender on the committee. He cherished his friendship with the president, he said, "but that friendship is not going to deter me one whit from doing what is right in this case according to the law, and I would hope that my colleagues share that conviction."

Wiggins stirred about in his chair as he spoke, as if the seat were uncomfortable.

He suggested that anyone who had preconceived notions about Nixon's guilt before he received the evidence should excuse himself from the inquiry. Then he took a swipe at Doar. He looked straight at Doar; Doar looked back, leaning to one side in his seat.

"It must trouble you, Mr. Doar, I am sure, as a possible assistant to managers in the Senate, to consider the evidence as distinguished from the material which we have made—been made available before this committee. Thirty-eight books of material. My guess, Mr. Doar, you can put all of the admissible evidence in half of one book. Most of this is just material. It is not evidence, and it may never surface in the Senate because it is not admissible evidence."

He related the requirements he thought evidence must meet and began a point-by-point refutation of the points that previous speakers had made against Nixon. He was in the middle of that when a note from Rodino was passed down to him. The note just said, "time."

Rodino let Wiggins complete his sentence and then turned to John

Conyers. "Now, in all candor," Conyers began, "I know that it is easier for some of us to discharge this onerous burden presented to us than it is for others, but we should be mindful that as we reached these judgments, we, too, must be judged by our fellow citizens today and for all time by history. Certainly, no one can accuse us of having rushed to judgment."

Conyers announced to no one's surprise that he favored impeachment, "not to punish Richard Nixon, because the constitutional remedy is not punitive, but to restore to our government the proper balance of constitutional power and serve notice on all future presidents that such abuse of conduct will not now or ever again be tolerated." He then called for impeachment based on the secret bombing in Cambodia and for Nixon's failure to comply with committee subpoenas.

David Dennis was next. In a raspy voice, he outlined the three principal articles, dismissed the second two as lacking any really serious value for the panel's decision. The first article, obstruction of justice, couldn't stand up in a court of law, Dennis said. There was nothing in the evidence to prove Nixon had made it a policy to mislead investigative officers, interfered with the Watergate investigation by the FBI, offered executive clemency as a bribe and then paid a defendant for his silence, or even attempted to cover up Watergate misdeeds.

Joshua Eilberg (D-Pa.) said it was his intention to vote for impeachment and ticked off the charges against Nixon, occasionally emphasizing a word, but mostly in a matter-of-fact tone that belied the importance of what he was saying. "The evidence presented during our hearings portrays a man who believes he is above the law and who is surrounded by advisers who believe they owe their allegiance to him and not to their country or the Constitution."

People were becoming paranoid, afraid to take a stand, looking out for themselves because of Nixon's actions, he said. "Mr. Chairman, it is my deep belief that not only is Richard Nixon guilty of bribery, high crimes, and misdemeanors, but he must be impeached and convicted by the Senate if we are to remain a free, courageous, and independent people."

Hamilton Fish, Jr., one of the seven swing votes, said he was "deeply troubled over evidence of presidential complicity in thwarting justice and in the alleged abuse of power of that great office, particularly the use of the enormous power of the U.S. government to invade and impinge upon the private rights of individuals.''

But he ended his speech without giving any further indication of his intentions. He removed his glasses and yielded the balance of his time to Wiggins, who had gone down the line of Republicans asking them for additional time if they didn't intend to take their entire fifteen minutes.

Inexperienced observers interpreted Fish's yielding to Wiggins as a sign he would vote against impeachment, but it was merely a common courtesy practiced by members of Congress.

Wiggins resumed where he had left off in his own speech, rebutting some of the charges. A committee investigation costing $1.5 million had come up with thirteen incidents charged against Nixon, Wiggins said, but "twelve of them have nothing to do with the president. . . . No evidence at all, ladies and gentlemen, of presidential involvement in those twelve incidents." The only one which contains it, he said, was testimony by John Dean that Nixon wanted the IRS used to punish persons on his list of enemies. But he said that a tape of that conversation revealed only that Nixon said, "Yeah," in answer to a Dean reference. Wiggins's time ran out again before he could satisfactorily complete his rebuttal.

Jerome Waldie and Wiley Mayne took expected positions, Waldie for impeachment and Mayne against.

At nine minutes before noon came the turn of Walter Flowers, the first of the three "swing votes" on the Democratic side. He, like his constituents, wanted to support Nixon, he said. But what if the panel failed to impeach, he asked rhetorically? "Do we ingrain forever in the very fabric of our Constitution a standard of conduct in our highest office that in the least is deplorable, and at worst impeachable?"

Like Railsback, Flowers listed the items which troubled him. He finished with: "I shall listen to these debates and only then shall I cast my vote." Bells rang, calling for a quorum in the House. Flowers ignored them. "And I can only vote as I am convinced in my heart and mind, based on the Constitution and the evidence." He still refrained from revealing his position.

At 12:08, Rodino recessed the session so members could answer the quorum call and take a lunch break.

Lawrence Hogan, who had called a news conference two days earlier to announce his decision to vote to impeach Nixon, referred to it in the opening speech of the afternoon session. "I read and reread and sifted and tested the mass of information and then I came to my conclusion, that Richard Nixon has beyond a reasonable doubt committed impeachable offenses which in my judgment are of sufficient magnitude that he would be removed from office." He described the evidence as similar to a mosaic that formed an image only when the pieces were put together.

Then came James Mann, another of the Democratic swing votes. He had worked on the drafting of the articles right up to the beginning of the session, so he had no chance to prepare remarks. He spoke extemporaneously, with tears in his eyes. His was to become one of the most memorable speeches of the debates, addressed to the American public. He looked into the television camera and addressed his unseen audience as "you," like a schoolteacher talking to his charges.

He reflected on the past weeks of deliberation and on the emotional critics of the Judiciary Committee. His own deep emotion showing, he said, "You know, some of the things that cause me to wonder are the phrases that keep coming back to me, 'Oh, it is just politics,' or, 'Let him who is without sin cast the first stone.' "

He spoke slowly and quietly. The audience was rapt. So were his colleagues. He sucked the inside of his cheek as he thought of the next phrase.

"Are we so morally bankrupt that we would accept a past course of wrongdoing or that we would decide that the system that we have is incapable of sustaining a system of law because we aren't perfect? . . . You will hear 'the system' used by each of us. . . . That system has been defended on battlefields and statesmen have ended their careers on behalf of the system. . . ."

He recalled the vote of Senator Edmund G. Ross of Kansas who voted to acquit President Andrew Johnson in 1868, but said twenty years later that he hoped his vote would not be construed as one against the constitutional power of impeachment and hoped that a future Congress would have the courage to fulfill its duty.

Even the buzzes for a quorum on the House floor could not dispel the drama or the emotion of the moment.

Mann said Americans were faced in the future "with a very, very serious problem, one that perhaps permits a president to escape accountability because he may choose to deal behind closed doors or to deal between two close, long-time, alter-ego trusted subordinates. We must examine our options to preserve our freedom. The president has the evidence. This committee is composed of Americans who are interested in national security, who have proposed and are ready to provide a mechanism for the screening of the evidence consistent with national security, that evidence taken in the office of the people of the United States at 1600 Pennsylvania Avenue at the expense of the taxpayers.''

He paused, fighting back tears. His voice quaked.

"I am starving for it," he said, pausing and letting his tongue dart between quivering lips, "but I will do the best I can with what I have.''

Exhausted, despite the slowness of his speech, Mann leaned back in his chair and brought his knuckles to his mouth.

After a short recess for a quorum call came M. Caldwell Butler, the most enigmatic of the swing votes to most observers.

Butler's was also a memorable speech, for its strength of conviction. Butler rebutted some of the thoughts expressed by his colleagues, disagreeing with Dennis's fear of rending the party, with Wiggins's opinion that a vote against Nixon should rest on the letter of the law and nothing else, with Mayne's contention that Nixon should not be impeached for doing what his predecessors may have done.

"There are frightening implications for the future of our country if we do not impeach the president of the United States. Because we will, by this impeachment proceeding, be establishing a standard of conduct for the president of the United States which will for all time be a matter of public record.''

He raced on, his voice revealing no emotion, save for the occasional raising of his black, arched eyebrows.

"If we fail to impeach, we have condoned and left unpunished a course of conduct totally inconsistent with the reasonable expectations of the American people; we will have condoned and left unpunished a presidential course of conduct designed to interfere with and obstruct the very process which he is sworn to uphold; and we will have condoned and left unpunished an abuse of power totally without justification. And we will have said to the American people: 'These misdeeds are inconsequential and unimportant.' ''

Butler had just become the first of the swing votes to announce for impeachment. It sent a stir through the audience, where some people were surprised by Butler's decision.

"Let me observe also that throughout the extensive transcripts made available to us of intimate presidential conversation and discussion there is no real evidence of regret for what occurred, or remorse, or resolution to change and precious little reference to, or concern for constitutional responsibility or reflection upon the basic obligations of the office of the presidency.

"In short, power appears to have corrupted. It is a sad chapter in American history, but I cannot condone what I have heard; I cannot excuse it; and I cannot and will not stand still for it."

He wound up: "The misuse of power is the very essence of tyranny. The evidence is clear, direct, and convincing to me that the president of the United States condoned and encouraged the use of the Internal Revenue Service taxpayer audit as a means of harassing the president's political enemies. And consider, if you will, the frightening implications of that for a free society."

At 2:55 P.M., Paul Sarbanes got his chance to speak. Like an "Oscar" recipient and with an equal sense of drama, he expressed thanks to Randolph Thrower and Johnnie Walters, successive commissioners of the Internal Revenue Service, "because they would not bend to the pressure that was brought to bear on them to use the tax system in a discriminatory manner against the citizens of this country, to use it against those who opposed the administration in political debate."

He thanked successive Attorneys General Elliot Richardson and William Ruckelshaus "because they knew that they had made a commitment as to how the special prosecutor would function and they had undertaken that he would not be discharged except for gross impropriety."

And Sarbanes expressed thanks to successive Special Prosecutors Archibald Cox and Leon Jaworski "who have pressed ahead to prove that no American stands above the law. . . ."

While Sarbanes spoke, Doar and Rodino were absent from the room. They were in a rear room taking part in the final drafting of the articles that would replace the pair Donohue had introduced to get the debate rolling.

Now wielding the gavel because he ranked just behind Rodino in seniority, Donohue read the usual instruction recognizing William S. Cohen "for the purpose of debate only . . . for a period not to exceed fifteen minutes." He dragged out the words interminably while Cohen fidgeted anxiously, finally erupting in nervous laughter when Donohue reached the end.

Cohen was the last of the Republicans who were members of the swing-vote coalition. He made a personal reference to another of the swing votes, Walter Flowers, when he noted that "I know that Mr. Flowers of Alabama has even developed an ulcer over this particular matter, but we take some consolation in the knowledge that throughout the ages men and women have always approached the impeachment process with the same apprehension and sense of awe."

He launched into a defense of the practice of using circumstantial evidence to impeach the president. "Well, first, let me say that conspiracies are not born in the sunlight of direct observation. They are hatched in dark recesses, amid whispers and code word and verbal signals, and many times the footprints of guilt must be traced with a searchlight of probability, of common experience.

"Second, I want to point out that circumstantial evidence is just as valid evidence in the eye of the law and that of logic as is direct evidence. In fact, sometimes I think it is much stronger."

He said the circumstantial evidence included Nixon's offer to use the CIA to help cover up Watergate and his orders to use the IRS to punish enemies. But it was strong circumstantial evidence, he said, stronger than a lot of direct evidence.

He answered the charge that other presidents had done just as much as Nixon: "The answer, I think, is that democracy, that solid rock of our system, may be eroded away by degree, and its survival will be determined by the degree to which we will tolerate those silent and subtle subversions that absorb it slowly into the rule of a few in the name of what is right."

By the time Cohen finished—still refraining from stating he would vote to impeach—and George Danielson was recognized at 3:28, nearly a dozen committee members were absent from the room, most of them Republicans. The speechmaking had become rather tedious.

Danielson left no doubt he would vote for impeachment. He reviewed selected bits of evidence that bothered him and hurriedly read from a transcript of a conversation between Bob Haldeman, John Dean, and Nixon. Then he snapped his fingers and turned to Rodino, who was back in the chair. Rodino, who had passed Danielson a note, said, "The chair is going to recess until four o'clock, and we are going to ask that the room be cleared."

Another bomb threat had been called in, this one to the impeachment inquiry headquarters in the Congressional Hotel up the street, by a male caller who said, "This is real." It wasn't and the debate resumed at four o'clock.

"I submit, Mr. Chairman," Danielson continued, "that [there] is enough direct and undisputed evidence to support a conviction of conspiracy in a criminal court. And that connects President Richard Nixon directly to conduct which is a clear breach of his oath of office and his duty to take care that the laws are faithfully executed."

As Rodino rapped the gavel, Danielson concluded: "I respectfully submit that rather than relying entirely upon circumstantial evidence, we have direct evidence coming out of the mouth of the president of the United States that he not only condoned, but directed these cover-up operations."

Trent Lott (R-Miss.) offered a strong defense of Nixon. John Seiberling (D-Ohio) followed with an outline of the patterns of conduct that made Nixon impeachable. It had been Seiberling's turn to speak after Sarbanes, but he had gone to the floor of the House to take part in the action on a strip-mining bill crucial to his home district.

Harold Froehlich (R-Wis.) was another Republican on the committee thought to be a possible vote for impeachment. He gave a strong hint that he would. He ticked off some of the accusations made against Nixon and then angrily discounted them as impeachable offenses.

"I am convinced that some of our previous presidents have engaged in shady, deplorable, and possibly illegal activities," Froehlich said. "But past misconduct cannot logically justify more of the same."

His voice broke and he came close to tears. "I am concerned about impeaching my president for his actions. My decision awaits final wording of the articles and the remaining debate." He pursed his lips to choke back the emotion and gathered up his papers.

Robert Drinan took his turn, delivering his prepared address in his normal, accusatory monotone.

There was a stir in the audience as he began. Not because of his speech, but because a celebrity of sorts, Caroline Kennedy, had walked into the room and taken a seat.

Drinan wound up his speech by paraphrasing Colonel George Mason, one of the authors of the Constitution, who "reminded the framers of the Constitution that the impeachment proceeding is designed to vindicate the rights of the people against a tyrant. But it is also provided so that there will be honorable acquittal for a public official should he be unjustly accused. Whatever the outcome of this proceeding, the American government will be purified and strengthened and in that process all of us will become as never before free men in a free society."

Carlos Moorhead (R-Calif.), Charles B. Rangel, and Joseph Maraziti (R-N.J.) delivered speeches of the sort that had been expected of them, the Republicans defending Nixon and Rangel attacking him.

Barbara Jordan already had made a reputation for herself as the gifted orator on the committee. Her speech was mostly extemporaneous, punctuated by a slight lisp. But she pronounced each word precisely.

A black, she stressed her color in her opening remarks: "Earlier today we heard the beginning to the Preamble to the Constitution of the United States—'We, the people.' It is a very eloquent beginning." The comment came from the corner of her mouth, as was her style.

"But when that document was completed on the seventeenth of September in 1787, I was not included in that 'We, the people.' I felt somehow for many years that George Washington and Alexander Hamilton just left me out by mistake. But through the process of amendment, interpretation, and court decisions I have finally been included in 'We, the people.'

"Today, I am an inquisitor. I believe hyperbole would not be fictional and would not overstate the solemnness that I feel right now. My faith in the Constitution is whole, it is complete, it is total. I am not going to sit here and be an idle spectator to the diminution, the subversion, the destruction of the Constitution."

That was her attention-grabbing rhetoric. Then came her unmatched ability to hone the issue. The House of Representatives had the jurisdiction of impeachment, she said. "The subject of its jurisdiction are those offenses which proceed from the misconduct of public men. That is what we are talking about. In other words, the jurisdiction comes from the abuse or violation of some public trust."

She reviewed some of the accusations against Nixon, some evidence to support them, and made another cogent point others had failed to make as succinctly. "The fact is that on yesterday, the American people waited with great anxiety for eight hours, not knowing whether their president would obey an order of the Supreme Court of the United States."

She emphasized the words "eight hours," raising her voice and pronouncing them crisply.

She concluded: "If the impeachment provision in the Constitution of the United States will not reach the offenses charged here, then perhaps the eighteenth-century Constitution should be abandoned to a twentieth-century paper shredder."

After she spoke, everyone else left had to know that their words would be anticlimactic. On top of that, thirty-two members already had delivered their fifteen-minute speeches. There was little left to say that hadn't been said.

Delbert Latta (R-Ohio) countered with a speech laced with anger and sarcasm. As he moved through his prepared speech, his voice rose.

"Yes, yes, the cries of 'impeach,' 'impeach,' 'impeach' are getting louder. But for these reasons alone one could easily be led to believe that the proper thing to do would be to vote to recommend impeachment."

He, too, asked for "hard evidence." He said, "This evidence must be clear and convincing. It cannot be based on inferences. We cannot make articles of impeachment against the president of the United States by attempting to infer that he had knowledge of wrongdoing that was going on in his administration and yes, lo and behold, in the Committee to Re-Elect the President, which was composed of Democrats, Republicans, and independents alike."

Ray Thornton, the remaining member of the seven swing votes, was next. "I started with the belief and the presumption of President Nixon's innocence of the charges that had been leveled against him.

. . . But, as I have reviewed the evidence and the testimony, it has become evident to me that while these offenses may have existed before, I know of no other time when they have been systematized, or carried on in such an organized and directed way.

"I can now say that on the basis of all of the evidence which has now been produced, I have reached the firm conviction that President Nixon has violated his oath of office by abuse of power, and by obstruction of justice, and that these offenses constitute high crimes and misdemeanors, requiring trial on these charges before the Senate of the United States of America," Thornton declared.

There were twenty-one Democrats on the committee and seventeen Republicans, reflecting the ratio in the House itself. Only Hutchinson's fifteen-minute speech remained from the Republican side. It had been decided that he would speak last, so that his fifteen-minute speech during the debate would not come on top of his opening remarks as ranking Republican.

So Rodino looked over the front of his desk at Elizabeth Holtzman seated below and recognized her.

"I am overwhelmed by the stark contrast [the Constitution] presents to the president's words and actions," she said. "Nowhere in the thousands of pages of evidence presented to this committee does the president ask, 'What does the Constitution say? What are the limits of my power? What does my oath of office require of me? What is the right thing to do?' In fact, those thousands of pages bring to light things that I never even dreamed of."

After Holtzman came Wayne Owens (D-Utah) and the most junior of the Democrats on the committee, Edward Mezvinsky. When they had finished, Rodino turned to his left again and recognized Hutchinson.

The hefty ranking Republican read from a prepared text. He gave his interpretation of the words, "high crimes and misdemeanors." The meaning of the phrase had been debated by the committee members, in articles and books and by scholars. Even semanticists got into the act. Was "misdemeanors" one of four crimes—i.e., treason, bribery, high crimes, misdemeanors—or was it an inseparable part of the phrase, "high crimes and misdemeanors," the word "high" modifying both crimes and misdemeanors?

Hutchinson said the meaning was simple, "that a president can be impeached for the commission of crimes and misdemeanors, which like other crimes to which they are linked in the Constitution, treason and bribery, are high in the sense that they are crimes directed against or having great impact upon the system of government itself. Thus, as I see it, the Constitution imposes two separate conditions for removal of a president. One, criminality, and two, serious impact of that criminality upon the government."

He said the proof of any criminal act by Nixon was lacking. "And I do not believe that we can strengthen that proof by stacking inferences, one upon another, or by making repeated demands for information from the president which we know we will not, and which he believes in principle he cannot, supply and then by trying to draw inferences from the refusal which we have fully anticipated before the demands were even made."

He finished and there remained only Rodino's fifteen-minute speech. The chairman of the committee traditionally speaks last and votes last not only to avoid any undue influence on the members of his committee, but also to have the final word.

Rodino looked up at the clock and opened extemporaneously. He announced that the process of amending the articles of impeachment charging obstruction of justice and abuse of powers would begin the next morning. He singled out members of the inquiry staff and his own committee staff for accolades. He looked directly at each as he addressed them and they looked back, somberly.

"This has to be and shall be one of the greatest experiences of my life," he said. By his own test of the facts in the case, he said, "I find that the president must be found wanting. And so tomorrow I shall urge, along with others, the adoption of articles of impeachment. I shall do so with a heavy heart because no man seeks to accuse or to find wanting the chief executive of this great country."

The evening and full day of oratory carried live to the American people by television had provided a great service to the committee, even if not one speech had changed a single mind.

For that debate had shown that an essentially random group of members of the U.S. Congress were rational, reasonably well-spoken men and women in the best traditions of the great oratory that had helped shape the nation two hundred years earlier. Congress could not have bought a more favorable image-producer than the debates had been. The committee's demeanor and impressiveness during ten and a half hours of speechmaking probably did more than anything else had up to that point to convince citizens that considering impeachment of Nixon was not part of a vendetta after all. Perhaps these were reasonable people who were deciding his fate and perhaps their judgment could be trusted.

But huge pitfalls lay ahead. Rodino knew there would be a serious effort when the committee sessions resumed in the morning to postpone further considerations of impeachment to give Nixon time to comply with the recent Supreme Court order. But he predicted to reporters that the first vote on an article of impeachment could come the next night.

Rodino was feeling proud as he left the committee room after the close of the speeches. Reality intruded immediately, however. Two bodyguards from the crew of city detectives assigned to the Capitol accompanied him as he walked down the hall to an elevator that would take him to his office.

Rodino had been assigned the guards earlier in the day because of the bomb threats. They would stay with him until impeachment ended.

CHAPTER X

Vote

Peter Rodino should have known better. He had been around Congress for more than twenty-five years. He had been extra cautious throughout the impeachment proceeding. So perhaps it was desire overwhelming reason when he predicted a vote on the first article of impeachment by the late afternoon of Friday, July 26, 1974.

Robert's Rules of Order, modified repeatedly by the U.S. Congress, have built into the parliamentary procedure myriad methods for the minority to hamper the majority. Republicans had been the minority in Congress for twenty consecutive years and had learned their parliamentary lessons better than their more secure Democratic counterparts. It might be said that the minority had adopted the motto: "If you can't beat 'em, hamper 'em."

Add to that tendency the committee's own rules allowing each member to speak for five minutes on each motion and the presence of television cameras encouraging politicians to grab all the time they could, and the likelihood arose that nearly four hours would be spent on each motion.

Room 2141 began filling well before 11:00 A.M., the scheduled start of the day's session. At 11:55, Rodino and others filed into the committee room. They had· been in chambers behind the committee room fashioning the final wording of the first article of impeachment. The careful wording was designed to satisfy most, if not all, of the swing votes without sacrificing the votes of the rest of the Democrats.

When the room settled, Rodino rapped once and, looking frustrated because he knew by then what was coming, recognized Robert McClory of Illinois. McClory offered a motion to delay consideration of articles for ten days to give Nixon time to supply the tapes the Supreme Court had ruled on the first day of the debates that Nixon must turn over to the special prosecutor's office.

Midway through the debate on McClory's motion, the committee experienced its first outburst from the audience. As Henry Smith finished a brief statement and two other Republicans shouted for recognition, a tall young man with wavy, long hair stood in the audience next to the central television stand and shouted toward the dais: "Mr. Chairman, why isn't the president being impeached for war crimes? Aren't lives more important than tapes?"

Rodino rapped the gavel and announced: "Please be in order, and be silent or otherwise you will be ejected, removed from the room." He rapped the gavel again. A detective who had been standing against the back wall moved to the end of the row the youth was in and glowered at the youth.

The discussion continued and George Danielson began speaking. He was interrupted as the youth jumped up again and shouted, "Mr. Chairman, I demand an answer."

David Dennis called, "Take him out," as the police moved in. As they led the youth through the door, his companion, a neat-looking young woman wearing a beige jacket over her dress, rose and, in an almost conversational tone, said, "We must speak for the people of Cambodia and the people of Vietnam, people who are still . . ." Murmuring in the audience drowned out her last words, spoken as Fifi Clay shoved her toward the end of the row where detectives intercepted her and escorted her from the room. The audience started laughing and Rodino pounded the gavel three times and said harshly, "The committee will be in order."

The chairman of a committee generally attempts to refrain from taking a stand during a debate, preferring to serve as a moderator between the contentious sides. Rodino had stated his position favoring impeachment the previous night, though, and everyone now knew exactly where he stood.

So Rodino had no difficulty in expressing opposition to McClory's motion. He could see that the debate was going to drag on, and he wanted to vote to get it over with.

Nixon's responses in the past to the committee's subpoenas for tapes had shown, Rodino said, "that the president has no intention whatsoever of complying."

"It has been a period of time since letter after letter was sent to the president. We have been fair. We have been patient. We have sought [the material] not only through letter, but through various requests, and I think it would be an idle, futile gesture for us to delay this matter of moment," Rodino said, particularly "knowing full well that we have the president's full response, which is unequivocal, categorical, and as decisive as anyone would want it to be."

It was an uncharacteristically caustic statement by Rodino and showed that he was tired of the wrangling the thirty-seven other lawyers on the committee had been engaging in for months. He saw the end a few days away and was anxious to hasten it.

For forty-five minutes the committee had argued the McClory motion to delay impeachment. Rodino let a few more members speak, rapped the gavel, ordered the vote to be taken and watched as it was defeated, 27–11.

The Donohue articles introduced to get the debate started were sloppy pieces of work, done hastily just before opening night. They were wordy and confusing in some parts, too general in others.

The two-paragraph preamble was acceptable, though. It said:

Resolved, that Richard M. Nixon, President of the United States, is impeached for high crimes and misdemeanors and that the following articles of impeachment be exhibited to the Senate.

Articles of impeachment exhibited by the House of Representatives of the United States of America in the name of itself and of all of the people of the United States of America, against Richard M. Nixon, President of the United States of America, in maintenance and support of its impeachment against him for high crimes and misdemeanors.

After that followed the language of Article I. Paul Sarbanes was selected to introduce a better-worded substitute. He had been identified with the moderates on the panel, was among the most articulate members, served a border state—Maryland—and had the intelligence to defend himself impressively in debate.

But when Sarbanes attempted to introduce his substitute, McClory objected. As per the usual procedure in Congress, he wanted the original Donohue resolution read in full. There ensued a long, involved argument during which everyone appeared to become confused over the procedure and even the issue. Rodino was one of them. He leaned back as Jerry Zeifman, acting as the committee's parliamentarian, whispered a long, involved explanation in his ear.

Many times the obligatory reading of a motion is dispensed with, but to do so either unanimous consent is obtained or, if that fails, a vote is taken on the issue. Jack Brooks asked for unanimous consent. McClory objected. Rodino then ordered Jim Cline to read the Donohue article, but Bob Kastenmeier interrupted, pointing out that actually, House rules only required that the title of a motion be read before a substitute motion was in order. Rodino leaped at the explanation and ordered Cline to read the title. He did, Sarbanes interrupted after ''Article I . . .'' and got his substitute introduced:

Article I. In his conduct of the office of President of the United States, Richard M. Nixon, in violation of his constitutional oath faithfully to execute the office of President of the United States and, to the best of his ability, preserve, protect and defend the Constitution of the United States, and in violation of his constitutional duty to take care that the laws be faithfully executed, has prevented, obstructed and impeded the administration of justice in that: . . .

It went on to list the separate charges in general terms, concluding with two paragraphs common to each of the articles eventually adopted.

In all of this, Richard M. Nixon has acted in a manner contrary to his trust as President and subversive of constitutional government, to the great prejudice of the cause of law and justice and to the manifest injury of the people of the United States.

Wherefore, Richard M. Nixon, by such conduct, warrants impeachment and trial, and removal from office.

Sarbanes then took the usual five minutes to explain what the article meant.

Edward Hutchinson accused those who had worked on the language in the back chambers of doing sloppy work. "I certainly do not believe that this substitute represents the caliber of legal work that should go into drawing an article of impeachment," he said.

Tom Railsback of Illinois, leader of the Republican swing votes, said he agreed with Hutchinson to an extent, that the substitute might be deficient in not including evidence to back up its nine separate charges. He and Sarbanes agreed the evidence could be outlined in the report accompanying the article, and the Sarbanes article on obstruction of justice could stand as written.

Each member was limited by committee rules to five minutes debate on each motion. Charles Wiggins of California, the leading legal mind on the Republican side and perhaps on the entire committee, rushed into his five minutes. Referring constantly to notes, he questioned Sarbanes closely on the relationship of the impeachment article against Nixon to criminal law governing obstruction of justice. It was a legal discussion, designed to create "legislative history."

The purpose of "legislative history" in law-making procedures was to make it clear in the report accompanying the bill and in the transcript of committee action just what Congress's intent was in passing a law. Congress cannot always be sure the laws it writes will be interpreted correctly and the courts generally rely on legislative intent when there is a substantial question about a statute.

Wiggins's purpose was to prepare the groundwork for later debate and for possible legal action to overturn the article. It was generally esoteric debate for the audience.

Rodino, Walter Flowers, John Doar, and Dick Cates were absent during the exchange, working with the committee members who were drafting the substitute for the second article, charging abuse of power. Charles Rangel and Barbara Jordan joined them later.

After Wiggins spoke, Charles Sandman was recognized by Harold Donohue for a speech he was to repeat and belabor for the next several days. He would become an embarrassment to the Republican side, which wished to present a reasoned, credible opposition to the articles. Sandman continuously came across as snide, belligerent, acerbic, whining, and petulant. At that point, however, he was extremely effective.

He launched into an unpleasant dialogue with Sarbanes and raised his central complaint, that the article as written lacked "specificity." Wiggins had alluded to the same thing, so it was clear that must be the Republicans' central defense against the charges—that the articles were too broadly written and did not accuse Nixon of the specific violations they felt the articles must include to be valid.

In the shrill voice that was to become his trademark during the televised sessions, Sandman said, "As I see this, you have about twenty different charges here, all on one piece of paper and not one of them is specific." He whipped his glasses on and off at a pace equaling his rapid angry words.

Sarbanes replied that the president had had a lawyer in the room since the beginning and had access to the same information the committee had. Sandman interrupted and loudly, bitingly said, "I do not yield any further for those kinds of speeches. I want answers and this is what I am entitled to. This is a charge against the president of the United States . . ."

Danielson got the floor and wrapped up the argument. "Well, at the risk of sounding frivolous, I would state that anyone who is in charge of the complicated business of this nation certainly would be able to understand the intendments of this proposed article of impeachment."

On that note, Donohue declared a recess from 1:30 to 3:00 P.M.

During the lunch period, Sarbanes and others worried that the Republican stalwarts were winning the opening round, perhaps making their points with the American audience where the Democrats, as prosecutors, were failing.

Sarbanes got the floor again when the committee session resumed and took great pains to spell out the specifics embodied in the first article's charges against Nixon. Sarbanes had used the five minutes he had coming to him as the opening speaker on his motion to introduce a substitute. But each member of the panel had five minutes and Sarbanes was yielded additional time by others. He stated the specifics in a staccato manner.

Sandman felt the sting of the extra Sarbanes time and arranged with other Republicans to get extra time. Rodino interrupted the exchange between Sarbanes and Sandman at one point to ask Doar whether specificity was necessary in the articles. Doar said it was not necessary beyond the degree embodied in the Sarbanes substitute.

McClory asked the same question of Sam Garrison, who had recently become chief Republican counsel. Garrison agreed that it wasn't a requirement of law but had been the uniform practice in the past. Rodino then asked Bert Jenner, Doar's right-hand man since being displaced by Garrison. Jenner agreed with Doar.

Don Edwards then got recognition and took up where Sarbanes left off, reading a litany of evidence supporting the obstruction of justice article. The debate went back and forth like that for more than an hour, members asking questions of each other, of counsel, trying to pin down just how much specificity was required.

Rodino decided to regain control and get the debate back on track. Impeachment rules were sparse, he said, especially concerning presidents. Rules in criminal proceedings do not have to apply and the president, therefore, doesn't have the automatic rights that are embodied in criminal law. The House, and the Senate if things got that far, would make their own rules.

Leaning forward on folded arms and referring to notes, Rodino said the issue of specificity "has long been settled. What we do here is to proceed with deliberations concerning the proposition that certain articles of impeachment be recommended by this committee to the House of Representatives."

All the necessary specificity will be furnished in the accompanying report, he said.

William Hungate got the floor and evoked laughter when he pretended to stumble over the word "specificity." Then he launched into one of the homilies that were to make Twain-like humor one of his trademarks, pronouncing Sarbanes's name as "sar-beans."

Deadpanning all the way, he said, "All the technicalities just remind me of the story of an old Missouri lawyer. The fellow was kind of a country fellow and got a case finally in the Supreme Court. He was nervous. He got up there and was arguing along and one of these judges looked down at him and he says, 'Well, young man, where you come from do they ever talk of the doctrine of "qui facit per alium facit per se?" '

"Well, he said, 'Judge, they hardly speak of anything else.' " It took a while for even the lawyers in the committee room to realize Hungate was saying that whoever does something through another, does it him-self—the doctrine of a person being responsible for the acts of his un-derlings.

After the laughter died, Hungate continued, "Let me tell you I think Mr. Haldeman faked it per alium and Mr. Ehrlichman faked it per alium. There is lots of evidence. If they don't understand what we are talking about now, a fellow wouldn't know a hawk from a handsaw anyway.

"Seriously, we know what we're discussing. It is really a question of pleading and I think we are . . . piling inference on inference. . . .

"We sit through these hearings day after day. I tell ya, if a guy brought an elephant through that door and one of us said, 'That's an ele-phant,' some of the doubters would say, 'You know, that is an infer-ence. That could be a mouse with a glandular condition.' "

Everyone understood that and the room shook with laughter. Still deadpanning, Hungate bounced in his seat and as the laughter con-tinued, leaned into the microphone and said, "You're on my time."

A little later, Harold Froehlich, who had been wavering, criticized some of the work of the staff and said he, too, had doubts about the ar-ticles without the specifics of wrongdoing on Nixon's part. Railsback leaned forward from the tier above to talk to him, to tell him that he was bothered too, but to coddle him, ease him into the proimpeachment fold.

Still later, after listening to several speakers argue the issues, Sand-man got the floor and said, "I am amazed that I have heard some of the arguments I have heard here today. I cannot believe this is the same group that made all of those speeches yesterday and the night before, every one of them making that Constitution, the Constitution, the most valuable thing that was ever made. And it is, and yet, [they are] so willing to cast aside the most important provision therein, the one known as due process."

Raising both hands in the air for emphasis, he filled his words with sarcasm: "Isn't it amazing? They are willing to do anything except make these articles specific. It is the same old story, you know, when you don't have the law on your side, you talk about facts. If you don't have the facts on your side, you just talk, and that is what a lot of people have been doing today.''

Sandman was continuing to make points with the American public that was still tuned in. Despite their contention they already had given Nixon far more latitude than they were required to give him in the impeachment proceedings, the impeachment proponents' case was being hurt by Sandman's approach. No matter how correct the proimpeachment forces might be according to the Constitution, the Congress, and the law, impeachment still had to be sold to the people. The proimpeachment forces had begun to lose sight of that. Sandman was bringing it back into their field of vision. His repetition of the need for specifics and the failure to provide them, contrasted with the arguments against specifics, was making the proimpeachment forces look like a vigilante group.

The committee members favoring impeachment had attempted to line up their troops to lay out the evidence against Nixon during the debate on the Sarbanes substitute. But their recital was haphazard, done after a sudden decision that Sandman was making points. The presentation was too scattershot. The proimpeachment forces faced the erosion of the swing votes and others who just could be persuaded by Sandman's arguments, or at least by the public perception that he was right.

Delbert Latta joined the lengthening debate, making points for Sandman's side. Speaking quietly, he held the audience rapt while he addressed Rodino: ''You are saying that we are going to send these articles of impeachment to the floor of the House, without being specific, without saying the time, the place, and say to the members of the House of Representatives who are not on this committee, 'Go through those thirty-eight or thirty-nine volumes. Try to sort out what we think as members of this committee are impeachable offenses, and make a judgment thereon.' Is that what we are saying? If you are, other members of the House, good luck.'' By the end of the sentence he had shifted his gaze from Rodino to the television camera.

''Well, Mr. Chairman, I think we ought to rethink what we are proposing. A common jaywalker charged with jaywalking any place in the United States is entitled to know when and where the alleged offense is supposed to have occurred. Is the president of the United States entitled to less?"It was an effective speech. But Latta was heating up. "Nobody is trying to delay the action here," he continued, his voice raising to a shout, "because I well know that anytime that the chairman puts down the gavel and says, 'Call the roll,' the votes are here to do exactly as you like."

Before he finished his speech, he launched a personal attack on Jenner. "Now, I can't agree with everything that Mr. Jenner does, who has been alluded to as an outstanding member of the bar, and he is.

"But I know that other members saw an article in the *Wall Street Journal* that they didn't agree with. A committee that he is chairman of has just reported that they recommended the repeal of the antiprostitution laws of the United States, [a committee] which termed the state laws 'one of the most direct forms of discrimination against women.' "

Jenner leaned back in his chair and smiled thinly as Latta spoke. Many of Latta's colleagues, including John Seiberling, were smiling when Latta finished. Demagoguery occurred on the Judiciary Committee just as it normally does in Congress.

After a couple more speakers, Seiberling got the floor and said, "I don't want to let any more time pass than I can help, to suggest that the other gentleman from Ohio owes this committee and Mr. Jenner an apology for what I consider to be an unprofessional and certainly an unjudicial comment on a completely extraneous matter with respect to Mr. Jenner.

"And I would hope the gentleman would reflect that it is unbecoming to the dignity of these proceedings and in all my time on this committee, it's the first time that I have ever heard that kind of thing indulged in."

Latta broke in and asked Seiberling to yield. Seiberling said he was speaking on someone else's time. Rangel said he had the floor and yielded to Latta.

"The gentleman is entitled to his opinion and that is all it is," Latta responded to Seiberling. "I think the American people are interested in what was in the article and here it is." He held up the paper again, leaned back and scratched his face with the ear piece of his eyeglasses.

Seiberling attempted to respond: "Mr. Chairman, I, I . . ." when Rangel broke in to yield back to the chair the rest of his time and ended the clash.

Tempers on both sides obviously were wearing thin. The debate had dragged on for hours with no relief in sight. Rodino, as tired as anyone else, rapped the gavel and declared a two-hour recess beginning at 6:00 P.M.

Rodino had predicted a vote on the first article that afternoon. That vote still appeared far away as the members straggled out of the room and headed for restaurants down Pennsylvania Avenue beyond the Capitol for a quick dinner before returning to the hot room for more grueling debate.

Rodino was aware that the exchange between Latta and Seiberling had made the committee look foolish. He had reveled along with the other committee members over the rave reviews given the committee for its previous two sessions of televised debate.

Rodino arranged for Barbara Jordan to be the first member recognized after dinner. He believed that she could lay out the case clearly in prime time, steal some of the Nixon stalwarts' thunder and get the viewing public back on the track of the case for impeachment. Her statement would center on fairness, the due process that Nixon was given in the committee's proceedings, but that his Republican supporters said was being denied him.

She was in good form again when the committee reconvened. Rodino was not disappointed.

"Mr. Chairman, this committee has spent two days receiving and listening to very eloquent arguments. We talked about the Constitution, and we talked about the serious nature of the impeachment process and [in] all which was said, we were telling the truth. We believed what we were talking about.

"Now, Mr. Chairman, this committee is called upon to get to the matter of the consideration of articles of impeachment. It apparently is very difficult for the committee to translate its views of the Constitution into the realities of the impeachment provisions. It is understandable that this committee would have procedural difficulties, because this is an unfamiliar and strange procedure.

"But, some of the arguments which were offered earlier today by some members of this committee, in my judgment, were phantom arguments, bottomless arguments." She spat out the words, "phantom," and "bottomless," leaning forward, using thrusts of her head for emphasis.

"Due process? Due process tripled. Due process quadrupled. We did that. The president knows the case which has been heard before this committee. The president's counsel knows the case which has been heard before this committee. It is a useless argument to say that what we would do is to throw thirty-eight or thirty-nine books at the House and say, 'You find the offenses with which the President is charged . . .' "

Flowers was recognized then and continued the theme: "I think the gentlelady from Texas makes some good points there. I have some concern, Mr. Chairman, that there might be a false impression being communicated here that this is too general and that we might be engaging too much in our own lawyerly tendencies. And we might convince the people in this audience and in the faraway audience that thirty-eight lawyers on one committee is simply too many lawyers, and I wouldn't necessarily disagree with that."

He turned the questioning to Doar to substantiate the idea that Nixon had been given great latitude by the committee and that the charges as listed were specific enough. Doar agreed that they were.

During the dinner break, Flowers had reached a decision about what he felt must be done before a vote was taken. He recognized the gains that Sandman had made and found that he didn't entirely disagree with him.

Flowers told the panel that he hoped the committee would discuss "the specific provable factual items of evidence that come under each one of the subparagraph heads of Article I, and determine for ourselves here, as I think we must, in an obviously unorchestrated manner, if anybody's been watching our proceedings here, exactly whether the facts fit the charges." He said the point of the proceedings was, after all, to see whether "the facts as charged here warrant the impeachment of the president of the United States."

Sandman soon was recognized to offer an amendment to the Sarbanes substitute. It merely was a motion to strike the first subparagraph of the substitute.

The subparagraph was one of the nine subparagraphs supporting the charge that Nixon had followed a policy of obstructing justice. It said, "The means used to implement this policy have included one or more of the following: (1) making false or misleading statements to lawfully authorized investigative officers and employees of the United States."

Sandman was trying to weaken the articles if he could, and cause a delay in the proceedings if he couldn't. Publicly, his purpose was to elicit the facts justifying the subparagraphs while gaining support for his contention the articles were too general.

Sandman had prepared nine amendments, one for each subparagraph. Three hours and ten minutes of debate could be spent on each amendment. That meant nearly thirty more hours could be consumed in debate on the first article of impeachment. Proimpeachment forces could refrain from participating to cut down the time, but then the debate would be one-sided.

Sandman charged into his argument in support of his amendment to strike the first subparagraph.

He called the charge "indefinite" and noted that "a simple parking ticket has to be specific. It has to say what you did that violated the law. It has got to have the license of your car; it has got to have the date that you did it. You want to replace that and say that does not have to apply to the president. Why, this is ridiculous and this is an altogether new ball game."

Sandman's tactic did not come as a surprise. Under the committee's procedures, each amendment that was to be offered had to be handed to the clerk in advance. In that way, each member knew beforehand what was to be offered and could prepare for it. Jim Cline had fourteen possible amendments in front of him at the dinner break.

To combat Sandman's tactic, Flowers and the other swing votes decided during the break that their best response would be to prepare a defense against Sandman's amendments, each swing vote using his five minutes of debate to lay out the specific evidence for each subparagraph for the television audience.

Railsback revealed part of the plan when he received recognition after

Sandman's defense of his amendment. "Let me say, Mr. Chairman, that I personally at this point in time think that perhaps it is a good idea to have a motion to strike on each of those counts so that those of us that are concerned about the various allegations have a right to submit our beliefs and our concerns. And this particular paragraph, which is item one in the Sarbanes substitute and has to do with false and misleading information, happens to be, as everyone knows, one of my major areas of concern."

He then proceeded with a chronology of the evidence behind the charge, laying it out in great detail. His time ran out but Flowers, taking advantage of the practice of alternating between a Republican and a Democrat, sought recognition and yielded three of his five minutes to Railsback so he could continue. Flowers used part of his remaining two minutes to get Doar to cover any areas Railsback might have missed.

The debate heated up and members clamored for attention. Rodino had to gavel them back to order and made a short speech on the need for decorum.

"The committee will be in order, and I believe that it is in order at this time to state that the view of one member does not express what is actually the law or the policy of this committee of the House of Representatives."

The usually judicious Wiggins broke in with: "Including the chairman."

Rodino heard the remark, stopped talking, held his temper and considered what he would say next. "I would hope that the members would recognize that the chair presides and the chair is attempting to be fair in recognizing each member. . . ." He added, "I don't mean to lecture in any way, but I think that this is serious enough that indulging in parliamentary maneuvers to delay a decision on this very important question, I think, serves to tell the people that we are afraid to meet the issue."

Rodino was exasperated by all the wrangling. He asked how many members wanted to speak on the Sandman amendment and counted twenty responses. He tried to get them to limit themselves to two minutes each, but Nixon stalwarts objected that the rules allowed five.

John Conyers turned to a colleague during the count of the members wanting to speak and wondered aloud whether a motion should be made to table the Sandman motion. A motion to table was not debatable, so it had the effect of choking off debate. But it was a heavy-handed maneuver and could have lost.

The debate droned on, back and forth from Republican to Democrat, from proimpeachment to Nixon stalwart.

The tedium was broken only by Latta, who wound up his five-minute speech on the Sandman amendment by asking Doar whether Nixon would have to go to the thirty-nine volumes of evidence and testimony the committee had issued thus far to flesh out his defense. Doar said yes, and that would not be unusual.

Latta responded by saying, "It might not be unusual, but in cases in criminal court these days we don't have thirty-eight or thirty-nine volumes of statements of information, and I would just like the American people to know what we are talking about." He put his glasses on while he reached back for four volumes tied together with a string, lifted them from the floor and plunked them atop five others already sitting on his desk.

He continued stacking, took his glasses off and received the rest from Joseph Maraziti, who lifted them in ones and twos from the floor behind Latta's chair. Latta had stacked twenty in one pile and the room was rocking with laughter when Rodino, also laughing, rapped the gavel and announced Latta's time had expired.

Latta leaned around the stack now higher than his head and toward the microphone. "I don't believe I need any more time, Mr. Chairman."

Finally, the speeches ran out and shortly after 11:00 P.M., a vote was taken on Sandman's amendment to strike the first paragraph. It failed on a 27–11 vote, with some strange alignments occurring. The vote did not accurately reflect impeachment sentiment since some of those who wanted to vote for the first article felt that the subparagraph that Sandman had proposed to strike created a flaw in an article they otherwise could accept. Others opposed the article but voted to keep the subparagraph in because they felt it would weaken an otherwise strong article.

Rodino rapped the session to a close at 11:35 P.M. and announced it would resume at noon the next day, Saturday, July 27.

During the intervening hours, committee and staff members were still working on the final wording of the second article, but the proimpeachment forces and swing votes, including Flowers and Railsback, thought the first could still use some improvements. They worried that Sandman was still controlling the progress of the proceedings. They felt uneasy about the Friday evening session.

The proimpeachment forces felt that a carefully organized litany of evidence would have an overwhelming effect, especially when, as lawyers, they considered that a debate in favor of evidence was a much stronger tool than a debate charging a lack of evidence. And they knew the president's defenders had no evidence to present that Nixon was innocent of the charges. They were relying as much on inference as was the proimpeachment force.

Typically, the Saturday session was forty-five minutes late getting started. The staff, which had been assigned to quickly line up all of the arguments in favor of each subparagraph, was just finishing up as the starting time arrived. Assignments were still being made to each proimpeachment member, and the members were polishing some of the arguments.

Rodino opened the session by announcing that after a reasonable period of debate on each motion to strike a subparagraph, he intended to choke off the discussion and move directly to a vote.

Sandman had learned what the proimpeachment force was up to and announced, ''There are amendments on the desk that have my name on them, and I would like to withdraw those because they are aimed at the same point of law that we discussed at great length yesterday.''

A cigar smoldering in front of him, Sandman spoke quietly this day. ''It is my hope, Mr. Chairman, that we will be able to proceed with Article I with the degree of discipline that existed yesterday and last night, no doubt continuing today. There is no way that the outcome of this vote is going to be changed by debate and I, therefore, hope that we can with dispatch cover the Sarbanes substitute and there will be no objections from me, no amendments from me, nor will there be any motions to strike from me.''

Sandman was trying to undercut the proimpeachment force's plans by denying them the forum they were prepared to use to lay out the evi-

dence. Sandman knew he was in the weaker position. An organized recitation of evidence would be devastating to his cause. He had gotten as
much mileage as he could out of the charge the first article lacked
specificity.

Flowers, a leader in the plan to lay out the evidence, saw that Sandman had outmaneuvered the proimpeachment side. Flowers got recognition and asked to have his name substituted for that of Sandman on the
amendments at the clerk's desk. This action required unanimous consent, but the fact that Flowers, who was thought to favor impeachment,
now proposed to strike the remaining eight subparagraphs from the
proposed article, took the Nixon stalwarts by surprise. None of them
objected. If Flowers had come over to their side, it was a valuable
switch they did not want to discourage.

In an exchange with Rangel, Flowers was able to explain to the television audience the plan for laying out the evidence for each subparagraph.

Latta, one of the Nixon stalwarts, tried to recover from the embarrassment: "We are certainly now bowing just because we want to be
bowing. We are bowing to the obvious and the obvious is that we do not
have the votes. We are not deserting our position. We think it was a
proper position." His side would have its chance on the floor of the
House, he said.

Then came several mostly technical changes in the wording of the
first article. Some of the changes proposed were very minor, but the
committee didn't challenge more substantive ones proposed by Republicans Lawrence Hogan and Railsback because they were still being
stroked to keep their votes in favor of impeachment.

One of Railsback's motions was to change some wording in the second subparagraph of the article. It read:

On June 17, 1972, and prior thereto, agents of the Committee for the Re-Election of the President committed illegal entry of the headquarters of the Democratic National Committee in Washington, District of Columbia, for the purpose
of securing political intelligence. Subsequent thereto, Richard M. Nixon, using
the powers of his high office, made it his policy and in furtherance of such policy did act directly and personally and through his close subordinates and
agents, to delay, impede and obstruct the investigation [of Watergate].

Railsback's language changed it to: "Subsequent thereto, Richard M. Nixon, using the powers of his high office, engaged, personally and through his subordinates and agents in a course of conduct or plan to delay . . . ," thus changing it to read that Nixon designed the obstruction of justice, rather than just making it his policy.

Nixon stalwarts joined with the proimpeachment forces in voting for the amendment because they felt it would be harder to prove a design than a "policy."

The only challenge came to an amendment offered by George Danielson to add congressional investigators to the list of those whom Nixon obstructed. The amendment won, however, 24–14.

After the "perfecting amendments" were disposed of, at 1:45 on Saturday afternoon, Flowers began the first of what was to become a long series of motions to strike the remaining eight subparagraphs in the Sarbanes substitute.

Flowers asked whether Doar could lay out the evidence for the subparagraph and Wiggins suggested that since Flowers introduced the amendment he should be the one presenting the evidence, not the staff. Flowers rejoined: "I would remind the gentleman that I made a motion to strike the subparagraph, not in support of the subparagraph, and I yield to the gentleman from Maine."

Cohen of Maine wasn't quite ready with his evidence defending the second subparagraph charging that Nixon had ordered false testimony to federal investigators. But he proceeded, finished his five minutes and got five minutes more yielded by Donohue.

Hardly anyone noticed that Cohen mistakenly had outlined the support that had been prepared for the fourth subparagraph, not for the second that was under consideration at the time.

After the second five minutes, Sandman was recognized and made it clear he did not understand what Flowers was up to. "I shall not use but seconds, and may I say to my friend from Alabama, if you were to stand on your head and do the fanciest of tricks, you would have twelve votes, no more" against impeachment.

Leaning into the mike while the audience laughed, Sandman's expression turned to a sneer as he said. "And there is no point in the continuation of this kind of an argument." He agreed with Flowers, Sandman said, believing they were on the same side. But he urged Flowers to save the fight for the House floor.

"So, please let us not bore the American public with a rehashing of what we have heard. We went through this for many hours yesterday and to those who favor keeping the Sarbanes substitute as it is, you've got twenty-seven votes. Let's go on with our business," Sandman said.

Sandman then was chided by Hogan for changing his tune, demanding specifics to back up the charges on one day and railing against them the next.

Doar was asked and confirmed that the staff was drawing up a bill of particulars to support each charge, as would be required in a criminal prosecution. Railsback replied, then, that perhaps the exercise the committee was currently engaged in might be a waste of time.

Railsback was ignored and David Dennis got the floor, stating that it was not the purpose of his side to state the evidence during debate, but to have it included in the article of impeachment before the committee. He then began an attempt to refute Cohen's evidence.

The debate continued until 2:30, when a voice vote defeated the motion to strike the second subparagraph. If Flowers held to his plan, there were seven subparagraphs to go and it appeared, as Rodino announced a recess from 2:41 to 4:00 P.M., that the historic first vote on impeachment would not come until the beginning of the following week.

During the lunch break, Flowers decided to continue with at least a few more motions to strike. He wasn't happy with the idea, but thought it necessary. If the committee went into the next article—Article II charging abuse of powers—he felt its chances for passage would be in trouble if it weren't accompanied by specifics.

When the late afternoon session convened, Flowers introduced the motion to strike the third subparagraph but asked unanimous consent to limit the debate on the amendment to twenty minutes. Everyone was tired of the haggling by that point and there was no objection. M. Caldwell Butler had been assigned the task of presenting the support for the third subparagraph, which charged Nixon with encouraging false or misleading testimony to courts and congressional committees.

Butler prompted laughter in the committee room when he finished the five minutes yielded to him by Flowers and, with a straight face, asked Rodino for five more minutes to speak in opposition to the motion.

Rodino was caught up short. He smiled and said, "I thought the gentleman was speaking in opposition to the motion." Butler replied, also with a smile, "I was, but I thought I was on Mr. Flowers's time, and he is the proponent of the motion." After the laughter, Rodino said the ten minutes would have to count against the side opposing the amendment.

The give-and-take on the motion continued, and when the voice vote was taken. Sandman demanded a roll call. Flowers, whose motion it was, voted "present," looking as though he expected a reaction that he didn't get. When his name was called for his vote, Dennis said, "I am quite puzzled. When the author of the amendment votes 'present,' I hardly know what to do, but I will vote 'aye.' " Rodino, appreciating the break in the tension, noted, "The gentleman made up his mind rather quickly." The motion was defeated, 25–12.

Flowers introduced the next motion, to strike the fourth subparagraph charging Nixon with impeding the investigations of the FBI, special prosecutor's office and congressional committees. He yielded to Hogan, a former FBI agent, who began his presentation saying, "Perhaps I feel the importance of this more than most." The first ten minutes were consumed by Hogan for the proimpeachment side.

When Sandman was recognized, he snarled, "The thing that amuses me the most today—what a difference twenty-four hours makes. Yesterday they had so much testimony they were afraid to put in nine simple sentences. Now today every other word they breathe is the word, 'specify.' Isn't that unusual? So unusual. Everything is so specific. But they have not changed one word in the articles, have they? Not a word."

The debate on striking the subparagraph charging Nixon with impeding investigations dragged on and another roll call was taken. The motion was defeated also, 26–11, with Flowers again voting "present."

To save time, Flowers skipped to the seventh subparagraph, explaining that the fifth and sixth had been adequately covered by the debate so far. The seventh charged Nixon with giving grand jury information to the subjects of the jury's investigation.

Rangel had the assignment for that one and proceeded. After nineteen minutes of the twenty-minute limit was consumed, Sandman got recognition. Reading from a paper, a pencil in his hand, he said, "My only purpose in seeking this one minute is, I have a question for my friend from Alabama. On my motion to strike, you voted 'no.' On the second one, of course, we had no vote. On three and four, you only voted 'present.' Five and six, we had no vote. Now, on seven, I am curious. Are you going to vote for your own amendment or are you going to continue to call on people to defeat your amendment?'' He grinned as he asked the question.

Flowers returned the grin, drawling, ''Well, the caliber of the debate is so outstanding, Mr. Sandman, that it leaves me undecided at the conclusion.'' Flowers was clearly enjoying his role. His colleagues guffawed and one of them said, ''Beautiful, beautiful, best comeback I've heard.'' Rodino rapped the gavel and pleaded for decorum.

Flowers voted ''present'' again on striking the seventh subparagraph and the motion to strike was defeated, 26–11. Flowers introduced the next two motions. Wayne Owens of Utah led the debate in favor of the eighth subparagraph charging deception of the people of the United States, and the ninth charging attempts to bribe Watergate defendants was led by William Hungate. The eighth lost, 25–12.

Sandman returned to the fray on the ninth subparagraph, which stated that Nixon was guilty of ''endeavoring to cause prospective defendants, and individuals duly tried and convicted, to expect favored treatment and consideration in return for their silence or false testimony, or rewarding individuals for their silence or false testimony.''

Sandman had finally realized what Flowers was up to and not quite able to mask his sarcasm, almost pleaded with his colleagues to listen to reason on that charge. He said the debate up to that time had been a waste of time. ''And two hundred and twenty million people know what you are up to. You did not kid anybody. You tried to sell them a bill of goods. And we did not, with all of our arguments, persuade a single vote. There is no way humanly possible to do that at this forum.''

As Sandman talked on, Flowers attempted to interrupt him. Sandman hurried on, telling Flowers, ''Let me try to get some votes on this one; I am reaching out.''

Flowers, laughing, responded, ''Well, you persuaded me already and you know, you may talk me back out of it.'' The room erupted in laughter again. Flowers did vote in favor of killing the subparagraph and was joined by two other swing votes, Fish and Railsback. They believed the evidence was too weak to support the charge. But the motion to kill it lost on a 23–15 vote.

So the ninth subparagraph remained, along with the other eight.

The time had come when each of the thirty-eight members was going to have to take a stand for or against an article of impeachment. Facing it and feeling he owed an explanation to his district, Flowers had used his position as a valuable swing vote to get Rodino to give him time for a speech at the end of the debate. His explanation was moving.

Reading from a prepared text in a somber voice, Flowers held the rapt attention of the room. No papers shuffled, there was no scribbling, not even whispers were exchanged.

"There are many people in my district who will disagree with my vote here," Flowers said. "Some will say that it hurts them deeply for me to vote for impeachment. I can assure them that I probably have enough pain for them and me. I have close, personal friends who strongly support President Nixon. To several of these close friends who somehow, I hope, will hear and see these proceedings, I say that the only way I could vote for impeachment would be the realization, to me anyway, that they, my friends, would do the same thing if they were in my place on this unhappy day and confronted with all of the same facts that I have. And I have to believe that they would, or I would not take the position that I do."

Before he finished, though, Flowers let his colleagues know that although he was voting for impeachment, he was still a conservative.

"Make no mistake, my friends, one of the effects of our action here will be to reduce the influence and power of the office of the president. To what extent will be determined only by future action in the House or in the Senate." After impeachment, he said, Congress would still face "the many hard choices that must be made for our nation, such as allocation of scarce resources, such as management of the forces of inflation and recession, such as balancing priorities and controlling the spending of taxpayers' money.

"In the weeks and months ahead I want my friends to know that I will be around to remind them when some of these hard choices are up, and we will be able to judge then how responsible we can be with our newly found congressional power."

It was the voice of a conservative saying to liberals, in effect, "All right, I am joining you this time because it is too important to shirk, but I want you to remember the hard decision I had to make when I ask you to make a hard one next time."

Flowers yielded to Fish, who announced for the first time in public that he would vote to impeach. When he finished, Rodino rapped the gavel. McClory wanted time for his own wind-up speech, but Rodino refused and rapped again.

The room became alert. The moment was at hand, the culmination of more than twenty-one hours of agonizing, debating, pleading, some joking and much soul-searching, all in front of a national television audience. The room was deathly silent at 7:00 P.M., July 27, 1974.

"The question is," Rodino said, stumbling over the words. ". . . the question occurs on the substitute offered by the gentleman from Maryland, as amended." The historic vote actually would be on Paul Sarbanes's substitute for the first article introduced by Donohue on Wednesday. It would reflect the impeachment sentiment.

"All those in favor of the substitute of the gentleman from Maryland, as amended, please signify by saying 'aye.' "

The room resounded with a chorus of ayes. Rodino asked for the noes and the room resounded again. That was pro forma. He already knew he was going to make that vote more official by calling the roll. It started at his immediate right.

The clerk, Jim Cline, in a sharp, clear voice, read the name of each member. The room was so still the only sound besides the names and the votes was that of the motorized still cameras.

"Mr. Donohue."

Harold Donohue of Massachusetts drew out an elongated "aayyee."

"Mr. Brooks."

Jack Brooks of Texas was writing on a pad and didn't even look up as he said "aye," loudly but without expression.

"Mr. Kastenmeier."

Bob Kastenmeier of Wisconsin said in a soft but deliberate voice, "aye."

"Mr. Edwards."

Don Edwards of California was leaning back in his chair when he said "aye," almost matter-of-factly.

Bill Hungate of Missouri, John Conyers of Michigan, Joshua Eilberg of Pennsylvania, and Jerry Waldie of California announced their expected "ayes."

"Mr. Flowers."

Walter Flowers of Alabama had sadness in his eyes but not in his voice as he said "aye" quietly, blinked, and looked at the television cameras while rolling a pen between his fingers.

"Mr. Mann."

Jim Mann of South Carolina looked down. He raised his head, displayed misting eyes and, almost in a whisper, said "aye."

"Mr. Sarbanes."

Paul Sarbanes of Maryland stared blankly into space and pronounced a soft "aye."

John Seiberling of Ohio, George Danielson of California, Father Robert Drinan of Massachusetts, and Charles Rangel of New York added their "ayes."

"Ms. Jordan."

Barbara Jordan of Texas was leaning forward, her head lowered. She raised her head, her face wore a "dare me" expression and she announced "aye" with contempt.

"Mr. Thornton."

Ray Thornton of Arkansas, sitting erect, his eyes lowered, said "aye" very softly.

Liz Holtzman of New York, Wayne Owens of Utah, and Ed Mezvinsky of Iowa quietly spoke their "ayes."

"Mr. Hutchinson."

Ed Hutchinson of Michigan rocked back in his chair, grinned and dragged out "nnooo," proudly and smugly.

"Mr. McClory."

Bob McClory of Illinois was interrupted while writing on a sheet of paper. He looked up, said a crisp "no," and returned to his writing.

"Mr. Smith."

Henry Smith of New York took a breath and pronounced a quick "no."

"Mr. Sandman."

Charles Sandman of New Jersey also was writing something, and he didn't even look up as he announced a matter-of-fact "no."

"Mr. Railsback."

Tom Railsback of Illinois looked at the clock with glistening eyes, said a soft "aye."

"Mr. Wiggins."

Charles Wiggins of California had his hand to his lips and removed it only long enough to say "no."

"Mr. Dennis."

David Dennis of Indiana dragged out his "nnooo" a bit, but without emotion.

"Mr. Fish."

Hamilton Fish of New York had misting eyes but said "aye" in a clear voice.

"Mr. Mayne."

Wiley Mayne of Iowa announced a soft but emotionless "no."

"Mr. Hogan."

Larry Hogan of Maryland stared straight ahead and said a soft "aye."

"Mr. Butler."

Caldwell Butler of Virginia moved as if he had been disturbed while doing something more important. He looked up and said a soft, but unemotional "aye" and looked back down at his desk top.

"Mr. Cohen."

Bill Cohen of Maine had his elbows on his desk and his hands were clasped at his chin when he said a very soft "aye."

"Mr. Lott."

Trent Lott of Mississippi pronounced a firm, crisp "no."

"Mr. Froehlich."

Harold Froehlich of Wisconsin showed no emotion and announced "aye" firmly.

Carlos Moorhead of California, Joseph Maraziti of New Jersey, and Delbert Latta of Ohio loudly and firmly completed the Republican vote with "noes."

"Mr. Rodino."

Peter Rodino, looking sad, said a soft "aye," shifted slightly in his chair and looked straight ahead.

Cline carefully tallied the votes.

"Mr. Chairman?"

"The clerk will report."

"Twenty-seven members have voted aye, eleven members have voted no."

"And the amendment is agreed to," Rodino read from a sheet in front of him, without emotion. "The question now occurs on Article I of the Donohue resolution as amended by the Sarbanes substitute as amended," he said, with just the slightest quake in his voice.

As often happens in Congress, the drama occurred on an amendment, a substitute, and not on the article of impeachment itself. The vote on the Sarbanes substitute told the story. But the article, as amended by the Sarbanes substitute, still had to be voted on. Under the procedures previously agreed to, a roll call would be conducted on it, too.

Cline read through the roll again and with less drama, fewer pauses for effect, the members answered just as they had before on the substitute, voting 27–11 in favor of the first article.

"And pursuant to the resolution, Article I, of that resolution is adopted and will be reported to the House and the committee will recess until ten-thirty Monday next, Monday morning," Rodino read quickly. He rapped once, and the committee recessed at 7:05 P.M., Saturday, July 27, 1974, having voted to impeach the president of the United States.

Peter W. Rodino, the son of an Italian immigrant, in his twenty-fifth year as a congressman and his first term as chairman of the House Judiciary Committee, had, however haltingly, led his charges to an impeachment vote, producing a bipartisan majority in favor of impeaching a president of the United States for the first time in 106 years.

Midway through the vote on Sarbanes's substitute article, Rodino had been handed a slip of paper telling him the Capitol police had received another threat. This one, bizarre as it sounded, said that a Kamikaze pilot had taken off from National Airport across the river and was going to fly his plane into the Rayburn Building.

Rodino had refused to recess the committee; the vote in progress seemed far more important than protecting people against some doubtful threat.

After he rapped the gavel ending the session, Rodino spoke briefly to

Hutchinson, accepted Brooks's hand in congratulations and headed for a door to the committee's offices, ignoring the reporters who clamored for his attention.

Past a row of telephone cubicles and his own, tiny glassed-in office, past well-wishing staff members and colleagues, Rodino walked glassy-eyed, to the windows on the far side of the office area. He pulled apart the Venetian blinds on the windows and peered out, almost as if he might be looking for the Kamikaze pilot.

After a few moments, Rodino turned to see Doar and Francis O'Brien standing there silently, looking at him expectantly, waiting for him to say something dramatic or historic. Rodino mumbled something incoherent, and walked past them into his little office. He shut the door, picked up the telephone and dialed his wife in Newark. He told her it was over. She replied that she knew, that she had watched him on television and was very proud of him. He broke down and cried.

A large crowd waited in the dark outside the Rayburn Building when, later, Doar walked out carrying his huge, battered briefcase. He walked down the curved driveway in his stoop-shouldered fashion as the crowd broke into spontaneous and sustained applause.

CHAPTER XI

Aftermath

The thirty-eight members of the House Judiciary Committee had taken the ultimate step. For good or ill, whether fatal to their political careers or not, all finally had decided whether Nixon should be impeached.

But one article would not be enough to lead the whole House to vote to impeach the president and send his case to a trial in the Senate.

Other complaints against him were not resolved by the first article charging him with obstructing justice by leading the cover-up of White House involvement in the Watergate break-in. Other charges, far more important from a historical point of view, remained.

And, although six of seventeen Republicans on the committee had voted for Article I, more GOP votes in favor of impeachment were possible on other allegations.

By Saturday, Bob McClory, who had voted against Article I, had worked with Frank Polk, the chief Republican counsel on the regular Judiciary Committee, to fashion a version of Article II that reduced the number of charges in the draft placed before Harold Donohue on Wednesday from eight to five. The draft charged Nixon with abusing the powers of the presidency, including failure to comply with the committee's subpoenas.

McClory had been bothered for weeks by the absence of ''the smoking gun'' tying Nixon directly to a criminal act. For that reason, he couldn't vote for Article I.

But it was clear to McClory that Nixon had violated a portion of his oath of office when he refused to comply with committee subpoenas. He also interpreted violation of his oath as covering the acts of subordinates whom the president allowed to abuse the powers of the presidency.

The draft of Article II by John Doar and James Mann accused Nixon of illegal surveillance, forming a special investigative unit in the White House (the "plumbers"), misuse of the Internal Revenue Service, misuse of the FBI, misuse of the Justice Department, misuse of the CIA, giving misleading information to Congress and agencies, and noncompliance with the committee's subpoenas.

McClory thought the Doar/Mann draft was overdone. His version put the misuse of the FBI, Justice Department, and CIA into one charge and dropped the last section charging noncompliance. He was drawing up a separate, third article embodying that abuse, he said. He contended that noncompliance went to the core of the House's ability to impeach the president and therefore the issue deserved the dignity of its own article.

The McClory version was presented to the swing votes when they met on Saturday morning before the debate and vote on the first article.

Several of the swing votes did not like the eighth charge in the Doar/Mann article because they thought Nixon's noncompliance was not an impeachable offense. The committee had not taken the extra step of getting the courts to back the legality of the subpoenas nor had it gotten the entire House to endorse its action by voting the president in contempt of Congress for refusing to supply subpoenaed material.

Some of the swing votes—now numbering nine with the inclusion of Larry Hogan and Harold Froehlich—felt the hastily written Doar/Mann version amounted to overkill; others thought that since two of the charges overlapped parts of the first article, the importance of Article II was weakened.

McClory's version strengthened those two charges by specifically citing Nixon for failing "to take care that the laws (are) faithfully executed." Acceptance of his version also would mean his vote for Article II, strengthening the ranks of the swing votes, so they agreed to write the article his way.

McClory had the endorsement of the swing votes, then, when he arrived at the Rayburn Building Sunday morning after the first impeachment vote. He joined a meeting in Rodino's office to work out the final wording of the article before it would be presented to a Democratic caucus set for 11:00 A.M. Doar, Mann, Polk, and another inquiry staffer, John Labovitz, also joined the meeting.

Nearly all the Democrats were present—so was Republican McClory—at the Democratic caucus. For several hours members discussed the advantages and disadvantages of the Doar and McClory versions. Their indecision lay primarily in whether Nixon's noncompliance with subpoenas would be included in Article II or offered as a third article.

They finally agreed to try for a third article, and offered McClory the chance to introduce both of them. It would look better to have a Republican offer an article. McClory said he wouldn't offer both, but would offer one and preferred that it be Article III, since it embodied his pet complaint.

None of the Democrats present offered to introduce Article II and Paul Sarbanes already had offered Article I. Bill Hungate of Missouri was absent, so the Democrats settled on him and told Rodino to call him and tell him he had the job.

Most of the Republicans were taking the Sunday off while the Democrats deliberated. Some attended tennis matches and others played golf. Bill Cohen flew to Maine that day for a fund-raising event where Nelson Rockefeller was the main speaker.

Cohen discovered the fears that Walter Flowers had expressed when he wanted all the votes saved until the end of the impeachment debate were justified. As he entered the meeting hall he was greeted with a chorus of boos and calls of "Judas" and "Brutus." His initial reaction was that his congressional career would end that fall.

Hungate arrived at the Capitol at 8:00 A.M. on Monday to work with Doar and Mann on his new assignment. In addition to carefully going over the wording, he had to be thoroughly grounded in less than three hours on the defenses for the article.

Just before the session set to begin at 10:30, McClory and the six Republican members of the swing group met in McClory's office to make sure they all agreed on the points in Article II. McClory also tried to do a selling job on Article III, which he and Polk had drafted.

Mann dropped in at the meeting to show the group the latest wording of Article II, finished after McClory and the Democrats met on Sunday.

The Republicans objected that the drafters had missed the point in two of the charges, one accusing Nixon of misusing the IRS, the other with setting up the "White House plumbers." They were not willing to impeach the president for acts of his subordinates that were unknown to him, they said. The president's knowledge of the acts committed in his name would have to be spelled out in the articles.

At the last minute, then, the drafting team now led by Mann added the phrase: "acting personally and through his subordinates and agents" to the two charges against Nixon. Because of that addition, the session was an hour late getting started.

Charles Wiggins, who had taken a stronger command of the Republicans since McClory's declaration the previous month that he probably would vote for impeachment, was ready with a new tactic.

It had been Wiggins's contention all along that a law must be violated for a high crime and misdemeanor to be committed. Article II as written did not cite such a criminal violation, he said. He raised a "point of order" to object to introduction of the article. By doing that he gained extra, valuable time for arguing against the article.

While waiting for an elevator with Rodino before the Sunday caucus, George Danielson had told Rodino he had gone along with him and used his debate time Thursday afternoon to lay out the evidence. Constituents complained, Danielson said, that everyone except him had spoken in lofty terms. "They didn't appreciate that I was trying to be a bricklayer," he said.

So Danielson leaped into the breach on the Wiggins point of order. He delivered an extemporaneous speech that summed up in five minutes his definition of impeachable offense.

Wiggins had argued that the term, "abuse of powers," which comprised Article II, was too imprecise to be the subject of impeachment.

The charges in Article II "are high crimes and misdemeanors," Danielson said, because "they are crimes or offenses against the very structure of the state, against the system of government, the system that has brought to the American people and has preserved for the American people the freedoms and liberties which we so cherish. This is uniquely a presidential offense . . . I submit that only the president can harm the presidency. No one but the president can destroy the presidency."

Rodino, as chairman, ruled against Wiggins's point of order, but the fight over Article II continued through the day and into the evening, often interrupted by votes and quorum calls on the House floor. Consideration of the article would have gone on longer, but there was general agreement that each amendment would be limited to forty minutes debate.

Some of the time was consumed debating Wiggins's amendment to strike out the new phrase that had been added to satisfy the GOP proimpeachers.

The phrase only made the article worse, Wiggins said, because it said nothing about whether the president had knowledge of the acts. Actually, Wiggins knew the phrase made the article stronger. He said, "I have no quarrel with impeaching President Nixon by reason of the acts of his subordinates and agents, so long as we know that we are talking about those acts of subordinates and agents which were done with his knowledge or pursuant to his instructions."

McClory answered, "The president can only act through his agents and subordinates, but is he tolerating and has he tolerated this kind of [illegal] conduct in the White House and in and around him? Well, it seems to me that that is the charge we are making."

The Wiggins amendment was rejected by a 28–9 vote. Trent Lott was absent during the vote.

Wiggins tried some more amendments to change wording and lost by lopsided votes. The proimpeachers picked up their strategy of Saturday and offered motions to strike subparagraphs so they could explain the supporting evidence.

Finally, shortly after 11:00 P.M., Article II charging that President Nixon had abused his powers of office, was approved by a 28–10 vote of the committee. Bob McClory joined the ranks of those voting in favor of impeachment.

Rodino announced the committee would return at 10:30 the next morning, July 30, for another day of impeachment votes.

Unknown to McClory, now that he had committed himself to impeachment, his coveted Article III was in jeopardy.

The next morning, the Democrats held a caucus in Jerry Zeifman's office to decide what would be done about Article III, which McClory would propose and which had been fashioned into its final form the previous day during the debate on the second article.

A surprising amount of opposition developed to the McClory article. John Doar, who rarely spoke out during caucuses, argued against Article III, although he had supported the removal of the noncompliance issue from Article II in favor of having it comprise a third article. "On reflection," he said, "I realize now that it has Fifth Amendment connotations."

Doar said he also didn't think it would be right for the legislative branch to put the president in the kind of position that "smacks of a star-chamber proceeding" and that the Senate could issue its own subpoena. "Scholars . . . will be writing articles in the *New York Times* critical of the committee and the House for making noncompliance with the subpoena a separate article," he said.

Zeifman's resentment of Doar and their constant disagreements reached a zenith at that point. Zeifman already had made soundings for another job and had decided it was his last year with the committee. He was going to have it out with Doar one last time.

Zeifman rebuked Doar for waiting until the eleventh hour to take a position against the article, "after six months of taking a contrary position, six months of lulling the committee into inactivity" by supporting the idea that Nixon's refusal to comply could itself constitute an impeachable offense.

He said the committee couldn't depend upon the Senate's subpoena power. If the House didn't send an article of impeachment based on noncompliance, he said, it would have no fall-back position if the first two articles failed because of a lack of evidence. And an article on noncompliance would stress the importance of a congressional subpoena.

Addressing the members present, Zeifman said, "Those of us who have worked for you for years and who have been in the position of being between you and the executive agencies, trying to get information from these agencies feel very strongly about this.

"If this committee is not willing to support its own subpoena authority, if you're going to be willing to let this go down the drain, this place will be unfit to work for and there never will be again another president who will be impeached unless he is so insane as to wire his office for sound and has a special prosecutor who goes to court.''

The caucus broke up in silence and headed for the committee chamber to consider Article III.

All thirty-eight committee members were tired and readily agreed to limit the debate on the article to two hours.

In a ten-minute speech in support of his article, McClory summed up the subpoena issue as it concerned the House's power to impeach. ''Now implicit in this authority to conduct an impeachment inquiry is the authority to investigate the actions that take place in [the president's] office. If we are without that authority, or if the respondent has the right to determine for himself or herself to what extent the investigation shall be carried on, of course, we do not have the sole power of impeachment. Someone else is impinging upon our authority. So it seems to me implicit in this authority that we have a broad authority to conduct an investigative inquiry.''

The effectiveness of future impeachments depended on passage of the article, McClory said. If the current Congress refused to impeach because of Nixon's defiance of the Congress, ''the future respondents will be in the position where they can determine themselves what they are going to provide in an impeachment inquiry and what they are not going to provide, and this would be particularly so in the case of an inquiry directed toward the President of the United States.''

Ray Thornton thought the McClory article had failed to tie Nixon's failure to comply with the subpoenas to the existence of impeachable offenses and that it implied the committee lacked proof. Thornton thought noncompliance was not impeachable in itself unless it was related to other impeachable offenses. He offered an amendment that would make the tie by substituting nearly half the words of the brief McClory article.

Wiggins, still riding shotgun for the president, then injected a salient point about the article. The McClory version had said the subpoenaed materials ''were deemed necessary by the committee to its inquiry . . . to determine whether sufficient grounds exist to impeach. . . .''

Thornton's amendment would change that to read: ''were deemed necessary by the committee in order to resolve by direct evidence fundamental, factual questions relating to presidential direction, knowledge, or approval of actions demonstrated by other evidence to be substantial grounds for impeachment. . . ."

Wiggins said, "This committee yesterday and the day before [actually Saturday] viewed the evidence and found it, I am told, overwhelming." It voted two articles of impeachment based upon that assumption "and now we seek to impeach him because he did not give us enough evidence to do the job." His colleagues couldn't have it both ways, he said.

Nonetheless, the Thornton amendment was adopted by a 24–14 vote and after another ninety minutes of debate and a lunch break, the panel voted, 21–17, for Article III. Flowers and Mann deserted the Democratic ranks and opposed the article. Larry Hogan was the only Republican to join McClory in favoring it.

Rodino recessed the session at mid-afternoon for a last-minute effort to try to talk John Conyers out of offering his article calling for the impeachment of Nixon because of the secret bombing of Cambodia beginning in 1969. Conyers would not yield. But he agreed to limit debate on the article to ninety minutes.

Conyers argued that his Article IV should be adopted because everything the committee had heard had its roots in the Vietnam war, and the bombing of Cambodia was the simplest of the articles to defend. No tape, no additional evidence was needed.

"The president unilaterally undertook major military actions against another sovereign nation and then consistently denied that he had done so to both the Congress and the American people."

Most of the committee members did not believe, however, that the bombing, which Cohen laid partially to "sloth and default on the part of the Congress," was an impeachable offense.

Conyers's article was defeated, as he knew it would be, by a large margin, 12–26. Rodino, the swing votes, and the rest of the Republicans voted against it.

At 6:30 the committee recessed for dinner and returned for what an exhausted Peter Rodino hoped would be the last session of the impeachment inquiry.

The article ready for the committee when it returned at 8:00 P.M. was one Rodino had drafted with Doar several weeks earlier. Ed Mezvinsky had adopted the question of Nixon's personal finances as his pet complaint against the president months earlier, so he introduced it. He had worked hard the previous days lobbying his committee colleagues for support.

The article sought Nixon's impeachment for spending huge sums of federal money on his two homes and for claiming income tax deductions worth $576,000 for a gift of his vice-presidential papers when such deductions were not authorized by law. Debate was limited to two hours. Jack Brooks, whose Government Operations subcommittee had conducted an investigation of the government expenditures on Nixon's homes, joined the freshman Mezvinsky in defending the article.

But the inquiry staff had not done much work beyond what Brooks's panel had done and had relied on another congressional committee to do the work on Nixon's allegedly specious tax claims. Committee members had no heart in voting yet another article of impeachment. The committee had voted for three and it was 10:30 P.M., July 30, at the end of nine, arduous months of discussing and wrangling, long hours and constant pressure.

Mezvinsky's article was defeated by a 12–26 vote, this time with Rodino voting for it. The swing votes and all the Republicans maintained the opposition.

Rodino repeated the vote, and after a few minutes of discussion on procedural matters, brought an end to the inquiry work at 11:08 when he said, "So, the committee stands adjourned until further call of the chair."

The committee had been the center of attention for ninety million television viewers for thirty-five hours and thirty-four minutes.

Sixteen blocks from the committee room the day the panel wound up its voting, a fateful step was taken by President Nixon. He sent his lawyer, James St. Clair to Judge John Sirica's courtroom with twenty of the sixty-four tapes that the Supreme Court had ordered him to hand over to Special Prosecutor Leon Jaworski.

Many of the tapes were the same ones the committee had subpoenaed for use in its impeachment investigation.

The following day, July 31, found the impeachment inquiry staff as busy as it had been for several weeks. It had less than three weeks to prepare what would have to be a voluminous report to accompany the articles of impeachment to the floor of the House and to prepare the arguments and supporting evidence that would be used to defend the articles.

Some Republicans already were calling for Nixon to concede impeachment by the House and seek a prompt Senate trial.

Committee members, meanwhile, slackened their workload a bit, though they did begin working out procedures for handling the floor debate set to begin on August 19. Much of the talk among committee members consisted of who might be floor managers for the articles.

Rodino already had decided who four of them would be. He met with Democrats Paul Sarbanes and Don Edwards, and Republicans Bob McClory and Tom Railsback in his office to work out assignments for presenting the arguments in favor of impeachment.

Nearly all the committee members were preparing additional views they wanted to insert into the historical report the staff was preparing. Ray Thornton, who voted for Article III, and Bill Cohen, who voted against it, began preparing to offer a motion on the floor that would add Article III charging noncompliance with the committee's subpoenas as the tenth charge in support of Article I charging obstruction of justice.

St. Clair returned to court on July 31 to submit a report to Sirica stating that the tapes he had given the court the previous day were "at variance" with Nixon's public statements and with the transcripts submitted to the Judiciary Committee.

Senators began studying the rules—already prepared by their parliamentarians—that might govern a presidential impeachment trial.

On Friday, August 2, a few House Republicans, still searching for ways to avoid a vote on impeachment and get themselves off the hook, circulated a petition calling for censure of Nixon for "negligence and maladministration." It received very little support.

Rodino circulated a letter to each of the 435 members advising that on each day of the following week they would be able to listen to the nineteen tape-recorded conversations the committee had listened to. A total of 204 "listening stations" would be equipped with earphones in four locations in the House office buildings, he said.

On that day St. Clair returned to Sirica's court a third time. This time he had ten more tapes to give Sirica. One was the tape recording of the conversations Nixon had with his chief of staff, H. R. Haldeman, on June 23, 1972. It was one the committee had subpoenaed.

St. Clair especially wanted Charles Wiggins to see a transcript of the June 23 tape. Wiggins had spent his time since the final impeachment vote planning how he and the nine other Nixon stalwarts on the committee would mount an informed defense during the impeachment debate on the House floor.

St. Clair called Wiggins Friday afternoon and asked if he would come to the White House to meet with him and General Alexander Haig, who had replaced Haldeman as Nixon's chief of staff.

When Wiggins arrived half an hour later, he was handed the June 23 tape transcript. He read it four times. But no matter how often he reread it, it said "guilty."

It was no longer a case of "adverse inference" that Nixon ordered the CIA to interfere with the FBI investigation of the Watergate break-in, it now was a case of solid proof he ordered it. The transcript was "the smoking gun."

"That's extremely damaging information to the president," Wiggins said sadly. "It's a bombshell. It established a count of obstruction of justice. You ought to be considering the possible resignation of the president."

They discussed the method of releasing the transcript to the public, and Wiggins said he had no intention of doing it for them. Haig and St. Clair said they hadn't decided how it would be released, but they intended to do it no later than Monday. Wiggins said he would keep his mouth shut until then, although he figured they were counting on him to leak it.

Wiggins asked how long Nixon had known about the tape. The two White House aides said he had last reviewed the tape back on May 2 in connection with the upcoming Supreme Court action. They said he came out of his office after listening to the tape and said, "Let's go to court."

Wiggins returned to his office, stared at the work on Nixon's defense that he had left to go to the White House, turned and walked out of his office, telling his staff he was going home for the weekend.

Without knowing about the conference Wiggins had at the White House, GOP Leader John Rhodes scheduled a news conference the following Monday to announce he would stick with Nixon. He had agonized over his decision and nearly decided at one time he would vote for impeachment. He didn't feel that confident about Nixon's innocence, but he knew that he would be carrying many Republicans along with him as their elected leader in the House if he opposed Nixon.

Al Haig called Rhodes at home on Sunday afternoon when he read press speculation that Rhodes would announce his continued support for Nixon the next day. He told Rhodes that the White House was planning to make some information available within twenty-four hours and that Rhodes should know about it before his news conference. Rhodes had an aide cancel the press conference, claiming Rhodes had a fever and sore throat.

On Monday, August 5, many members took advantage of their first chance to listen to the Oval Office tape recordings. Many expressed the same shock as the committee members had at how much more offensive the discussions sounded than they looked on paper.

Nixon's two chief counsels, Fred Buzhardt and James St. Clair, and Bill Timmons, Nixon's congressional liaison, went to the Hill Monday afternoon to meet first with the House Republican leadership and the ten Judiciary stalwarts, and then with the Senate GOP leadership. They told the congressmen the gist of the June 23 tape, a transcript of which was soon to be made public.

The House committee members weren't prepared for the devastating news. Many were disbelieving. Wiggins, whom they had chosen as their unofficial leader, said it was true, he had read the transcript. As far as he was concerned, it was all over. He already had prepared a news release to announce his new position as soon as the transcript of the tape was made public.

As promised, the transcript of three Nixon-Haldeman conversations on June 23, 1972, was released.

To John Doar's copies, St. Clair added a note saying, "These conversations first came to my attention a few days ago . . . and I believe they are necessary to more accurately and competely describe the events involving the relationship between the FBI Watergate investigation and the CIA in 1972 than has been previously furnished the committee."

At a morning meeting with Haldeman, according to the first of the transcripts Nixon released:

H: Now, on the investigation, you know the Democratic break-in thing, we're back in the problem area because the FBI is not under control, because Gray doesn't exactly know how to control it and they have—their investigation is now leading into some productive areas—because they've been able to trace the money—not through the money itself—but through the bank sources—the banker. And, and it goes in some directions we don't want it to go. Ah, also there have been some things—like an informant came in off the street to the FBI in Miami who was a photographer or has a friend who is a photographer who developed some films through this guy Barker and the films had pictures of Democratic National Committee letterhead documents and things. So it's things like that that are filtering in. Mitchell came up with yesterday, and John Dean analyzed very carefully last night and concludes, concurs now with Mitchell's recommendation that the only way to solve this, and we're set up beautifully to do it, ah, in that and that—the only network that paid any attention to it last night was NBC—they did a massive story on the Cuban thing.

P: That's right.

H: That the way to handle this now is for us to have Walters call Pat Gray and just say, "Stay to hell out of this, this is ah, business here we don't want you to go any further on it." That's not an unusual development, and ah, that would take care of it.

P: What about Pat Gray—you mean Pat Gray doesn't want to?

H: Pat does want to. He doesn't know how to, and he doesn't have, he doesn't have any basis for doing it. Given this, he will then have the basis. He'll call Mark Felt in and the two of them—and Mark Felt wants to cooperate because he's ambitious—

P: Yeah.

H: He'll call him and say, "We've got the signal from across the river to put the hold on this." And that will fit rather well because the FBI agents who are working the case, at this point, feel that's what is . . .

P: This is the CIA? They've traced the money? Who'd they trace it to?

H: Well they've traced to a name, but they haven't gotten to the guy yet.

P: Would it be somebody here?

H: Ken Dahlberg.

P: Who the hell is Ken Dahlberg?

H: He gave $25,000 in Minnesota and, ah, the check went directly to this guy Barker.

P: It isn't from the Committee, though, from Stans?

H: Yeah. It is. It's directly traceable and there's some more through some Texas people that went to the Mexican bank which can also be traced to the Mexican bank—they'll get their names today.

H: And [pause]

P: Well, I mean, there's no way—I'm just thinking if they don't cooperate, what do they say? That they were approached by the Cubans. That's what Dahlberg has to say, the Texans too, that they—

H: Well, if they will. But then we're relying on more and more people all the time. That's the problem and they'll stop if we could take this other route.

P: All right.

H: And you seem to think the thing to do is to get them to stop?

P: Right, fine.

H: They say the only way to do that is from White House instructions. And it's got to be to Helms and to—ah, what's his name . . . ? Walters.

P: Walters.

H: And the proposal would be that Ehrlichman and I call them in, and say, ah—

P: All right, fine. How do you call him in—I mean you just—well, we protected Helms from one hell of a lot of things.

Nixon had given instructions, then, six days after the burglary to use the CIA to halt the FBI investigation of the laundered money that would lead to his reelection committee. Dick Cates had guessed correctly what must have been said on that date..

The tapes revealed more. Nixon asked Haldeman at one point, "Well who was the asshole that did [know about the break-in plans]? Is it Liddy? Is that the fellow? He must be a little nuts!'' G. Gordon Liddy wasn't even approached by the FBI until five days after the June 23 conversation and his name wasn't publicly linked to Watergate until more than a month later.

Nixon and Haldeman continued discussing the break-in, including the possible involvement of John Mitchell and Charles Colson.

H: The FBI interviewed Colson yesterday. They determined that would be a good thing to do. To have him take an interrogation, which he did, and that—the FBI guys working the case concluded that there were one or two possibilities—one, that this was a White House—they don't think that there is anything at the Election Committee—they think it was either a White House operation and they had some obscure reasons for it—nonpolitical, or it was a—Cuban and the CIA. And after their interrogation of Colson yesterday, they concluded it was not the White House, but are now convinced it is a CIA thing, so the CIA turnoff would—

P: Well, not sure of their analysis, I'm not going to get that involved. I'm [unintelligible].

H: No, sir, we don't want you to.

P: You call them in.

H: Good deal.

P: Play it tough. That's the way they play it and that's the way we are going to play it.

They discussed the explanation the CIA would use for requesting the FBI to halt its probe, citing the danger of exposing matters involved in the abortive "Bay of Pigs" invasion of Cuba in 1961. That part of transcript covered the period from 10:04 to 11:39 A.M. The second tape recorded a nine-minute conversation, from 1:04 P.M. to 1:13 P.M., during which the two men discussed their cover-up story again.

Haldeman's logs, which the committee already had, showed that at 1:30 that day he met in Ehrlichman's office with CIA director Richard Helms and his deputy, Vernon Walters. They acknowledged discussing an approach to FBI Acting Director L. Patrick Gray about possible CIA involvement in the Watergate money they had traced.

At 2:30, the third tape recorded still another Nixon-Haldeman conversation:

H: No problem.

P: [Unintelligible.]

H: Well, it was kind of interesting. Walters made the point and I didn't mention Hunt, I just said that the thing was leading into directions that were going to create potential problems because they were exploring leads that led back into areas that would be harmful to the CIA and harmful to the government [unintelligible] didn't have anything to do [unintelligible].

Nixon answered the telephone and then the conversation resumed:

H: [Unintelligible] I think Helms did to [unintelligible] said, I've had no—

P: God [unintelligible].

H: Gray called and said, yesterday, and said that he thought—

P: Who did? Gray?

H: Gray called Helms and said I think we've run right into the middle of a CIA covert operation.

P: Gray said that?

H: Yeah. And [unintelligible] said nothing we've done at this point and ah [unintelligible] says well it sure looks to me like it is [unintelligible] and ah, that was the end of that conversation [unintelligible] the problem is it tracks back to the Bay of Pigs and it tracks back to some other the leads run out to people who had no involvement in this, except by contacts and connection, but it gets to areas that are liable to be raised? The whole problem [unintelligible] Hunt. So at that point he kind of got the picture. He said, he said we'll be very happy to be helpful [unintelligible] handle anything you want. I would like to know the reason for being helpful, and I made it clear to him he wasn't going to get explicit [unintelligible] generality, and he said fine. And Walters [unintelligible]. Walters is going to make a call to Gray. That's the way we put it and that's the way it was left.

In a statement accompanying the public release of the June 23 transcripts, Nixon recounted his televised statement of April 29 and the release the following day of the set of transcripts. He said he listened to two of the tapes of June 23 shortly after that, in May, and

although I recognized that these presented potential problems, I did not inform my staff or my counsel of it, or those arguing my case, nor did I amend my submission to the Judiciary Committee in order to include and reflect it. At the time, I did not realize the extent of the implications which these conversations might now appear to have. As a result, those arguing my case, as well as those passing judgment on the case, did so with information that was incomplete and in some respects erroneous. This was a serious act of omission for which I take full responsibility and which I deeply regret.

That was taken as a statement to let St. Clair and Nixon's staff off the hook. Since the July 24 Supreme Court ruling, Nixon said, he had reviewed many of the sixty-four tapes subpoenaed. "This process has made it clear that portions of the tapes of these June twenty-third conversations are at variance with certain of my previous statements." He tried to explain it away as faulty recollection.

The June twenty-third tapes clearly show, however, that at the time I gave those instructions I also discussed the political aspects of the situation, and that I was aware of the advantage this course of action would have with respect to limiting possible public exposure of involvement by persons connected with the reelection committee.

The House debate was set to begin in two weeks.

It is highly unlikely that this review [of the rest of the sixty-four tapes] will be completed in time for the House debate. It appears at this stage, however, that a House vote of impeachment is, as a practical matter, virtually a foregone conclusion, and that the issue will therefore go to trial in the Senate. In order to ensure that no other significant relevant materials are withheld, I shall voluntarily furnish to the Senate everything from these tapes that Judge Sirica rules should go to the Special Prosecutor.

I recognize that this additional material I am now furnishing may further damage my case, especially because attention will be drawn separately to it rather than to the evidence in its entirety.

Nixon urged those considering the tapes' implications to keep in mind that two weeks later he told Gray to "press ahead vigorously" with his investigation after Gray complained there was no CIA involvement. The record in its entirety, he said, didn't justify his impeachment.

"The second point I would urge is that the evidence be looked at in its entirety and the events be looked at in perspective."

Twenty-eight members of the House Judiciary Committee already had the perspective. And now Charles Wiggins felt he had the facts and issued a press release: "I am now possessed of information which establishes beyond a reasonable doubt that on June 23, 1972, the President personally agreed to certain actions" to interfere with the Watergate break-in. "After considerable reflection, I have reached the painful conclusion that the President of the United States should resign," he said, and if not, "I am prepared to conclude that the magnificent career of public service of Richard Nixon must be terminated involuntarily." He would vote for impeachment based on certain portions of Article I, he said.

Months earlier, Hamilton Fish had told a reporter, "Watch Wiggins. If he votes for impeachment it'll be unanimous." Fish was correct.

One by one the ten stalwarts announced their defection from Nixon's defense. The committee's vote on impeachment would be presented on the House floor as unanimous. The House schedule for two weeks of debate was cut to one. The senators who would be serving as judge and jury made it clear they would convict Nixon and remove him from office.

After releasing the damning transcript, Nixon was greeted with a flood of calls for his resignation. Members of Congress began dreaming up ways to encourage his exit. One was an offer of immunity if he resigned.

Peter Rodino probably was the member of the House most relieved by the release of the June 23 transcript. It not only would make his work much easier, it was unlikely that Nixon would choose to remain in office in the face of his obviously imminent impeachment and Senate conviction.

When Senate Democratic Leader Mike Mansfield suggested that impeachment be carried to its conclusion even if Nixon resigned, the House balked.

After meeting with the House leadership on August 7, Rodino told reporters that some questions could be answered by continuing with the impeachment process. The Constitution left as an option to the Senate a decision on whether the person removed could be barred from ever holding public office. Once Nixon was removed, he could be tried on criminal charges. The June 23 tape responded only to Article I. There were still the other two articles to be confirmed by House and Senate votes.

But if Nixon resigned, Rodino said, the practical considerations would have to be taken into account. "I believe in the fullest sense we would have served the full purpose of the Constitutional requirements by his resignation. . . ."

He said, "Tomorrow, tomorrow, and tomorrow there will be others who will look back and see how we handled this." Even if Nixon resigned and impeachment stopped, the report being prepared by the staff would be carefully done to tell the entire story.

That afternoon, Rodino met with McClory and Edwards to go over plans for handling the floor debate. The talk turned to the possibility Nixon would resign. Rodino said he hoped Nixon would and spare the nation the continued trauma of House impeachment and a Senate trial. No one would want to carry on the case against him if he quit, Rodino said, not the courts and certainly not Congress. Edwards said he agreed.

McClory interpreted that as an inducement for him to tell the White House that no further action would be taken against Nixon if he resigned. McClory told that to Bill Timmons and Timmons said he would relay the message to Nixon as soon as the three leading Republicans in Congress, John Rhodes, Senate GOP Leader Hugh Scott, and Senator Barry Goldwater, finished their talk with the president in the Oval Office. They were there to give him a reading of the House and Senate sentiment on impeachment. It was overwhelming, they reported.

Two days later, on August 9, 1974, Nixon resigned. His replacement, Gerald Ford, who had been confirmed as vice-president by the committee only eight months earlier, pardoned Nixon for all impeachment-related crimes one month later.

Except for its report on the inquiry, the House Judiciary Committee's impeachment role was over. The 528-page committee report laid out the case for impeachment and concluded that Richard M. Nixon left the presidency for good reasons—he had lied, violated laws, and subverted the Constitution.

The strongest language was in the draft circulated to members on August 14 to use in preparing their individual views, to be included in the report: "For more than two years, the President engaged in a course of conduct which involved deliberate, repeated and continued deception of the American people."

Rodino and Doar worked together to fashion softer language, more in keeping with what they thought proper for a historical document. The wording, in the conclusion of the presentation of evidence supporting Article I, was changed to say that since June 17, 1972, Nixon engaged in a course of conduct or plan

to cover up, conceal and protect those responsible; and to conceal the existence and scope of other unlawful activities.

This finding is the only one that can explain the President's involvement in a pattern of undisputed acts that occurred after the break-in and that cannot otherwise be rationally explained.

The conclusion then listed thirty-two Watergate-related events it laid directly or indirectly to decisions by Nixon.

The conclusion's strongest language was:

President Nixon's course of conduct following the Watergate break-in, as described in Article I, caused action not only by his subordinates, but by the agencies of the United States, including the Department of Justice, the FBI, and the CIA. It required perjury, destruction of evidence, obstruction of justice, all crimes. But, most important, it required deliberate, contrived, and continuing deception of the American people.

In the conclusion to Article II charging abuse of powers, the committee wrote that Nixon

on many occasions has acted to the detriment of justice, right, and the public good, in violation of his constitutional duty to see to the faithful execution of the laws. This conduct has demonstrated a contempt for the rule of law; it has posed a threat to our democratic republic.

The conclusion in support of Article III charging noncompliance with subpoenas was short:

Unless the defiance of the committee's subpoenas under these circumstances is considered grounds for impeachment, it is difficult to conceive of any President acknowledging that he is obligated to supply the relevant evidence necessary for Congress to exercise its constitutional responsibility in an impeachment proceeding.

The committee filed its final impeachment report with the House on August 20, 1974. The House accepted it, 412–3.

Conclusions

Our gratitude for his having by his resignation spared the nation additional agony should not obscure for history our judgment that Richard Nixon, as President, committed certain acts for which he should have been impeached and removed from office.

So wrote Nixon's ten stalwart defenders on the House Judiciary Committee in their "minority views" in the committee's report to the House on its impeachment inquiry.

They also said

We know that it has been said, and perhaps some will continue to say, that Richard Nixon was "hounded from office" by his political opponents and media critics. We feel constrained to point out, however, that it was Richard Nixon who impeded the FBI's investigation of the Watergate affair by wrongfully attempting to implicate the Central Intelligence Agency; it was Richard Nixon who created and preserved the evidence of that transgression and who, knowing that it had been subpoenaed by this Committee and the Special Prosecutor, concealed its terrible import, even from his own counsel, until he could do so no longer. And it was a unanimous Supreme Court of the United States which, in an opinion authored by the Chief Justice whom he appointed, ordered Richard Nixon to surrender that evidence to the Special Prosecutor, to further the ends of justice.

To be sure, the stalwarts' statement insisted that only the release of the June 23 transcript supported the conclusion that Nixon should be impeached because he obstructed justice, the allegation in Article I. They still didn't agree that Nixon had abused his powers or unconstitutionally flouted the committee's authority to investigate his actions, as the other two articles concluded. But, the Republicans' statement that he deserved to be impeached and removed from office, plus the House vote of 412–3 in accepting the committee report on impeachment and its conclusions, left no doubt that Richard Nixon was guilty of impeachable offenses.

The statement by the stalwarts was written in August 1974. Nearly three years later, in May 1977, Nixon had a chance to admit his guilt and express contrition when he was interviewed by David Frost on a series of television programs. It was Nixon's first national statement since his exile to San Clemente.

He offered no admission of guilt, no apology for wrongdoing, no contrition. In the vernacular he helped create, Nixon was still "stonewalling."

During one interview, he said, "I did not commit, in my view, an impeachable offense."

As close as he came to contrition was to say, "I let down my friends. I let down the country. I let down our system of government and the dreams of all those young people that ought to get into government, but who now will think it's all too corrupt . . .

"Yep, I, I, I let the American people down, and I have to carry that burden with me for the rest of my life. . . . And, so, I can only say that in answer to your question, that while technically, I did not commit a crime, an impeachable offense . . . these are legalisms. As far as the handling of this matter is concerned, it was so botched-up. I made so many bad judgments. The worst ones, mistakes of the heart rather than the head. . . ."

Several national polls taken shortly after that interview showed that a majority of those responding believed that Richard M. Nixon, their former president, was still lying to them.

The irony is that if Nixon had said as early as September 15, 1972, for instance, that he had learned of White House involvement in the break-in, would not condone it, and was firing everyone involved, the scandal probably would have halted right there. Those fired could have talked later, but the scandal would not have developed into a constitutional crisis. Nixon would have finished his term in office in 1976 as another respected, if somewhat tainted, former president, and no one would have cared much what he had said on June 23, 1972.

There remains a core of Americans, however, who still believe Nixon was "hounded from office," that he had done no more than any other president had done and should not have been singled out for punishment.

The case for Nixon's ouster might have been better served had the impeachment inquiry staff supplied, as Charles Wiggins once asked for, a review of abuses by previous presidents. He never received it.

It can be said that other presidents have abused the power of their office and that it had been an increasing tendency—snowballing from the days when Franklin D. Roosevelt tried to pack the Supreme Court and ordered the internment of Japanese-Americans during World War II, through international incursions and domestic intelligence-gathering in the Kennedy, and certainly the Johnson, administrations.

Nixon and his men, possessed of the accumulation of successive layers of power built up by previous presidents, thought they were unanswerable to anyone for their actions. And they never would have to give up the White House tapes, they thought. The heady world of having a jet, a helicopter, a limousine, and hundreds of thousands of federal workers at beck and call doesn't tend to instill humility in those who never possessed any.

The power of the presidency is immense. It tends to attract sycophants ready to do the president's bidding, right or wrong. It is that combination of power and sycophancy that corrupts. Nixon took the use of presidential power a step further. But it was a giant step. Somewhere in the series of presidential abuses, the American people had to shout, "Stop!"

They finally did that in 1973 and 1974 and the House Judiciary Committee members, to their credit, responded as should good representatives of the people.

Thirty-eight men and women, ranging from one member who had trouble paying the monthly mortgage to a millionaire, from reactionary to radical, from those who relished their decision to those who anguished over it, all cut him down in an attempt to bring sanity back to the government and to preserve the democracy that a further accumulation of unchecked abuses of power surely would have destroyed.

Many of those who still believe Nixon innocent express reverence for the flag, the Constitution, and the American democracy. All of the evidence compiled against Richard Nixon could not be presented in this book. The evidence comprised forty-three volumes published by the committee. The evidence quoted here has been selective, but representative. By itself, however, the evidence paints a picture of overwhelming disdain for the democratic process, in favor of a fascistic concept of governing a nation. Nixon's supporters have never realized that his governance would have destroyed everything they professed to believe in.

Their representatives in the U.S. Congress arrived at a conclusion that was correct, just, necessary, and desirable.

After watching the Nixon-Frost interviews, Rodino called the former president's performance, "A sad commentary for me to see a former president of the United States attempt to explain away offenses that he'd committed then and attempting to rewrite history. We know the record is there on the report that we brought out. . . . That's what I believe history will judge Mr. Nixon on . . . and you can't rewrite that history."

History also will have to judge Peter Rodino's performance, and John Doar's and that of everyone else with a role in impeachment. In the circumstances of 1973 and 1974, someone like the ever-cautious Rodino probably was essential to the success of impeachment, someone willing to give a free rein to the meticulous, plodding type of inquiry a person like Doar would conduct, totally impervious to the efforts by the White House to provoke the committee to commit some foolish and precipitous act.

The impeachment process also probably needed someone like Jerry Zeifman, who would challenge the course of the inquiry—he quoted from Jeremiah, 48:10: "Cursed is he who does the work of the Lord with slackness"—and help steer it back from a purely legalistic course onto one that would take cognizance of the political necessities accompanying the process.

Again, someone like Rodino, whose unwillingness to pressure the thirty-seven other committee members or strike political bargains with them, allowed the sort of interplay that eventually produced the bipartisan vote for impeachment that Rodino knew would be needed. Emanuel Celler undoubtedly would have flexed his muscles and had an impeachment vote in February. But Celler probably would have lost in the committee and certainly would have lost in the House and in the public eye.

History also will have to judge whether the committee did enough. The impeachment staff really did no investigating on its own; it merely collated the work of other government entities, "an investigation by Xerox" as one participant described it. Jim Mann, facing the prospect he would be a manager of the articles of impeachment in the House and Senate, worried about whether the evidence as presented to the Judiciary Committee by the staff would be sufficient to win the case in a Senate trial. "We just kind of got that evidence by osmosis," he said. "To present that type of case before the Senate would be very difficult."

Many questions were never answered. Why did the White House have a "Gemstone" plan for White House intelligence? What was the relationship between the CIA and FBI that Nixon thought he could exploit? What prior illegal activities had they engaged in? Why did Nixon indicate the White House had protected the CIA even before Watergate? And why didn't all those government employees who could see the abuses of power as they were being used speak up and cry "foul"?

Rodino is reluctant to say this soon how history will view the impeachment inquiry he chaired. But so far, he is proud. The ultimate goal of impeachment is the removal of a president from office, he says, and that was accomplished by Nixon's resignation in the face of an obviously imminent impeachment and conviction.

The process proved, he states, that "the system not only works, it works rather well." Had the totality of Nixon's actions gone unchecked, "it could ultimately have meant the subversion of our whole system." And, he says, it proved that "no man, no matter how powerful, can escape and avoid being called to account." The faith of the American people in their system of government was restored, and the phrase, "a government of laws and not of men," was not just rhetoric any more.

One of the marvels of getting the top man involved in the Watergate scandal was that every branch of government played a key role. The Senate Watergate Committee gave official sanction to the *Washington Post* revelations by eliciting the details of the scandal throughout months of hearings that in themselves raised the consciousness of the American public. The special prosecutor's office gathered the evidence that linked the scandal with criminality and connected the president to it. The Supreme Court backed up the special prosecutor's demand for tapes. And the White House helped by botching its handling of the scandal and its ramifications for two years.

But, given all of those events and the enormity of them, separately or collectively they would not have driven Nixon from office. Only the Judiciary Committee's vote, which made a House impeachment a reality and Senate conviction a probability, could force Nixon to resign or be thrown out. He took the easier way.

Had those outside events involving the Senate panel, the special prosecutor, the Supreme Court and the White House activities, not happened as they did, and more importantly, when they did, the Judiciary Committee's vote to recommend impeachment could have failed.

Rodino became a national figure after impeachment. So much so that he was considered as a possible vice-presidential candidate by Democratic presidential nominee Jimmy Carter at the 1976 convention in New York. Rodino didn't want the job. His excuse was that he was suffering from glaucoma that eventually could lead to blindness. But Rodino isn't the sort of person who would be comfortable as vice-president.

Carter's people were impressed, however, with Rodino's administrative assistant, who served as liaison between the two. Francis O'Brien was appointed press secretary to vice-presidential candidate Walter Mondale, and after the election O'Brien went to work for a New York–based conglomerate, rising quickly to become a vice-president of its film division.

Rodino suggested John Doar as a candidate for attorney general, but

Doar didn't get the job. He joined a prestigious New York law firm. Jerry Zeifman became a law professor at a San Francisco–area university; Dick Cates returned to his Madison law firm, Bert Jenner to his Chicago firm, and St. Clair to his in Boston. Sam Garrison set up a law partnership in Roanoke, Virginia.

Walter Flowers, Jim Mann, and Hamilton Fish, who remained in Congress, changed their minds after impeachment and regretted that they had voted against Article III charging Nixon with noncompliance with committee subpoenas. Their votes at the time would have made it a more decisive, 24–14 vote, instead of 21–17.

Jack Brooks became chairman of the Government Operations Committee. Ray Thornton left Judiciary for a spot on the Agriculture Committee, and then gave up his seat in the House to consider running for the Senate. Mann also said he would retire from the House.

Tom Railsback and M. Caldwell Butler remained. Edward Hutchinson retired and Bob McClory became ranking Republican on the committee. Charles Wiggins decided to retire from Congress and William Cohen decided to run for the Senate.

The most important question, though, is not how the participants viewed the process. It is, "Did we learn anything? Did things improve?"

Most persons would agree that Gerald Ford was a decent and honest president who did not abuse the powers of his office. At least in his first year, neither did Jimmy Carter.

The dangers are that lessons are too often forgotten. George Santayana, said, in effect, that those who don't know history are doomed to repeat it.

Nixon showed in one of his interviews with Frost that he never understood what all the fuss was about. He still didn't understand why he had to leave office. He was asked about the Huston plan for domestic surveillance, a plan that would have violated several federal laws and a variety of constitutional rights:

NIXON: Well, when the president does it, that means that it is not illegal.
FROST: By definition.
NIXON: Exactly. Exactly. If the president . . . approves an action because of

the national security, or in this case because of a threat to internal peace and order of significant magnitude, then the president's decision in that instance is one that enables those who carry it out, to carry it out without violating a law. Otherwise, they're in an impossible position.

In a long explanation he sent to the *Washington Star,* Nixon tried to justify presidential discretion in obeying or disobeying the law. He hadn't read James Madison 191 years earlier, nor had he read Don Edwards in the House Judiciary Committee's report just three years previous. Edwards, who also remained in Congress, pointed out in his remarks in the report that one essential point almost was overlooked in the search for the "smoking gun" of the cover-up:

> In his attempts to subvert the processes of representative government and the guarantees of the Bill of Rights, Mr. Nixon and his associates used repeatedly the justification he described as "national security."
>
> It was a familiar theme, referred to by James Madison in a letter to Jefferson in 1786. "Perhaps it is a universal truth," wrote the author of the Bill of Rights, "that the loss of liberty at home is to be charged to the provisions against dangers, real or pretended, from abroad."

The committee's evidence, Edwards said, pointed to a continuous pattern of such conduct:

> Congress, the press, and indeed all of the American people must be vigilant to the perils of the subversive notion that any public official, the president or the policeman, possesses a kind of inherent power to set aside the Constitution whenever he thinks the public interest, or "national security" warrants it. That notion is the essential postulate of tyranny.

Both Gerald Ford and Jimmy Carter have invoked the phrase, "national security" during their White House terms. The invocation of "national security" should, after Nixon, send shudders up every American's spine and raise doubts in every American's mind.

Appendix

Resolution

Impeaching Richard M. Nixon, President of the United States, of high crimes and misdemeanors.

Resolved, That Richard M. Nixon, President of the United States, is impeached for high crimes and misdemeanors, and that the following articles of impeachment be exhibited to the Senate:

Articles of impeachment exhibited by the House of Representatives of the United States of America in the name of itself and of all of the people of the United States of America, against Richard M. Nixon, President of the United States of America, in maintenance and support of its impeachment against him for high crimes and misdemeanors.

Article I

In his conduct of the office of President of the United States, Richard M. Nixon, in violation of his constitutional oath faithfully to execute the office of President of the United States, and, to the best of his ability, preserve, protect, and defend the Constitution of the United States, and in violation of his constitutional duty to take care that the laws be faithfully executed, has prevented, obstructed, and impeded the administration of justice, in that:

On June 17, 1972, and prior thereto, agents of the Committee for the Re-election of the President committed unlawful entry of the headquarters of the Democratic National Committee in Washington, District of Columbia, for the purpose of securing political intelligence. Subsequent thereto, Richard M. Nixon, using

Article I

COMMITTEE ON THE JUDICIARY
HOUSE OF REPRESENTATIVES
93D CONGRESS

ROLL CALL

No. *Obstruction of Justice* **DATE** *7/27/74*

H. _____ **S.** _____

7p,

Present	COMMITTEE	Sarbanes			Donohue	
		Ayes	Nays	Present	Ayes	Nays
____	MR. DONOHUE	✓			✓	
____	MR. BROOKS	✓			✓	
____	MR. KASTENMEIER	✓			✓	
____	MR. EDWARDS	✓			✓	
____	MR. HUNGATE	✓			✓	
____	MR. CONYERS	✓			✓	
____	MR. EILBERG	✓			✓	
____	MR. WALDIE	✓			✓	
____	MR. FLOWERS	✓			✓	
____	MR. MANN	✓			✓	
____	MR. SARBANES	✓			✓	
____	MR. SEIBERLING	✓			✓	
____	MR. DANIELSON	✓			✓	
____	MR. DRINAN	✓			✓	
____	MR. RANGEL	✓			✓	

The House Judiciary Committee roll call votes as recorded by the author, July 27, 1974.

___	MS. JORDAN	✓		✓	
___	MR. THORNTON	✓		✓	
___	MS. HOLTZMAN	✓		✓	
___	MR. OWENS	✓		✓	
___	MR. MEZVINSKY	✓		✓	
___	MR. HUTCHINSON		✓		✓
___	MR. McCLORY		✓		✓
___	MR. SMITH		✓		✓
___	MR. SANDMAN		✓		✓
___	MR. RAILSBACK	✓		✓	
___	MR. WIGGINS		✓		✓
___	MR. DENNIS		✓		✓
___	MR. FISH	✓		✓	
___	MR. MAYNE		✓		✓
___	MR. HOGAN	✓		✓	
___	MR. BUTLER	✓		✓	
___	MR. COHEN	✓		✓	
___	MR. LOTT		✓		✓
___	MR. FROEHLICH	✓		✓	
___	MR. MOORHEAD		✓		✓
___	MR. MARAZITI		✓		✓
___	MR. LATTA		✓		✓
___	MR. RODINO, *Chairman*	✓		✓	
___	TOTAL	27	11	27	11

7:02   7:05

the powers of his high office, engaged personally and through his subordinates and agents, in a course of conduct or plan designed to delay, impede, and obstruct the investigation of such unlawful entry; to cover up, conceal and protect those responsible; and to conceal the existence and scope of other unlawful covert activities.

The means used to implement this course of conduct or plan included one or more of the following:

(1) making or causing to be made false or misleading statements to lawfully authorized investigative officers and employees of the United States;

(2) withholding relevant and material evidence or information from lawfully authorized investigative officers and employees of the United States;

(3) approving, condoning, acquiescing in, and counseling witnesses with respect to the giving of false or misleading statements to lawfully authorized investigative officers and employees of the United States and false or misleading testimony in duly instituted judicial and congressional proceedings;

(4) interfering or endeavoring to interfere with the conduct of investigations by the Department of Justice of the United States, the Federal Bureau of Investigation, the Office of Watergate Special Prosecution Force, and Congressional Committees;

(5) approving, condoning, and acquiescing in, the surreptitious payment of substantial sums of money for the purpose of obtaining the silence or influencing the testimony of witnesses, potential witnesses or individuals who participated in such unlawful entry and other illegal activities;

(6) endeavoring to misuse the Central Intelligence Agency, an agency of the United States;

(7) disseminating information received from officers of the Department of Justice of the United States to subjects of investigations conducted by lawfully authorized investigative officers and employees of the United States, for the purpose of aiding and assisting such subjects in their attempts to avoid criminal liability;

(8) making false or misleading public statements for the purpose of deceiving the people of the United States into believing that a thorough and complete investigation had been conducted with respect to allegations of misconduct on the part of personnel of the executive branch of the United States and personnel of the Committee for the Re-election of the President, and that there was no involvement of such personnel in such misconduct; or

(9) endeavoring to cause prospective defendants, and individuals duly tried and convicted, to expect favored treatment and consideration in return for

their silence or false testimony, or rewarding individuals for their silence or false testimony.

In all of this, Richard M. Nixon has acted in a manner contrary to his trust as President and subversive of constitutional government, to the great prejudice of the cause of law and justice and to the manifest injury of the people of the United States.

Wherefore, Richard M. Nixon, by such conduct, warrants impeachment and trial, and removal from office.

Article II

Using the powers of the office of President of the United States, Richard M. Nixon, in violation of his constitutional oath faithfully to execute the office of President of the United States and, to the best of his ability, preserve, protect, and defend the Constitution of the United States, and in disregard of his constitutional duty to take care that the laws be faithfully executed, has repeatedly engaged in conduct violating the constitutional rights of citizens, impairing the due and proper administration of justice and the conduct of lawful inquiries, or contravening the laws governing agencies of the executive branch and the purposes of these agencies.

This conduct has included one or more of the following:

(1) He has, acting personally and through his subordinates and agents, endeavored to obtain from the Internal Revenue Service, in violation of the constitutional rights of citizens, confidential information contained in income tax returns for purposes not authorized by law, and to cause, in violation of the constitutional rights of citizens, income tax audits or other income tax investigations to be initiated or conducted in a discriminatory manner.

(2) He misused the Federal Bureau of Investigation, the Secret Service, and other executive personnel, in violation or disregard of the constitutional rights of citizens, by directing or authorizing such agencies or personnel to conduct or continue electronic surveillance or other investigations for purposes unrelated to national security, the enforcement of laws, or any other lawful function of his office; and he did direct the concealment of certain records made by the Federal Bureau of Investigation of electronic surveillance.

(3) He has, acting personally and through his subordinates and agents, in violation or disregard of the constitutional rights of citizens, authorized and permitted to be maintained a secret investigative unit within the office of the President, financed in part with money derived from campaign contributions,

Article II

COMMITTEE ON THE JUDICIARY
HOUSE OF REPRESENTATIVES
93D CONGRESS

ROLL CALL

No. _____ *Abuse of Powers* DATE _7/29/74_

H. _____ S. _____

Present	COMMITTEE	Hungate Substitute Ayes (11)	Nays (6)	Donohue Abuse of Powers Present	Ayes	Nays
___	MR. DONOHUE	✓			✓	
___	MR. BROOKS	✓			✓	
___	MR. KASTENMEIER	✓			✓	
___	MR. EDWARDS	✓			✓	
___	MR. HUNGATE	✓			✓	
___	MR. CONYERS	✓			✓	
___	MR. EILBERG	✓			✓	
___	MR. WALDIE	✓			✓	
___	MR. FLOWERS	✓			✓	
___	MR. MANN	✓			✓	
___	MR. SARBANES	✓			✓	
___	MR. SEIBERLING	✓			✓	
___	MR. DANIELSON	✓			✓	
___	MR. DRINAN	✓			✓	
___	MR. RANGEL	✓			✓	

The House Judiciary Committee roll call votes as recorded by the author, July 29, 1974.

___	MS. JORDAN	✓				✓	
___	MR. THORNTON	✓				✓	
___	MS. HOLTZMAN	✓				✓	
___	MR. OWENS	✓				✓	
___	MR. MEZVINSKY	✓				✓	
___	MR. HUTCHINSON		✓				✓
___	MR. McCLORY	✓				✓	
___	MR. SMITH		✓				✓
___	MR. SANDMAN		✓				✓
___	MR. RAILSBACK	✓				✓	
___	MR. WIGGINS		✓				✓
___	MR. DENNIS		✓				✓
___	MR. FISH	✓				✓	
___	MR. MAYNE		✓				✓
___	MR. HOGAN	✓				✓	
___	MR. BUTLER	✓				✓	
___	MR. COHEN	✓				✓	
___	MR. LOTT		✓				✓
___	MR. FROEHLICH	✓				✓	
___	MR. MOORHEAD		✓				✓
___	MR. MARAZITI		✓				✓
___	MR. LATTA		✓				✓
___	MR. RODINO, *Chairman*	✓				✓	
___	TOTAL	28	10			28	10

which unlawfully utilized the resources of the Central Intelligence Agency, engaged in covert and unlawful activities, and attempted to prejudice the constitutional right of an accused to a fair trial.

(4) He has failed to take care that the laws were faithfully executed by failing to act when he knew or had reason to know that his close subordinates endeavored to impede and frustrate lawful inquiries by duly constituted executive, judicial, and legislative entities concerning the unlawful entry into the headquarters of the Democratic National Committee, and the cover-up thereof, and concerning other unlawful activities, including those relating to the confirmation of Richard Kleindienst as Attorney General of the United States, the electronic surveillance of private citizens, the break-in into the offices of Dr. Lewis Fielding, and the campaign financing practices of the Committee to Re-elect the President.

(5) In disregard of the rule of law, he knowingly misused the executive power by interfering with agencies of the executive branch, including the Federal Bureau of Investigation, the Criminal Division, and the Office of Watergate Special Prosecution Force, of the Department of Justice, and the Central Intelligence Agency, in violation of his duty to take care that the laws be faithfully executed.

In all of this, Richard M. Nixon has acted in a manner contrary to his trust as President and subversive of constitutional government, to the great prejudice of the cause of law and justice and to the manifest injury of the people of the United States.

Wherefore Richard M. Nixon, by such conduct, warrants impeachment and trial, and removal from office.

Article III

In his conduct of the office of President of the United States, Richard M. Nixon, contrary to his oath faithfully to execute the office of President of the United States and, to the best of his ability, preserve, protect, and defend the Constitution of the United States, and in violation of his constitutional duty to take care that the laws be faithfully executed, has failed without lawful cause or excuse to produce papers and things as directed by duly authorized subpoenas issued by the Committee on the Judiciary of the House of Representatives on April 11, 1974, May 15, 1974, May 30, 1974, and June 24, 1974, and willfully disobeyed such subpoenas. The subpoenaed papers and things were deemed necessary by the Committee in order to resolve by direct evidence fundamental, factual questions relating to Presidential direction, knowledge, or approval of actions demonstrated by other evidence to be substantial grounds for impeachment of the President. In refusing to produce these papers and things, Richard M. Nixon, substituting his judgment as to what materials were necessary for the inquiry, interposed the powers of the Presidency against the lawful subpoenas of the House of Representatives, thereby assuming to himself functions and judgments necessary to the exercise of the sole power of impeachment vested by the Constitution in the House of Representatives.

In all of this, Richard M. Nixon has acted in a manner contrary to his trust as President and subversive of constitutional government, to the great prejudice of the cause of law and justice, and to the manifest injury of the people of the United States.

Wherefore Richard M. Nixon, by such conduct, warrants impeachment and trial, and removal from office.

Articles Not Approved

Cambodia Bombing

In his conduct of the office of President of the United States, Richard M. Nixon, in violation of his constitutional oath faithfully to execute the office of President of the United States, and in disregard of his constitutional duty to take care that the laws be faithfully executed, on and subsequent to March 17, 1969, authorized, ordered, and ratified the concealment from the Congress of the facts and the submission to the Congress of false and misleading statements concerning the existence, scope and nature of American bombing operations in Cambodia in derogation of the power of the Congress to declare war, to make appropriations and to raise and support armies, and by such conduct warrants impeachment and trial and removal from office.

Emoluments and Income Taxes

In his conduct of the office of President of the United States, Richard M. Nixon, in violation of his constitutional oath faithfully to execute the office of the President of the United States, and, to the best of his ability, preserve, protect and defend the Constitution of the United States and in violation of his constitutional duty to take care that the laws be faithfully executed, did receive emoluments from the United States in excess of the compensation provided by law pursuant to Article II, Section 1, Clause 7 of the Constitution, and did willfully attempt to evade the payment of a portion of Federal income taxes due and owing by him for the years 1969, 1970, 1971, and 1972, in that:

Article III

COMMITTEE ON THE JUDICIARY
HOUSE OF REPRESENTATIVES
93D CONGRESS

ROLL CALL

No. ....   DATE *7/30/74*

H. ....   S. ....

Present	COMMITTEE	Thornton Amendment			McClory noncompliance	
		Ayes	Nays	Present	Ayes	Nays
___	MR. DONOHUE	✓			✓	
___	MR. BROOKS	✓			✓	
___	MR. KASTENMEIER	✓			✓	
___	MR. EDWARDS	✓			✓	
___	MR. HUNGATE	✓			✓	
___	MR. CONYERS		✓		✓	
___	MR. EILBERG	✓			✓	
___	MR. WALDIE	✓			✓	
___	MR. FLOWERS		✓			✓
___	MR. MANN	✓				✓
___	MR. SARBANES	✓			✓	
___	MR. SEIBERLING	✓			✓	
___	MR. DANIELSON	✓			✓	
___	MR. DRINAN	✓			✓	
___	MR. RANGEL	✓			✓	

The House Judiciary Committee roll call votes as recorded by the author, July 30, 1974.

MS. JORDAN	✓			✓	
MR. THORNTON	✓			✓	
MS. HOLTZMAN	✓			✓	
MR. OWENS		✓		✓	
MR. MEZVINSKY	✓			✓	
MR. HUTCHINSON	✓				✓
MR. McCLORY	✓				✓
MR. SMITH		✓			✓
MR. SANDMAN		✓			✓
MR. RAILSBACK		✓			✓
MR. WIGGINS		✓			✓
MR. DENNIS		✓			✓
MR. FISH	✓				✓
MR. MAYNE		✓			✓
MR. HOGAN		✓		✓	
MR. BUTLER	✓				✓
MR. COHEN	✓				✓
MR. LOTT	✓				✓
MR. FROEHLICH		✓			✓
MR. MOORHEAD		✓			✓
MR. MARAZITI		✓			✓
MR. LATTA		✓			✓
MR. RODINO, *Chairman*	✓			✓	
TOTAL	24	14		21	17

3:27

Article IV

COMMITTEE ON THE JUDICIARY
HOUSE OF REPRESENTATIVES
93D CONGRESS

ROLL CALL

No. .... Cambodia   DATE 7/30/74

H. .... S. ....

Conyers

Present	COMMITTEE	Ayes	Nays	Present	Ayes	Nays
____	MR. DONOHUE		/			
____	MR. BROOKS	/				
____	MR. KASTENMEIER	/				
____	MR. EDWARDS	/				
____	MR. HUNGATE	/				
____	MR. CONYERS	/				
____	MR. EILBERG		/			
____	MR. WALDIE	/				
____	MR. FLOWERS		/			
____	MR. MANN		/			
____	MR. SARBANES		/			
____	MR. SEIBERLING		/			
____	MR. DANIELSON		/			
____	MR. DRINAN	/				
____	MR. RANGEL	/				

The House Judiciary Committee roll call votes as recorded by the author, July 30, 1974.

___	MS. JORDAN	✓							
___	MR. THORNTON		✓						
___	MS. HOLTZMAN	✓							
___	MR. OWENS	✓							
___	MR. MEZVINSKY	✓							
___									
___	MR. HUTCHINSON		✓						
___	MR. McCLORY		✓						
___	MR. SMITH		✓						
___	MR. SANDMAN		✓						
___	MR. RAILSBACK		✓						
___	MR. WIGGINS		✓						
___	MR. DENNIS		✓						
___	MR. FISH		✓						
___	MR. MAYNE		✓						
___	MR. HOGAN		✓						
___	MR. BUTLER		✓						
___	MR. COHEN		✓						
___	MR. LOTT		✓						
___	MR. FROEHLICH		✓						
___	MR. MOORHEAD		✓						
___	MR. MARAZITI		✓						
___	MR. LATTA		✓						
___									
___	MR. RODINO, *Chairman*	✓							
___	TOTAL	12	26						

Article IV

COMMITTEE ON THE JUDICIARY
HOUSE OF REPRESENTATIVES
93D CONGRESS

ROLL CALL

No. ....   DATE 7/30/74

Taxes and Emoluments
H. .... S. ....

Mezvinsky

Present	COMMITTEE	Ayes	Nays	Present	Ayes	Nays
......	MR. DONOHUE		/			
......	MR. BROOKS	/				
......	MR. KASTENMEIER	/				
......	MR. EDWARDS	/				
......	MR. HUNGATE		/			
......	MR. CONYERS	/				
......	MR. EILBERG	/				
......	MR. WALDIE		/			
......	MR. FLOWERS		/			
......	MR. MANN		/			
......	MR. SARBANES		/			
......	MR. SEIBERLING	/				
......	MR. DANIELSON	/				
......	MR. DRINAN		/			
......	MR. RANGEL	/				

The House Judiciary Committee roll call votes as recorded by the author, July 30, 1974.

___	MS. JORDAN	✓			
___	MR. THORNTON		✓		
___	MS. HOLTZMAN	✓			
___	MR. OWENS		✓		
___	MR. MEZVINSKY	✓			
___	MR. HUTCHINSON		✓		
___	MR. McCLORY		✓		
___	MR. SMITH		✓		
___	MR. SANDMAN		✓		
___	MR. RAILSBACK		✓		
___	MR. WIGGINS		✓		
___	MR. DENNIS		✓		
___	MR. FISH		✓		
___	MR. MAYNE		✓		
___	MR. HOGAN		✓		
___	MR. BUTLER		✓		
___	MR. COHEN		✓		
___	MR. LOTT		✓		
___	MR. FROEHLICH		✓		
___	MR. MOORHEAD		✓		
___	MR. MARAZITI		✓		
___	MR. LATTA		✓		
___	MR. RODINO, *Chairman*	✓			
___	TOTAL	12	26		

(1) He, during the period for which he has been elected President, unlawfully received compensation in the form of government expenditures at and on his privately-owned properties located in or near San Clemente, California, and Key Biscayne, Florida.

(2) He knowingly and fraudulently failed to report certain income and claimed deductions in the year 1969, 1970, 1971, and 1972 on his Federal income tax returns which were not authorized by law, including deductions for a gift of papers to the United States valued at approximately $576,000.

In all of this, Richard M. Nixon has acted in a manner contrary to his trust as President and subversive of constitutional government, to the great prejudice of the cause of law and justice and to the manifest injury of the people of the United States.

Wherefore Richard M. Nixon, by such conduct, warrants impeachment and trial, and removal from office.

Index